PRAISE FOR *RON CAREY AND THE TEAMSTERS*

"Reiman's book is both a history of Teamster members' struggles to reform their union and a guidebook for younger activists determined to revive the union movement. Ron Carey was GUILTY—guilty of fighting courageously for over forty years, for union democracy and against both corporate bosses and union corruption. And a jury of his peers in a federal trial made it clear that Carey was INNOCENT, of all fake, trumped up, fraudulent charges against him. Read *Ron Carey and the Teamsters*, the tale of one of America's great working-class heroes."—BOB MUEHLENKAMP, TEAMSTER ORGANIZING DIRECTOR; ASSISTANT TO PRESIDENT RON CAREY

"The '97 UPS strike that Ron Carey led revived a dead labor movement with action, not bluff. Reiman shows us that Carey didn't suddenly morph into a reformer—he was the real deal from the beginning."—TOM LEEDHAM, 1996 RUNNING MATE TO RON CAREY; FORMER DIRECTOR OF WAREHOUSE WORKERS

"A sympathetic and frank portrait of the former Teamster president who in 1997 led one of the country's largest strikes and was then driven from union office by the powers he had challenged. Reiman has talked to everyone, read everything, and provides a comprehensive account of Carey's life as he dealt with the challenges of the Mafia, the Teamster old guard, UPS, and the government. We come away having met an honest man who was ensnared in the net woven by big business, government, and the Teamster old guard. If he was defeated, still we admire him for having worked to create a union that fought for its members."—DAN LA BOTZ, FOUNDING MEMBER, TEAMSTERS FOR A DEMOCRATIC UNION; AUTHOR, *RANK-AND-FILE REBELLION TEAMSTERS FOR A DEMOCRATIC UNION*

RON CAREY

——— AND THE ———

TEAMSTERS

How a UPS Driver Became the Greatest Union
Reformer of the Twentieth Century by
Putting Members First

KEN REIMAN

MONTHLY REVIEW PRESS
New York

Library of Congress Cataloging-in-Publication data
available from the publisher

ISBN 978-1-68590-058-8 paperback
ISBN 978-1-68590-059-5 cloth

Typeset in Minion Pro and Brown

MONTHLY REVIEW PRESS, NEW YORK
monthlyreview.org

5 4 3 2 1

Contents

Contents

Foreword

BY TIM SYLVESTER

Ken Reiman has taken on the task of telling the story of the greatest Teamster President in history—Ron Carey. Ken tells this story from the perspective of an insider. He was a UPS package driver and an activist. Ken prided himself on telling the truth first through his own newsletter the "Local Agitator" and later by running for and winning office in Local 804. He brings that experience and honesty to this book,

In this, he follows the trail blazed by Ron Carey himself. As Ken writes, Ron was a fundamentally honest and decent leader. He took on UPS, corporate America, and a culture of "go along get along" among many teamster Locals and officers, and he won. For this, he had to be punished. Ken tells the story of the vendetta launched against him by corporate America and specifically UPS.

Why such a vendetta, you may ask. Simply follow the story, the story of a man who "put the members first," and who made other Teamster officers look ineffective in comparison.

Ken has conducted exhaustive research to write this book. He has spent many hours on interviews with those who were there from the start of the effort to reform the Teamsters union until the end. Sadly, this is also a story of those who were part of the good fight, but who would later betray Carey .

When historians or journalists in the future write about what happened after the 1997 UPS strike, and how this strike played a central role in the rebirth of the labor movement, they will come back to the pivotal role played by Ron Carey. I knew Ron, and it was my honor to work with him and learn from him. He was an honest, courageous, and selfless union activist who stood up for rank-and-file workers no matter the cost to himself.

The book begins by including the entire acceptance speech that Ron Carey gave at the 1991 convention. Known as the "Forgotten Teamster" speech, it was the first speech to address the excesses of the Teamster leadership. These included huge salaries and multiple pensions, private jets, and unlimited vacation time, among other perks. He spoke of the frustration of a membership that felt estranged from their so-called leaders, the "forgotten Teamsters."

Today, at Teamster conventions, delegates in their red vests get up and walk out when someone opposes them. Most of them sat down this time when Carey spoke. You could see it in their faces; they knew there was big change imminent. I remember seeing them exchanging looks. They were shocked to see Carey being carried on the shoulders of his supporters as he came off the stage. But more importantly, he refused such treatment and quickly got off their shoulders and walked to the rear of the hall where rank-and-file members were seated. The hall burst into thunderous cheering that went on unabated for the duration of time it took for Carey to shake every hand in the members' section in the rear.

"CAREY, CAREY, CAREY" was the chant of the day!

When the convention came to order, a delegate for an opposing candidate rose on a point of order and complained to the chair (old guard Vice President Weldon Mathis) that the Carey contingent was allowed more than the twenty minutes allotted for demonstration, a violation of convention rules. Mathis to his credit responded, "I guess time doesn't pass when you ain't having fun."

Ron Carey came into that convention as an upstart who stood

no chance of winning the leadership. Yet he left as a candidate who had electrified the members.

This was one of the most important days of my life. I was there with my wife and my brothers from local 804. Our hands hurt from clapping and our throats were sore from cheering, but we were proud. My shop steward, Joe Fazio, said to me that day, "We made history."

Ken's book is a beautiful encapsulation of Ron's story. It sets the record straight and details the history of the Teamsters in the Carey era. There have been numerous attempts to smear Carey and to rewrite history. Those who once supported him turned their backs on him later. This book, with its detailed research and firsthand accounts by key players, is an important one for all who want to learn how to reform the labor movement.

It is unfortunate that some of those who stood by Ron like Bob Hauptman and Aaron Belk are no longer with us.

Sadly, those who betrayed Carey or didn't stand up for him contributed to his banishment from the labor movement. Instead of being celebrated for leading one of the most important strikes of the 1990s, he was ousted from the Teamsters.

Ten years after the strike, Professor Deepa Kumar wrote a book, *Outside the Box*, about the way the media covered the UPS strike and how the incredible organizing by the Teamsters was a turning point in how labor struggles were covered. Today, strikes are covered more sympathetically by the corporate media, but it was the UPS strike and the Teamsters contract campaign that was instrumental in creating this pro-labor framework. She interviewed Ron for her book and ran the full interview at the end of it.

At first, the Teamsters offered to write about her book in the magazine. When they saw that she had included the interview with Ron, they refused to mention the book or have anything to do with it. Ron didn't like this, and he decided to speak at the book launch event in Manhattan to show his support for her. This was the first time he had spoken about the strike. In attendance was Jim Reynolds, the only other 804 member to attend Carey's trial, and me. Ron introduced us to those in attendance and commented on the loyalty and support he had received from us both.

This was the last time we saw him alive. Ron Carey died about a year later, on December 11, 2008. I miss him every day. He was my friend. I am so glad Ken has decided to tell his story in this powerful book.

—TIM SYLVESTER
SEPTEMBER 2023

TIM SYLVESTER was a longtime friend of Ron Carey who worked under Ron as shop steward and Teamsters organizer.

Preface

People have asked me why I wanted to write this book. And why me? First, Ron Carey's story needs to be told. It's a remarkable story of a man who, through hard work and passion, rose from truck driver to president of the most powerful union in the country, a real-life David beating Goliath. Sometimes, leaders do tell the truth, do devote themselves to their members' cause, do put members first.

U.S. workers need a good, positive story about union leaders. In the mainstream media, there are way too many stories that are negative, focusing, often with condescension, on criminality and corruption. Labor in general gets limited coverage. Newspapers rarely have a labor "beat." Unions are now covered mainly in the business section. History seems to be that of the so-called great industrialists, the powerful, and the politicians, who have thousands of articles and books written about them. It is rare that a book about a fighter for the rank and file gets published, especially if the fighter is a union leader.

Back when I was a UPS driver, the name Ron Carey only came up when the old-timers spoke of him. I observed the blank stares on too many young faces at the mention of his name. I assumed that if you were a Teamster, you would have heard the name and been aware of who the man was and his legacy. I was wrong. I remember thinking our Local union and the International need to educate their members about their own history. It would be a pity if this man's achievements were forgotten.

Why me? Frankly, I took on this project because no one else was doing it. I asked around if any professional writer, someone like the labor reporter Ken Crowe, author of *Collision: How The Rank and File Took Back the Teamsters*, or someone from Teamsters for a Democratic Union (TDU), was writing a book on Ron. I was disappointed, but at the same time elated by the answer. No one was, but maybe I could. A spark was lit!

For a short time, I worked as an elected Business Agent (BA) in Local 804's (New York City) union hall. During my short tenure, I was told many amazing stories about Ron. It was like getting a weekly oral history lesson about Ron Carey, the Local, and the International told by several smart and experienced union men in the offices Ron had once occupied. Looking at the many photos on the walls, I pictured him sitting behind his desk talking on the phone to a UPS Division Manager, working long hours. I could almost visualize Ron walking into a BA's office and sitting on the couch and asking about what was going on in their buildings.

I felt a great yearning to tell that story. His spirit was in those offices, and it inspired me to write this book.

It is no exaggeration to say that writing this book has been a monumental task. It took me a long time to put together. Starting in early 2014, I began with an outline of what I wanted to say, the story I wanted to tell. After reading every book that even mentioned Ron Carey's name and countless newspaper articles and videos on Ron and his tenure, I decided I wanted Ron's family members, associates, rank-and-file drivers, and friends, the people who knew him best, to help me tell Ron's story. I then went about interviewing more than fifty people who knew or worked with Ron. Some were family, some were friends. Most were Ron's associates. There are many endnotes because I use their words, their phrases. I also spoke to several others who had important roles to play in Ron's life, but these were off-the-record and so cannot be named.

Under normal circumstances, this book would have been completed a long time ago. But working a full-time job with long hours was not conducive to writing a book quickly. I had to wait until I retired from UPS to find the time to finish the research and start writing.

Though retired, I worked part-time as a school bus driver. During my down time between shifts, I spent countless hours in three libraries in Suffolk County, those in Elwood, Deer Park, and Harborfields. I also spent many hours at New York University's Tamiment Library and Robert F. Wagner Labor Archives where I read all of Ken Crowe's files on Ron and the Teamsters. It seemed overwhelming. I also visited the U.S. District Court's (Southern District of New York) archives where I ordered and read the transcript of Ron's 2001 trial. Most records are sent off-site to a place in Missouri. It took a few days for Ron's records to arrive; it cost about $100 to have them delivered.

I requested and received a copy of Ron Carey's FBI File. It was mostly filled with old newspaper articles where Ron's name appeared. Before Ron and his team took over, Local 804 was mob infested. So the government had looked into his early years when he was in control of the Local. Later, when Ron ran for General President of the Teamsters, the government investigated his real estate holdings. On all accounts they found nothing. I detected an inherent anti-union bias on the part of the FBI. They seemed to assume that all Teamster leaders were corrupt. I guess they didn't bother to read Steven Brill's book, *The Teamsters*,[1] in which an entire chapter was devoted to the incorruptible president of Local 804, Ron Carey.

Ron Carey was different things to different people. Some, like Dennis Skelton, called him Mr. Carey. Others, like Tim Sylvester, called him Boss. Most just called him Ron or Ronnie. Over the years of putting this book together, I felt that I got to know Ron Carey. Well enough to call him Ron, even though my only encounter with him was at a New York Labor Day Parade in 1996. That is why when I write his name, I prefer to use just his informal first name, Ron.

I'm sure people will say, "You forgot this story" or "You got this particular thing wrong." It's part of what kept me from actually finishing the book for so long. I'm a stickler for accuracy. But some issues are just the nature of people's recollections. It's what they remember at the point when asked about a topic. For many, it's been around twenty-five years ago, for others fifty-five. I acknowledge that over time people's memories fail. They forget or remember falsely or differently. I've tried to portray the wonderful career of a man loved and admired by many people. I'm simply a chronicler, putting together a narrative that began before I came along. Though I never was honored to hang out with the man or even interview him for this project, I think I got it right.

Sadly, a few people didn't want to help me with this project; some of them were right in the middle of things. I can't speak for their intentions not to cooperate. A few spoke off the record. Maybe they just wanted to move on. Maybe they didn't know me or feel comfortable speaking to me. Maybe they were embarrassed in the role they played back then. I wish they had cooperated, because I wanted every voice heard. I wanted all insights included, whether by friend or foe. Alas.

In the end, I spoke with many people, ranging from Ron's immediate family to men and women he worked with and socialized with in the late '60s and '70s to people he campaigned with in 1990–91 to the people he surrounded himself with in Washington to his legal team in 2001. So many gave me their time and contributed all they could. They too believed that this book needed to be written. They might have been skeptical about my ability to make it happen, but in the end they became cheerleaders and, in a way, co-writers.

I wanted this book to be written mostly by the people who contributed, the people who knew Ron. I wanted the voices of the rank and file as well as the activist and the professional to be heard. My role was to craft a coherent narrative written by those voices. I hope I accomplished that, that I "got it right."

Before the story of Ron Carey begins, I want to share with you Ron Carey's speech from the 1991 Teamsters Convention, better known as "The Forgotten Teamster Speech":

Mr. Chairman, brothers, sisters of this Teamster union, guests and friends, thank you for the opportunity to address this convention as a nominee for the General Presidency of all of the Teamsters.

I ask you today to bear with me. I will not give a long speech. There is little that hasn't already been said and stated. Give me the courtesy to give my remarks that you would want me to give of my supporters and to grant to other speakers.

My journey to this day began more than a year and a half ago with the solid support of over 7,000 members of Local 804, the men and women in my local who have worked hard to bring me here today. To them and to all others who have joined me during the many and often lonely months of crisscrossing North America in an effort to bring to Teamsters a vision of what a trade union can be, what a trade union should be, I thank you from the bottom of my heart.

But my acceptance of this nomination is not an acceptance of victory. It is an acceptance of only the beginning of a victory, and not even for me. It is the beginning of a victory for the members of many local unions who know what it means and what can be won by having hard-working union officers, principal officers whose only concern is the interests of its members.

It is the beginning of victory for them, just as it is for our sister Teamsters, like Diana Kilmury, throughout North America, who total about 30% of our union's membership, but who have never had a representative on the General Executive Board, much less an elected at-large vice president.

And just as it is in the beginning of the victory for my other running mates on the Carey Slate, folks like Tom Sever of Jeannette, Pennsylvania, our candidate for secretary-treasurer; Mario Perrucci of Hillside, New Jersey; Sam Theodus of Cleveland,

Ohio; John Riojas if San Antonio, Texas; Jim Benson of Phoenix, Arizona—all candidates for Vice President-at-Large; and our Conference Vice President candidates: Tom Gilmartin, Jr. of South Windsor, Connecticut; Gene Giacumbo of Sea Bright, New Jersey, for the Eastern Conference; Bill Urman of St. Paul, Minnesota; Dennis Skelton of St. Louis, Missouri; and Leroy Ellis of Chicago Heights, Illinois, for the Central Conference.

Doug Mims of Atlanta, Georgia; and Aaron Belk of Walls, Mississippi, for the Southern Conference; and Tom Shay of Springfield, Oregon; and Ken Mee of San Jose, California, for the Western Conference.

But most important, today is the beginning of a victory for hundreds of thousands of Teamsters, men and women, part-timers, full-timers who have lost faith in their union, Teamsters who do not believe it can be reformed, that it can and will work and represent the concerns for their families, for their futures.

Yes, they're Teamsters, but too many are Teamsters in name only, and we all know that. You know them. They don't attend the meetings. They don't participate in the local union elections. They pay dues. They follow the rules, and each month they throw away their Teamster magazine which writes about faraway people and about faraway events which really have no meaning in the lives of our members.

They continue to believe in the promise of the labor movement, but no longer believe in the promise of the Teamster union.

They are forgotten Teamsters. Forgotten by the top leaders who travel about this nation and the world in private jets paid for with your dues money and whose huge multiple salaries let them take home more in a single month than some of our members who pay the dues will earn in a year.

Forgotten by leaders who will retire on pensions paying more in a single week than the pensions our Forgotten Teamsters will be paid in an entire month. The beginning of our victory for them is that we have an opportunity to make it possible to believe that

are no longer forgotten and that there is truth and meaning
ery word of solidarity, that together and always together we
can share each other's burdens and successes, that together and
only together we can shape our future to provide the lifetime of
dignity, fairness that working men and women deserve.

Our victory for the Forgotten Teamsters will be when they
can once again see the huge resources of this great union used to
reach out, to organize, to educate, to build the union it once was,
organizing the oppressed workers everywhere. It will be when we
restore the strength in the membership, the numbers, regain the
power that we once had, numbers in power which make it possible for us to provide these lifestyles for our members and not
the country club lifestyles that we see our leaders enjoying today.

It will be that day when the Forgotten Teamsters know that if
we promise to negotiate good contracts, good wages, good working conditions, good health care benefits, good pensions, and a
good secure future for Teamster families, then they'll know that
we deliver on our promises because we can and because we have.

Our victory for them will be on the day when they know there
is no more Marble Palace, no union official, no union abuse, no
union corruption beyond their power to correct, change, and
clean up, and no dream for a better tomorrow that we cannot
obtain.

It will be when the Forgotten Teamster no longer feels embar-
rassment of a government takeover of this once-proud union, a
takeover forced on the membership which has done absolutely
no wrong.

It will be when they know they are partners in a strong, united
union, a growing union, not declining, with strength, with commitment, with determination to mold government policy and
not be molded by government policy.

None of these things will be easy to achieve. We face powerful roadblocks from within our union and from without our
union. From within our union, by those who are so comfortable,
so arrogant in the unchallenged leadership positions, that they

no longer remember what it's like to be at a jobsite some freezing cold morning at 7 o'clock, or the humiliation of an unwarranted, unfair decision handed down by a kangaroo grievance system which was negotiated by this union.

And from without—I heard it. A motion was put on the floor today about excluding employers from our business and we had folks standing up there including folks... Shouldn't we include the membership, not the employers who all of us agree...

The enemy from without, multinational employers, runaway shops, the so-called free trade, scabs which now are politely and disgustingly called "replacement workers," and last, but not least, a union-busting government.

As Teamsters—and we all know it—I've been a Teamster for thirty-six years, a president of a Local for twenty-three. We've allowed ourselves to be out-gunned, to be out-thought, to be out-spent, and most of all, to be to be out-hustled by the enemies of labor on Capitol Hill, in the corporate board rooms and in the federal courtrooms. Our members are not asking for miracles. They don't expect miracles. But they have an absolute right to ask for hard work, honesty, accountability from their leaders. They have a right to know that their working conditions, their standard of living, will not decline; and they have a right to know and no longer be asked to accept weaker contracts with evaporating job security. They have a right to know that their union stands committed to one principle, that only honest men and women who work hard for members will have a place in this union.

They have a right to know that they will never again be Forgotten Teamsters, that they are only Teamsters, brothers and sisters, working men and women, part-timers, full-timers, who stand tall and say, "I'm a Teamster and I'm damn proud of it!" Thank you very much.[2]

CHAPTER 1

Son of a UPS Driver

Ronald Robert Carey was born on the East Side of Manhattan on March 22, 1936, to Joseph and Loretta Carey. A few years later, they moved across the East River to Queens. The Careys had six children, all boys: Carl, Ron, Allen, Bruce, Eric, and Joel. They all lived in a six-room "railroad flat" (an apartment with a series of rooms connecting to each other in a straight line) at 45-25 Davis Street in Long Island City, a neighborhood on the east coast of Queens, right up the block from where the subway entered a tunnel.[1]

It was a blue-collar neighborhood surrounded by numerous industrial factories and warehouses. Immigrants of Irish, Polish, and Italian descent together took the subway to work, Monday through Friday. The Careys were from Scottish, French, Irish, and possible American Indian stock.[2] They lived in a union neighborhood in a union city. Ron was always proud of that, as was his dad.

His father was a UPS driver, and he took his son to his first Local 804 meeting when Ron was very young. The Local is where he was introduced to unions and the idea of solidarity. He listened to the members' grievances and watched guys like his dad stand up and speak at the mic and be heard. It inspired him. "My father was my guiding light. He taught me the importance of family and to care about working people," Ron later recalled.[3]

While the rest of the Carey boys attended the local Queens high school, Ron's parents sent him across the river to Haaran High School in Manhattan. A vocational school, it was noted for programs that taught the workings of the internal combustion engine. (The original school building is now part of John Jay College and was used as the setting for the movie *Fame*.)

Those who knew Ron say he was a hard worker, committing himself to his studies. Ron was also a swimmer. According to Ron's wife, Barbara, he and his brothers were introduced to swimming by their father at the YMCA. "Ron loved to swim," Barbara said, "he won many medals in competition."[4]

Ron had a very close relationship with his brothers. "They spent most of their time together, whether they were on vacation or swimming," Barbara said. "Al, Ron, and Carl were the big swimmers," says Bruce Carey, Ron's younger brother. "They swam for Madison Square Boys Club in Kip's Bay on the East Side of Manhattan by the Third Avenue El train. There were always practices and meets. Their coach's name was Bill Fredericks. Carl was the stronger swimmer, but Ronnie was more a diver and swam the back stroke/breaststroke."[5]

Bruce remembers that "Ronnie spent most of his time with Al and Carl. They were very competitive. They argued at times, but not many fights. Lots of passing things down to younger brothers. You know, bikes, baseball gloves, clothing. Ronnie was the more subdued and studious of the three. He had good grades. Al and Carl were more wild."

Ron was different. He recognized early to appreciate hard work. "Ron saw how hard Daddy had to work bringing up six kids, educating us, clothing us. He even had to work on Christmas Day," Bruce added.[6]

Ron's dad worked out of the Bronx facility as a driver for United Parcel Service. His route was in the Harlem area of Manhattan;

it ranged from 116th Street to 125th Street between Park and Pleasant Avenues. Pat Pagnanella, later Ron's right-hand man in Local 804, described Joe Carey: "I go back to 1948 with his father, Joe. He was a very quiet man, a straight arrow."[7]

According to Bruce Carey, their father was a disciplinarian. "With Mom, it was usually, 'Wait till your father gets home.' Though she wouldn't let you go everywhere, anytime. You had to be home for dinner at a certain time. And if someone was smoking, she knew. Then we caught hell with Dad. He was pretty strict with us. He saw to it that we went to school, brushed our teeth. Dad got braces for Ronnie."[8]

Ron's childhood consisted of school, chores, sports, family, and friends. One of those friends was a Murphy, of the family that lived upstairs from the Careys. Through that friendship, he was introduced to Barbara Murphy, the girl upstairs. Barbara was one of thirteen children. She later said, "Our families got along very well. We knew each other for about a year before we started dating. Before that he was very friendly with my brothers. They used to tease and joke around." Ron eventually married her, his childhood sweetheart.

It seems Ron had a special gift. At a young age, he had "drive" and "perseverance" for what was best for people, recalled his daughter, Sandra. He was big on fairness, equality, and was always empathetic to the plight of others.

In 1953, when it came time to decide on what to do after high school, Ron decided to join the United States Marine Corps. He could have gone to St. John's University on a swimming scholarship, but instead he felt he needed to serve his country. Ron Carey was always a team player. Now he wanted to play on Team America. "He was not interested in college. Ronnie wanted to serve. He went into the Marines, which influenced me. I admired Ronnie. I also joined the Marines," said Bruce.[9]

He was stationed at Quantico, Virginia, and was part of the Special Services. He used his swimming skills to his advantage while in the Marines, getting assignments as a lifeguard and swimming instructor. He also worked in Motor Transportation. As a

Marine he learned discipline, hard work, and teamwork, reinforcing what he had already learned in his childhood.[10]

But he still had a girlfriend back home. "Shortly after we started dating, he left for the service. We corresponded through letters. He would come home to see me. We were always in contact with each other. We never stopped speaking to each other," said Barbara.[11] According to Bruce, when "Ronnie would come home on weekend furloughs, he usually brought home some friends from the base. One guy, Chick, I remember, was from California. The others were more local guys. He'd show them the town."[12]

Ron and Barbara were married at Quantico in a small ceremony in 1954. He also learned how to cook. By the time Ron left the Marines, he was a Private First Class, where he was expected to serve as a model for newly enlisted troops.

Ron realized that he couldn't support a family on Marine wages. After finishing his two- year enlistment, Ron returned home and looked for a solid job. The young couple found a nice little apartment in Greenpoint, Brooklyn. They were both eager to start a family. Ron Jr. was their first-born, on June 12, 1956, followed by Daniel on August 12, 1957. A year later, Ron and his father chipped in and bought a two-family house in Kew Gardens, Queens, for $15,500.

In the summer of 1953, Ron and his brother Allen started a construction business, Carey Brothers Construction. "They did mainly small household jobs like bathrooms and concrete work. Ronnie was always very handy and skillful like that," said Bruce.[13]

The business provided Ron and his family some income, but he realized that he needed regular work now that he had a family to support. Ron decided to follow his father and brother Al's example by taking a steady job as a driver at UPS. UPS was still small, but it was growing nationwide. While Ron had no intention of moving up the corporate ladder, he did foresee a long future with the company. He "saw his future with UPS because he thought he could go far."[14] His route was on Roosevelt Ave in Jackson Heights, Queens. "I was looking for a good job. I worked with my father on the UPS truck without management knowing. Teaching me the ropes. The working conditions were not good. They demeaned people," Ron Carey told Deepa Kumar in her book *Outside the Box*.[15]

According to Ken Crowe, author of *Collision: How the Rank and File Took Back the Teamsters*,[16] Ron, after hearing his father speak about UPS management over the years, "made an early decision not to move into management but to make the union into something better." Within two years he ran for and won the position of shop steward of his center in the Woodside Building off of Northern Boulevard.[17]

It wasn't long before Ron noticed the grievances and injustices at UPS. His fellow drivers were not getting the services that their union dues were paying for. The "go along to get along" attitude with management angered Ron. He recalled years later that "Many times I found myself biting my tongue, trying not to strike out at the manager. I felt like shouting 'Wait a minute! That's a human being you're talking to. My God! Give the guy a chance to answer, and get out of his face.'"[18]

The Teamsters union then was not responsive to the members. "These six-foot-two union characters would come down but they never really cared. The first place they went was into the office to talk to the manager and find out what his beef was, so they could straighten us out when they came outside. That's what we had to contend with," Ron recalled. "I hated it, I despised it. All my life I had fought for what was right. So I ran for shop steward." He continued:

At that point in time, the policy book talked about how employees were the most important product in their company, but that philosophy never trickled down to lower management. The result was daily frustration and anger in the way management dealt with the hourly employees, which was very difficult for me to deal with.

The steward I first ran against, in 1958, was a guy who didn't want to rock the boat. His response was "What are you complaining about? You're lucky to have a job."[19]

CHAPTER 2

The UPS Driver

R on was meant for the job of shop steward. He immediately began addressing his members' grievances and started to hear familiar phrases from the union hierarchy above him: "You're lucky to have a job," and "Sit down and shut up!" That only inspired Ron to fight even harder for his members. "As a shop steward, he was very aggressive," recalled Ken Spillane, who ran on Ron's original slate in 1967. "He made sure you went by the contract. He made sure you gave a 'fair day's work for a fair day's pay.' His Marine toughness really stood out. I too was a Marine. They called us the Queens North Marines."[1]

There was lots of corruption in the local: tough guy operators and characters like Louis Sunshine were actual Business Agents. Mike Moroney, former Department of Labor and Justice investigator, commented that Louis Sunshine was the brother-in-law of Harry "Pittsburgh Phil" Strauss, the right arm of Lepke Buchalter, the mobster who led Murder Inc. during the 1930s.[2]

According to journalist and lawyer Steven Brill, soon after becoming a shop steward, Ron "enrolled in college labor-relations courses at night school."[3] Over the years, Ron began to get a reputation. Management got alarmed. Recalling an earlier time, Ron told Crowe: "I remember one time standing outside the UPS building and we had a problem. A UPS manager had been kicking a rock. He said to me, 'I wish this was your fucking head.' I just ignored it. He said, 'You're nothing but trouble.'"[4]

On the home front, the Carey family was expanding. Their first daughter, Sandra, was born on August 14, 1959. On January 31, 1961, another baby, Barbara, was born, followed by the birth of Pamela on January 16, 1963.

THE LOCAL 804 CHARTER WAS first granted in 1937 under the jurisdiction of mostly UPS and Macy's delivery drivers, the Merchandise Delivery Drivers and Employees. By 1941, Local 804 had 3,325 members.[5] Ron inherited a local that had been through numerous strikes, work stoppages, and a great deal of corruption.

In 1949, Macy's worker and union officer Leonard Geiger ran and won the presidency of the local. The members were granted a new charter known as Delivery and Warehouse Workers. The *New York Times* described Geiger as a "virtual Czar in the local." In the 1950s, the United States Post Office decided to stop delivering packages weighing more than twenty pounds. This allowed UPS to expand and become a national company.[6] Local 804 grew to 10,000 members.

The original office of Local 804 was in Manhattan on Forty-Second Street. (Note that later in the book, Forty-Third Street is mentioned. This was a UPS building, not to be confused with the Local's actual building. UPS had numerous buildings throughout the Local. Today there are close to eighteen.) It subsequently moved to 24-01 Jackson Avenue, Long Island City, Queens. Changes were also made to the Charter. Shop stewards were now to be elected, and the top four officers in the Local now had terms of three years instead of one year.[7]

In 1957, Geiger negotiated a contract that gave the members "25 and out" pensions if one served twenty-five years or more and was over fifty-five years of age. It offered $141/month until the age of sixty-five when it dropped to $33/month. The $33/month plus Social Security brought it back up to $141/month.[8]

It was an Old Guard local. Geiger was very pro-Hoffa, this being James Hoffa, Sr. Geiger died of a heart attack in August 1957. Jack Mahoney was elected later that year as Local 804's president. Jimmy Hoffa also won election as International Brotherhood of Teamsters (IBT) president. This led to the AFL-CIO's expulsion of the Teamsters that same year for failing to make reforms and not removing Hoffa.[9] This occurred in the wake of congressional hearings into labor union corruption.

Meanwhile, in 1958, Local 804 had twenty wildcat strikes (strikes not sanctioned by union leadership) with their employers. Mahoney served only one term, after which his vice president, Thomas Simcox, was first elected president in 1960. During Simcox's tenure, Local 804 had numerous strikes.[10]

In 1962, UPS wanted to start hiring part-time workers to load and unload trucks on the evening shift.[11] With the contract expiring on March 31, negotiations continued for weeks as Simcox gave the company an extension. Both Local president Simcox and IBT General President Hoffa didn't want a strike.[12] (Jim Casey, the founder of UPS, retired as CEO in 1962. He remained on the Board of Directors until his death in 1983.)

Hoffa sent a representative of the national union's Eastern Conference to try to prevent a strike. But his representative was shouted down at a special union meeting of 1,500 angry Local 804 members. Days later, by a vote of 2,273 to 93, the members of Local 804 rejected UPS's final offer. At midnight, May 13, service was halted at UPS as 3,200 drivers and loaders struck.[13] "During that strike we were all working wherever we could. I worked for Canada Dry and Ron with Schaeffer Beer," remembered Ken Spillane.[14] The strike lasted six weeks. In the settlement, the members won a contract that raised wages totally by $6 to $8 a week along with better benefits.

In 1965, however, Simcox avoided a strike for the first time in twelve years. Possibly feeling the heat from being seriously challenged, Simcox agreed to a contract with UPS that increased pay to around $135 per week, improved health and pension contributions, as well as adding three paid sick days. However, this happened at a time when there were rival factions and a burgeoning rank-and-file movement. Even before this, Ron had become "concerned about the way things were being handled by the union." He felt someone needed to challenge the leadership. That someone was Ron himself. So, in 1961 he ran for Business Agent (BA). It was "something I had always dreamt about." But he lost. Two years later he ran for a Trustee spot and lost again.[15]

In late 1966, Ron decided to put together a well-organized campaign slate, the Security and Future slate, to run against Simcox and his executive board. "I ran as an independent," Ron said in an interview with labor reporter Ken Crowe. "I was always vocal, talking to others about grievances over production and working conditions. Our union officials didn't do shit!"[16]

But UPS management was content with the current Executive Board. They even tried to intervene in the local election to get Ron to back out. A few months before the election, management called Ron into the office. Ron suspected that something was not right. He placed a tape recorder in his shop steward brief case just in case.

He was right to be suspicious. His manager wanted him to resign "because we have evidence that you've been having an affair with another woman. And if you don't resign, we're going to have to turn that evidence over to your wife." Ron asked him to repeat what he had just said but louder and proceeded to show the manager the recorder. He stood up and then walked out. There was no resignation. As a matter of fact, that tape played well on the campaign trail.[17]

Pat Pagnanella ran on the original slate with Ron. Pat spoke Old School New Yorkese: when he said the word *term* it sounded like "toym." "I met Ron in 1966," recalled Pagnanella,

> he said he was gonna put together a slate for the '67 local election. I was surprised he called me. He says to me on the phone, "I heard about you from the steward, Sal Marina," in the Furniture Division. I came out of Furniture with Macy's. Ron asked, "Are

you interested, I wanna put you on my slate." But he wanted to meet me in person so we could talk. I was excited. I mean I heard of the guy. He was known all over the local even though he was only a shop steward.

All his men loved and admired him. He was a real fighter. Ron's name was always coming up. Guys saying, "Did you hear what that guy, that steward, in Queens is saying?" So we met up in a little restaurant, we talked for while about the things going on in the local and his plans. He officially asked, and I said Yes.[18]

They had to go up against an entrenched Old Guard incumbent who had become "remote and invisible." According to Ken Spillane, "Simcox was very impressive on the stage. He could give a good speech. But he never accomplished much. They were out of touch with the drivers. Almost his entire slate came out of tractor trailer. People said he was corrupt, but I think it was mostly incompetence."[19]

Simcox also had a reputation as a "big spender and playboy," spending Local funds, thousands of dollars, on "entertainment." "We took on the Old Guard Simcox," Pat Pagnanella said, with pride in his voice. "He was so corrupt. And he had girlfriends all over the place. He spent more time with his girls than on the job with the members. I ran as a Trustee. Sal Marina was to be on the slate, but his dues were missed [dues were not paid] so Ron later made him a BA."[20]

The Security and Future slate consisted of Ron Carey, John Long, Doc Dougherty, Gene Dugan, Pat Pagnanella, Ken Spillane, Lenny Morata, Maxie Moynihan, Tom O'Connor, and Sal Marina. They campaigned for over a year. "Ron had us campaigning over at Maspeth, then over to Melville at midnight then ending up at Forty-Third Street at 3 a.m.," remembered Pat.[21]

"The incumbents didn't know how to run an election campaign because no one ever ran against them!" recalled Ron. "They were out at bars, shaking hands, and associating with the old-boy's network. I held job-site meetings and spoke out against what was wrong with the union and what needed to be done. I told the members I had a plan as to how we get there. And I had the courage to go out there and say what had to be said." "We put together a strong slate with some courageous members and strategized the whole election. We campaigned day and night, and we won, the whole slate! And what we promised was that from then on, it was going to be all about the members!"[22]

They ran on better representation, ending "go along to get along," and a true 25-and-out pension at any age. When the ballots were counted that December 1967 they were declared the winners. A few weeks later, at the first general membership meeting, the entire slate took the oath of office. Ron and the other nine officers and business agents raised their right hands and recited the oath: "I solemnly swear to uphold the International Union Constitution and, more so, to uphold the Local 804 Constitution."

According to Ken Spillane, a member of the 1967 slate, "We took office in 1968, it was so strange. We were just truck drivers, now we were going up against these guys. The bosses. We looked to Ron for guidance. He had such a head on his shoulders. His concern was always for the members. We all tried to follow in his footsteps." [23]

Upon taking office, Ron and his Executive Board implemented reforms such as barring officers from putting their relatives on the payroll and insisting every officer and Business Agent visit their buildings. Each BA had one or two UPS or Macy's buildings to represent throughout the Local. There was one union hall and around twelve buildings to cover/visit/represent daily. Ron mandated that none of their drivers would EVER cross a picket line. He also banned union credit cards and required his board to take labor classes. He made sure that all meals had to come out of the officers' pockets and all travel had to be authorized beforehand and must be related to necessary union business.[24]

Ron's Executive Board made cuts to union officers' salaries, set up 24-hour representation so that if a part-timer working the overnight shift needed assistance, there would always be a member of

the Executive Board to have their back created educational programs for the shop stewards, set up retirement seminars and the
credit union.

They also moved Local 804's union hall from 24-01 Jackson
Avenue. "The place was a shithole," remarked Ron. "It really
looked like what you'd expect a Teamsters hall to look like in the
movies—a few chairs falling apart in a dark, dirty room." He found
a nicer place, on the ground floor across the street at 24-20 Jackson
Avenue, a small brick building, three stories high. It had a large
anteroom where three clerks and a secretary worked, a small conference room, and five offices.[25]

Ron had his own office, while the rest of the board shared
the others. He decorated his office with union bowling trophies
and numerous certificates from taking labor courses at night
school. He also had a poster of a wave breaking with the caption:
"Momentum. Once you are moving in the direction of your goals...
nothing can stop you."[26]

After Ron and his team took office in January 1968, International
General President Frank Fitzsimmons—who became interim president in March 1967 when James Hoffa was sentenced to a long
prison term for various forms of corruption—appointed former
Local 804 president Simcox to Joint Council 16 headed by Old
Guard boss Joe Trerotola. It was a not-so-subtle move to annoy the
new leader of Local 804 and keep a watchful eye and control over
him during negotiations with employers such as Macy's, Lord &
Taylor, Gimbels, and UPS. [27]

Fresh off the truck, Ron and his team went into negotiations
with UPS. Their contract expired March 31, 1968, so he didn't have
much time. He was eager to deliver on their campaign promises.
He wanted to push the 25-and-out pension as well as end the company's tactic of "piggyback runs," which was transporting trucks
on railroads instead of tractor trailers. UPS also wanted to hire
more student part-timers, who were not union members.

But when he got to the bargaining table, he found he also had
to deal with a hostile union hierarchy. Other Teamsters from Joint

Council 16 and the International were in the room to "help" him. They urged the "kid" to take a softer line with the company. The Teamster hierarchy never treated Ron with respect. They repeatedly referred to him as "the kid," "the tough kid," or the "naïve kid." It bothered Ron. He didn't want to be perceived as a sucker. "That's what I hate. Because I've never been a sucker. I can't tell you how much that gets to me," Ron told Brill. [28]

Ron asked them to leave the negotiations. He told them. "Take a walk, it's our contract not yours."[29] They didn't leave. But negotiations continued until Ron told his members to hit the picket lines on May 2. Joint Council 16's representative stormed out of the room, calling Ron "a psycho."[30]

The Old Guard was upset that Ron was pushing for a true 25-and-out pension regardless of age when retiring. They pressed Ron that no other Teamster plan had such a plan. They all had 30-year retirement clauses. The Old Guard leaders did not want to be outplayed by some naïve kid. Again, they urged Ron to settle, even telling him that Fitzsimmons also wanted it settled. But the strike continued. [31]

Two months into the strike, things started to get dirty. Someone had planted a fake news story in the New York *Daily News* claiming that an investigation, overseen by U.S. Attorney Robert Morgenthau, was going on into whether the strike against UPS was part of a "mob-dominated conspiracy."[32] The article alleged that Ron Carey was controlled by the mob, extending the strike so that mob-owned trucking companies could get the business that UPS was losing.[33] Ron told the press that he would cooperate with the probe. But the planted story worked. As a rebuke to Carey and his dissenting reformers, on July 5, Fitzsimmons ordered Local 804 to vote on UPS's latest weak offer. Their offer consisted of a $10 per week increase in wages in the first year of the contract, $6 per week in the second, and $6 per week in the final year.[34]

During the strike, Ron was awakened by a late-night phone call at his home. An anonymous voice warned him to "check his car before he started it in the morning." Ron was warned to "watch out for your family." It really "shook Ron up."[35] Ron's family members were not aware of such threats. According to Sandra Carey, Ron's daughter, "There were threats. We didn't know at the time what was going on. But we always had to be home by dark."[36]

Ron didn't have a choice. He put the offer up for a vote, telling members that it was the International's idea, not his. On Tuesday, July 9, the vote was taken. The members of Local 804 voted in person at the Marc Ballroom at 27 Union Square West at 16th Street, with voting taking place from 9 a.m. until 5 p.m. The offer was rejected overwhelmingly.[37]

The next day, UPS conceded. Local 804 had won a new contract that included the 25-and-out pension at any age as well as some work-rule language changes that benefited the members. They also agreed to a 55 cents an hour raise over the length of the three-year pact. The members went back to work happy, empowered, and glad they had voted for change in the previous election.[38]

Ron displayed a unique understanding of the needs of his members. He practiced what he preached. While mandating that his Business Agents visit their buildings in the local every day, Ron visited different buildings to meet with his members. He was up at 6 a.m. in order to see "the men" before they went out with the day's deliveries. He believed that "taking the pulse and looking for problems" was a big part of the job.[39]

Ron put together a strong and experienced legal team, hiring Cohen, Weiss for legal and arbitration cases. While his law firm was filled with elitist, liberal intellectual types, Ron was more of a working-class populist. He believed in "Americanism," voted for Richard Nixon in 1972,[40] and had an old-fashioned view of women. He regularly called the secretaries in the hall "the girls" and thought certain chores around the house were "reserved for the women."[41]

Yet, on July 28, 1970, Ron led a militant wildcat strike against UPS over the symbolic issue of flag pins/buttons. Brill described it: "Some of Carey's deliverers, heeding President Nixon's call to the 'Great Silent Majority' [42] began wearing lapel pins to show their support for the Vietnam War."[43]

It began with a limited strike out of the 43rd Street building in Manhattan after the company said that several drivers would not be allowed to work if they continued to wear the flag pins. The contract with UPS stipulated that only union buttons could be worn on the uniforms. Over time, they turned a blind eye when drivers started wearing the American flag pins. However, when many African American drivers began wearing "Black Power" buttons and then there appeared "Irish Power," "Italian Power," and other buttons with obscenities on them, customers started to complain, which made management object.[44]

UPS won an arbitration ruling that stated that no pins or buttons were to be worn on the uniforms.[45] Regardless, Ron ordered his men to stop working to protest the arbitrators' ruling. UPS went to court to have it stopped, and Judge Irving Ben Cooper held Local 804 in civil contempt for striking in defiance of an arbitration ruling. He placed a fine on Local 804 of $25,000 each day the strike continued. He also placed a penalty of $2,500 a day each on Ron Carey and John Long, Local 804's secretary-treasurer. The penalties started at 9:55 p.m. on July 28, a Thursday. [46]

The next day there was a rally at City Hall in Manhattan. Hundreds of Local 804 members rallied and marched peacefully to the federal courthouse in Foley Square. Ron climbed on top of the roof of a newsstand. Using a bullhorn, he told his members: "That's the American flag they're talking about. I spent three years in the Marines and I'm not going to give it up that easily." Ron said he was prepared to go to jail over this issue because "the local was not prepared to pay the fine." He went on: "We are striking for the American flag and the pride of a man in his country or his race. Never has it been a question of black or white but just of pride." He finished by noting that the police around the perimeter of the rally were even allowed to wear the flag.[47]

On August 3, the wildcat strike spread across the river. Some drivers in New Jersey's Local 177 walked off the job in sympathy with Local 804. UPS was beginning to fear it would spread to even more areas of the country.[48]

On Sunday, August 9, Local 804 held an emergency general membership meeting at 311 West 34th Street, the Manhattan Center. Ron told his members that he wanted a new arbitration hearing to settle questions about wearing other buttons on their uniforms. But Ron's own lawyers were telling him to throw in the towel. "Sam Cohen, of Cohen, Weiss, was the big boy at the law firm for us," recalled Pat Pagnanella. "He said, 'You can't keep this up. They have the right. It's in their rules that you can't wear anything on the uniform, but if you continue they are gonna sue you.'"[49]

Later that day, Day 11, the strike was over. The two sides agreed to allow all UPS employees to wear an American flag pin as well as their union pin on their uniforms. As part of the agreement, UPS agreed to vacate the original arbitration award and would allow the twenty drivers who were fired for wearing the flag pins to return to work. It was also agreed that Ron and his secretary-treasurer each had to pay a $500 fine out of their own pockets, and a new arbitrator, from the pool of arbitrators, would be appointed to investigate the issue of wearing other buttons, lockout pay, and UPS's claims for damages against Local 804.[50]

Ron Carey had again proved himself to be a real fighter for the members. But even when it wasn't about the members, Ron always seemed to do the right thing. In 1971, the members of Local 804 authorized their officers to give themselves salary increases matching the percentage that Ron had won for them in the new UPS contract. But Ron and his board never used that authority. They only made a few thousand dollars more annually than the average driver in the Local. Ron didn't want his officers and BAs to lose touch with the rank and file. [51]

After a few months on the job, Ron and his men experienced outright corruption by several employers. Ron commented, "No one had ever offered him a bribe straight out," in his first few years in office, though there had been several "overtures." [52] Pat Pagnanella recalled a story:

One day Ron tells me he wants to put me in charge of the Macy's negotiations. It had to be 1968 or '69. He said take Sal Marina with you. So, we're in negotiations at the table and the lawyer for Macy's wants to speak with me outside. He says, "When the previous guy was in charge we had an arrangement." He says, "You go on vacation a lot? I'll supply the airfare to Bermuda and some cash, all we ask is to not go heavy on us for a big raise." I said, "Go fuck yourself!"[53]

Another time, an employer negotiator told a Local 804 trustee that "Ron and I should be his guests for a Florida vacation 'if this contract gets settled quickly.'"[54] Greedy, underhanded employers assumed that Ron and his green crew would be susceptible to easy money under the table. But they soon realized that Ron was incorruptible.

Ron was straitlaced. He didn't want to have any appearance of corruption. Sam Begleiter, a shop steward at Macy's, remembered that while on a break in negotiations with the company, their lawyer acknowledged Ron's ongoing problems stemming from the flag pin strike and innocently offered Ron some assistance. Sam tells us, "Ron immediately told the shop stewards what the lawyer had said. He of course refused any help." To Ron Carey, trust was everything. [55]

In the summer of 1971, Ron experienced his first IBT Convention in Miami. He and his wife, Barbara, looked forward to attending. It was supposed to be his "planned emergence in national Teamsters affairs."[56] But it turned into a huge disappointment. When Ron had the opportunity to hit the mic during the convention to speak against a proposed dues increase, the Teamster hierarchy cut him off. He and Barbara left two days before the convention ended.

This was the convention in which acting IBT president Fitzsimmons was elected by the delegates as the official president. Fitzsimmons, aware of Hoffa's continued popularity with the rank and file yet comfortable in his new position as president, made a deal with President Nixon. Nixon would commute Hoffa's sentence—he was supposed to serve thirteen years—to time served in exchange for an IBT endorsement for Nixon's reelection in 1972. Fitzsimmons attained a condition stating that Hoffa could not participate in Teamster affairs until 1980. Upon release on December 23, 1971, Hoffa reneged on his part and vowed to run again for General President and to rid the union of the mob. The mob preferred the status quo. On July 30, 1975, Hoffa disappeared from a parking lot of a restaurant in Oakland County, Michigan, and was never seen alive again.[57]

In his personal life, Ron was able for a while to balance his time between his family and his members. He coached his children's softball team at Queen of Peace Roman Catholic Church. He was also elected vice president of the Queens' Boys Club, where he was very active. Moreover, Ron was active in the community as well. He was on the boards of the American Parkinson's Disease Association, the Central Labor Rehabilitation Council of Greater New York, the American Cancer Society, and the Teamsters Medical Centers of the New York area.[58]

Over the years, Ron maintained his popularity with his members. People rarely challenged him for reelection. But in 1973, three influential shop stewards, Billy Pritchard, Howard Redmond, and Buster Calura, ran as independents and challenged three of Ron's officers and trustees. Pritchard ran against John Long, Local 804's secretary-treasurer; Calura ran against Ken Spillane; and Howard Redmond ran against trustee Maxie Moynihan.

According to Ken Spillane, a trustee at the time, "Maxie was having some problems. We didn't back Maxie."[59] Redmond was the only insurgent to win. "Ron welcomed me in and gave me more responsibility than I expected. He let me make my own decisions and mistakes, and then helped me out of them," recalled Redmond. [60] Quietly, Ron was rooting for Pritchard to take out John Long. There was always tension between the two. Both their personalities and philosophies clashed. That tension kept brewing over the years. To the rank and file, all appeared fine. But it was mostly a marriage of convenience.

On May 10, 1974, Local 804 began contract talks with UPS. The contract expired June 30. A major issue this time was UPS's use of part-time sorters and loaders. The company wanted to open decentralized package sorting centers in the New York suburbs and staff them with part-time workers, who could sort the packages in just a few hours instead of a full eight-hour shift.[61] Pat Pagnanella remembered:

> Ron put me in charge of negotiations that year. He asked me what the next date with the company was because he wanted to attend that day. I told him August 28. Well, the next day we were having a board meeting so I knew something was up. At that board meeting, Ron says, "We are not getting anywhere with negotiations with the company and they're not gonna move, so we are gonna hit them. We're gonna be at negotiations and our stewards are gonna be pulling the men out of 43rd Street or Maspeth." No one on the board objected.[62]

It was now August 28, four months and two extensions later. "So, we are at negotiations and Ron says to management, 'Why don't you guys ask your managers in the buildings what's goin' on?' The lead negotiator, I forget his name, he gets on the phone and a few minutes later he's like, 'You son of a bitch!' It was on!"[63]

Pickets went up in Westchester, the Bronx, Manhattan, Brooklyn, Queens, and Long Island. But Ron heard that the company was sending supervisors and managers from the 43rd Street building in Manhattan and the Maspeth, Queens, buildings over to one of their New Jersey hubs in Secaucus. The workers at the Secaucus building were members of Local 177, which was run by the mobbed-up, Old Guard Provenzano brothers. It seemed the Local 177 Teamsters were helping UPS to break a Local 804 strike.[64]

Ron responded by sending pickets to the Secaucus building the next day, August 29. He was fuming because the New Jersey Teamsters had announced that they would not handle any of Local 804's work. Ron felt deceived. According to Pat Pagnanella, Ron said, "Let's go over there and break some balls, slow them down."

So, he sent over about twenty men to "take charge of the situation." That group of men included Ed "Doc" Dougherty, a trustee in Local 804 and a close friend of Ron's. Some of that crew attempted to block the trucks as they arrived at the building by forming a human wall.[65]

At around 9:15 that night, a UPS feeder driver out of Local 177, Ernest Henry of Hackensack, New Jersey, behind the wheel of a tractor-trailer, turned into the driveway at the Secaucus building. The truck sped up wildly, forcing the picketers to disperse as fast as they could. Doc Dougherty was the only one who wasn't able to move fast enough. He was "killed instantly as his head was crushed under one of the tires." No charges were ever brought against the driver.[66]

Pagnanella, who was also at the scene that night, believes it was just an accident: "The guy in the truck didn't really see him because it's so high up there in the cab. I think he panicked and just hit the gas, threw Doc and then drove over his body. It was horrible. The ambulance arrived. I went with Doc to the hospital. He passed away on the way to the hospital."[67]

Doc's death devastated Ron. But he had to be a leader. He announced the cancellation of a rally that was planned and withdrew the pickets from Secaucus after the Eastern Conference of Teamsters advised Local 804 to cease and desist picketing in New Jersey.

He drove out to Doc's house to tell his wife the news directly and to comfort her. Distraught, sleepless, and agitated, Ron then drove to the scene of the crime in Secaucus where he got into a shouting match with a Local 177 member. He pulled in front of a UPS tractor-trailer as it was about to enter the UPS driveway and he slammed on the breaks causing the truck to hit his car in the rear. "Police cars drove up from all sides. Ron was pushed around, then handcuffed and arrested for drunk driving. He had had one beer with a sandwich that night. He spent the rest of the night in jail crying for Doc Dougherty."[68]

No one from the International union attended Dougherty's

wake. An angry Ron called General President Fitzsimmons to ask his assistance to prevent New Jersey from continuing to undermine Local 804's strike. The hierarchy told him he would need positive proof that New Jersey locals were processing Local 804's work. Ron proceeded to obtain that proof. He personally sent packages to addresses that he already knew would cause them to go through New York first, and received them on the other end with labels proving they had gone through New Jersey.[69]

With the evidence in hand, Ron traveled to Washington for a meeting with Fitzsimmons, his Executive Secretary Walter Shea, and Sal Provenzano, who was a powerful official of New Jersey's Local 560. The Provenzano family controlled Local 560 for decades and were closely affiliated with organized crime.[70] At the meeting, Fitzsimmons stared out the window, while Provenzano denied it all. Ron suspected that once again Local 804 was out front in taking on an important issue, part-timers, and the International was slow to address it. They didn't like a young upstart showing them up. A federal mediator was called in. The strike continued.[71]

On Sunday, November 17, the striking Local 804 members, faced with a threat by UPS to cease operating in New York City if they did not end the strike and resume work by Wednesday, overwhelmingly rejected the company's latest offer. It was a "non-binding vote" taken at a General Membership meeting at the Manhattan Center on 34th Street called by Ron in order to keep his members informed of the latest offer and get their reaction. Some members reacted by actually tearing up the proposed contract into little pieces and tossing them in the air like confetti. Others stood on chairs and shouted epithets at the company.[72]

But on Tuesday night, with the help of federal mediator William Usery, the two sides reached an agreement. The company won its original goal to replace through attrition its full-time inside workers with part-timers in the decentralized small buildings it planned to open in the New York suburbs. Local 804 won a slowing down of the phasing out of the full-timers to a limit of 180 replacements a year. It also won raises, a "cost of living escalator" clause, and improved benefits. The next day, again at the Manhattan Center, 2,500 members overwhelmingly voted to approve the three-year agreement by voice vote. They were smiling and happy to be going back to work. At the meeting, Ron admitted that he was "not 100 percent satisfied with what we got. But it is much better than what was offered to us before—with unlimited attritions." The 87-day strike was finally over.[73]

Ron not only always put his members first, but he also did the right thing by his staff, the Business Agents and women in the office. In 1975 the country was still in the depths of a recession and many businesses were laying off workers. Hundreds of Local 804 members were subsequently furloughed along with their union dues. Ron decided that he and his fellow officers would cut their own salaries by $100 a week for the rest of the year to avoid reducing staff. His philosophy always embraced the common good.[74]

It was a struggle to balance making your family a priority and putting members first. Ron's wife, Barbara, recalled:

> He was always there for our family when we needed him. But I knew his members were very important to him, so at times we had to give him up. The most important thing for Ron was to be there for the members. They really came first. It was OK with me because they really looked up to him. He felt equally compassionate about them, and I never minded. I got used to it, like they were his own children. Sharing him was something I got used to. It was a way of life.
>
> Ron was mostly there for all the events that our children had. He spent a lot of time helping with their schoolwork. The kids, when they were young, never really knew what he really did. He never came home with work or things to do.[75]

"We lived on a block with many children," remembered Barbara, "so every Sunday they were all out there on the corner playing football or something with Ron, the only adult out there."[76]

"We always had a pool in the backyard," recalled Sandra Carey,

Ron's oldest daughter. "Dad loved to do laps in the pool. He wasn't home a lot but we made the best of his time home with us. Mom would be in charge, but I remember when we acted up her saying, 'Wait till your father gets home!' We were fearful of the consequences. We wouldn't see him until later in the night. On rainy weekends we'd play board games."[77]

Ron tried to separate his two lives. "I think he told Mom certain things about work and threats, but he basically kept her out of it. We as kids didn't know what was going on. Our parents made sure that we were home before dark."[78]

"Our lifestyles haven't changed a bit since Ron took office," Barbara said. "He's the big union leader, right? Even the mailman asks him to get his son a job, but he doesn't have any power like that. The only change in the last ten years is that Ron seems to keep looking more and more tense when he comes home at night." Ron's salary was only about $5,000 more than he made as a driver.[79]

His brother, Bruce Carey, added, "The labor movement inspired Ron. He had a good handle on what was happening and what to do. He did a lot of Dale Carnegie stuff for public speaking and things like that."[80]

With his family, Ron was a homebody. He enjoyed cooking for them on Sundays. "My dad was always busy, but Sunday was family day," recalled Sandra Carey. "We were brought up to go to church. We were religious. But before church, Dad made breakfast for seven: twelve eggs, sausage, and home fries. Remember, he was a chef in the Marines. He cooked the Sunday family meal, which might have been a meat, a potato, and a vegetable. We didn't have a lot of pasta or bread."[81]

Sundays also meant playing sports with his children, Sandra said. "After dinner was a football game with the family and some neighborhood kids, our friends. We'd play on the corner, girls and boys. My father would take on some of my girlfriends who were tough, to make it fair."[82]

Sandra remembers, "My dad was always doing some project. And he was very handy. I picture him in those blue shorts and maybe a yellow shirt working on our basement or helping a friend or neighbor on redoing their bathroom."[83] The Careys rarely took vacations in these years. The only place they went to escape was to Ron's father's New Jersey bungalow. Ron said, "Where else could I afford to go with five kids?" [84]

In 1976, after forty years with UPS, Ron's father, Joseph, finally retired. He "became fastidious" and Loretta, his wife, couldn't handle it. They separated, but remained close. His mom moved to a place about fifteen minutes away, while his father continued to live on the second floor of the Careys' two-family home in Kew Gardens. "My grandparents stayed married but didn't live together," remembered Sandra. "My grandfather always lived upstairs with us. Holidays, of course, we had to split it up: New Year's Eve, Christmas Day, Christmas Eve Mass. I sometimes saw my grandmother. She was a strong person. I think that's where my father got his motivation from. She was a fighter. He took after her."[85]

The 1970s for the Carey family were busy times. Barbara Carey took a job at Macy's to help make ends meet. Ron, of course, worked long hours. "We didn't see him until later at night. But we knew we had to share him with his members. I realized that later how much his members actually loved him," recalled Sandra.[86]

At one point, Ron smoked a lot. His brand was Lucky Strikes, the perfect brand name for a union leader whose favorite tactic was the wildcat strike! He more or less stopped when he turned fifty. He told his daughter that "he didn't want anything to take him over."[87]

He was a big reader. He loved to read the newspaper. Ron spent two years taking correspondence courses at Xavier Institute for Labor Management Relations and took Cornell Labor Management Relations courses for six months. "We would sit together and he'd talk about the techniques for remembering people's names and how important it was to look people in the eye," Sandra reflected.[88]

CHAPTER 3

The Leader

In the mid-1970s, the journalist Steven Brill spent several days following Ron Carey around in his daily routine in Local 804. He eventually gave Ron a full chapter in his 1978 book *The Teamsters*. He witnessed how in control Ron was in his Local; how the members loved and respected him; how straight and incorruptible he was.

During a visit at a UPS facility, Brill described Ron to his audience: "Although Carey's double-knit gray suit, white shirt and black tie didn't match, it didn't outdo the uniforms either. Carey looked like one of the deliverymen dressed up: which is what he was." He went on:

> Carey moved that way too. He didn't glad-hand his men or overdo it with a wide smile that would have intruded gratingly on their dull winter Monday morning. He gave each of them a subdued "Hello," a quiet nod, or a wink of recognition. He was one of them. The members addressed him as "Ron" or "Ronnie," never Mr. Carey. He listened to his members, took notes on small scraps of paper and promised them he or a Business Agent would get back to them or "I'll see what I can do."[1]

Ron never tried to sound any different from the way he always spoke. When he spoke about the members, it sounded like "membas." He regularly dropped the "*g*" on words like striking, negotiating, and fighting. He pronounced the word "none" like most people would pronounce the word "nun."

Laying out his methods, Ron said, "The key is using your time well. Even if you're locked in negotiations, you have to use the early morning to get around to some shops. Otherwise, the guys will think you're on the golf course or something, even if you were up until four in the morning before, negotiating for them."[2]

Over time, Ron got more frustrated with the International hierarchy. He didn't even attend the 1976 Teamsters Convention. Ron told Brill: "What is wrong with so many people in the Teamster leadership is that they see themselves as different once they get elected. They start wearing pinky rings and talking out of both sides of their mouths." He continued, "If they ever do visit a shop they stand off in a corner as if to say, 'I'm calling the shots here.' Well, I don't call the shots. I work for these guys. These drivers' dues pay my salary." He never forgot that.[3]

Furthermore, Ron felt disrespected by the occupants of the Marble Palace, the nickname union reformers gave to the Teamsters' Washington, D.C., headquarters. "The International thought I was some kind of joke, a fluke," Ron told Brill. "They didn't take me seriously."[4] But over the years, after getting reelected again and again and delivering strong, groundbreaking contracts, they began to take notice, then fear him, and finally despise him.

The hierarchy never mentioned Ron in its magazine, the *International Teamster*. Yet it never got to Ron. He continued to carry on and remain incorruptible and independent of the International. When General President Fitzsimmons invited all local leaders to Washington to denounce the media and refused to resign over corruption charges, Ron didn't attend. Instead, he sent two delegates.[5]

The Brill book made people take notice of Ron Carey. As Ken Crowe describes in his book *Collision*, the Brill book "depicted

Carey as a diamond in the dung heap of an International union rife with corruption. . . . The Carey chapter was a touchstone proving his reputation as an aggressive, honest union leader with a sterling character."[6]

Though he was straight and independent, Ron was not a very vocal critic of the International. He had "allowed a kind of tacit détente to set in between Local 804 and the International." Every five years, Local 804 would send its delegates to the Convention and its per capita dues to Washington, and in return the International would send strike benefits if Local 804 had a strike. He was unhappy but carefully and cautiously waged a cold war that never turned hot.[7]

Over the years Ron negotiated robust wage increases and expanded benefits and pension rights for his full-timers, with more days off and health care coverage for his part-timers. But in 1977, for the first time in decades, Local 804 settled a contract with UPS without a strike. It consisted of another $1.79 an hour for full-timers and $2.68 for part-timers, as well as other fringe benefits increased over the three years of the contract.[8] Furthermore, the old contract allowed for pensions of $475 a month only for those with twenty-five years of service and had reached age 55, then decreasing to $235 when Social Security payments kicked in at 65. The new contract provided $500 a month for life, with no reduction at 65.[9]

However, this contract included a major concession. By making the contract retroactive to 1976, it guaranteed that it would expire April 30, 1979, the same expiration date of the Eastern Conference contract. This meant that Ron was no longer able to negotiate exclusively with UPS. Instead, Local 804 would have to negotiate as one of the seventy-five locals in the fourteen states of the Eastern Conference. Though he had given up some autonomy, Local 804 was given the right to bargain for a supplement to the area agreement.[10]

Numerous people admit that Ron was outmaneuvered in the next round of negotiations in 1979. By agreeing to what appeared to be a generous settlement, "Local 804, from 1982 on, would fall under the national agreement. In one fell swoop, UPS had eliminated the aggressive Carey from the bargaining table."[11] That year, General President Fitzsimmons coaxed Local leaders like Ron and others to give away their bargaining rights by allowing almost two-dozen local supplements and riders to the National Master UPS contract on issues that weren't specifically covered by the national contract.[12] Going forward, independent locals like Local 804 that once bargained solely for their own members were now represented by the International. As a consolation, these locals attained some autonomy in negotiating specific issues that concerned their own locals.

In the 1982 National Contract, UPS was able to nationalize its move toward becoming a mostly part-time workforce. UPS eliminated the cost-of-living (COLA) pay increases and cut the starting pay for part-timers from $11 an hour to $8 an hour. All this came with the complicity of the Teamster hierarchy, who agreed to these changes and pushed for passage of the concessionary contracts. According to Rick Gilberg, Ron's then legal counsel, "There was a view that a national contract would give you more strength if you trust the people who are negotiating for you. There's a certain value to having a national contract: you won't get picked off if you are one of these small locals with less resources. It made sense, plus there were still the local supplements."[13]

Moreover, the International hierarchy led Ron to believe that he would be on the national negotiating committee in 1982. But that was just a lie to make Ron feel better about losing independence. For when it came time to start negotiating with UPS on the 1982 contract, Fitzsimmons appointed the entire contract negotiating committee and Ron Carey's name was nowhere to be found. The contract they agreed to was filled with concessions. That agitated Ron into actively campaigning against the national contract all over the country. Nevertheless, it passed.[14]

Once again in 1985, another weak, concessionary contract was agreed to by the International union. And once again, Ron was denied a place on the national negotiating committee. Although he campaigned nationally against it, it passed.

Ron waited. He bided his time. He did his job and fought the Battle of Review Avenue (Local 804 had bought a building at 34-21 Review Avenue in Long Island City). At times that battle got physical. For years Ron and his secretary-treasurer, John Long, had not gotten along. "Union politics had brought the two together, but they had come to despise one another," wrote Crowe.[15] They were different kinds of union leader. Ron was the regular guy who brought his own lunch to work and didn't wear expensive suits. John Long was more the old type of union leader: tough guy, glad-hander, who "fitted into the mold of the swaggering, tough Teamster out to make a deal wherever he could."[16]

There was bad blood going back to the early 1970s. For a while, there was a controversy over who would be the Principal Officer. In certain locals, the president was the Principal Officer whereas in others it was the secretary-treasurer. John Long, thinking that he should be the top guy, petitioned Joe Trerotola ("Joe T"), the leader of Joint Council 16. Joe T sided with Ron. Ron and Long had tolerated each other because they had to, but once you start fighting, the "ship breaks down."

That ship momentarily broke down one day when "the hulking Long and the smaller Carey slugged it out outside their union hall, with Carey coming out bloodied. They managed to coexist after that, but not happily."[17] Pat Pagnanella, who never liked Long, saw him as a thug like the "king of the hill." That is, he was a tough guy who fought his battles with his fists. He witnessed the fight. "Long comes charging down the stairs and without warning, he hits Ron and knocks him flying back."[18] Ken Spillane recalls the fight as well: "Yep, there was a little fisticuffs. Long came down to the front of the office, a couple of blows were thrown and then me and Doc jumped in and we got them separated."[19] According to Gilberg, Ron and Long "were always an odd couple. Ron was so dedicated to the members and handling grievances. John was sort of a back slapper, not a Carey kind of guy. Different style of union politics."[20]

The specific reason for the fight is still unclear, but Pat thinks it was over dues. "In those days, we had to go around to the members to collect the initiation dues. You said to the member, 'You got your 30 days in, you're in the union.' Long would deny members gave him the $50 dues—and pocket the money. It happened a few times. Ronnie would get pissed."[21]

Also in 1979, John Long conspired to get some shop stewards to join him to unseat Ron in a Local 804 palace coup. Long was upset because in 1976 Ron didn't attend the Teamsters Convention. He felt embarrassed and thought Ron was making the Local look bad. Long was close to the corrupt Teamster hierarchy. The coup failed because the shop stewards refused to go along. They were committed to Ron Carey.[22]

Another UPS contract year was 1987, and of course since UPS contracts were now bargained by the International, Ron Carey was not on the bargaining committee. This time the bargaining committee agreed to a contract offering less than 2 percent a year in base wage hikes. They tried to sell the deal by adding a $1,000 lump-sum payment, with $600 for part-timers.[23] Ron called the entire contract a "sellout" and traveled the country campaigning against it. A 53 percent majority of the members rejected the contract. Regardless, the new General President, Jackie Presser, imposed it on the 140,000 rank and file. He ruled that approval was automatic unless there was a two-thirds negative vote, which there was not.[24]

An angry Ron spoke with his lawyers, Rich Gilberg and Susan Davis, and filed a lawsuit in federal court against the "2/3s Rule." Though he wasn't looking for a strike, Ron did want to force the company back to the bargaining table. He personally took on Presser: "I have no idea why [they did this] other than they think they are above the law. Above what is right, above rules of this country that the majority rules!"[25]

Ron financed his organization, Teamsters for a Fair Contract, by asking UPSers around the country to contribute $20 each. He used that organization to fight the 2/3s Rule. A few months later, the

National Master Freight Agreement was rejected by 63.5 percent of voters, a drop less than the 2/3s required to defeat a contract. Once again, Presser imposed the contract on the 200,000 truck drivers and warehouse workers.[26]

That was the final straw. Now other Local officials nationwide joined Ron's crusade to end the undemocratic 2/3s Rule. Two powerful Chicago Teamsters, Gerry Zero and John McCormick, heard about a New York Teamster Local leader challenging the 2/3s rule. They sent Ron $20 to help cover some legal expenses. Fitzsimmons summoned his Chief Negotiator with UPS, Al Barlow, to meet with Ron to strike a deal: if Ron withdrew his lawsuit, the Teamsters would amend their constitution and provide majority rule. They also promised to put Ron on the UPS contract committee in 1990.[27]

On October 17, 1988, the General Executive Board officially approved the rule change.[28] After he won his case, Ron sent Zero and McCormick a check for $14 with a note that said: "Thanks, I didn't need it all." It was a striking gesture in a union notorious for officers who abused their expense accounts and had multiple salaries.

In sum, the Ron Carey years in Local 804 were exciting and scandal-free. And that is some accomplishment, given that that New York City unions were a stew of corruption and mob connections. The only thing close to a scandal was the relationship between John Long and Jesse Hyman.[29] John Long was Local 804's secretary-treasurer, and Jesse Hyman was the head of an investment group, Resource Capital, a dentist, and a mob associate. He "carried bags of money from Cleveland for distribution to mobsters in Buffalo, New York City, and all of New England. When Long hooked up with him, he was raising money for a loan-shark operation."[30]

In 1983, two FBI agents came into Local 804's offices at Review Avenue with a subpoena for all documents, correspondence, and records between Long and Hyman from 1980 to 1982.[31] Unbeknownst to all involved, Rudy Giuliani and the Southern

District of New York were investigating a loan-sharking ring in the New York City area that used union money, which involved Hyman.[32]

That investigation, which began in 1982, led to the convictions of eight people in April 1985, including Jesse Hyman and Melvin Cooper, Hyman's partner at Resource Capital. They were convicted of a loan-sharking operation run by organized crime figures. Hyman then cooperated with Giuliani's office.[33] But Vincent Rotondo, a member of the New Jersey–based De Cavalcante family and a member of Local 814 of the International Longshoremen's Association (ILA), was acquitted.

Hyman told Giuliani that around 1980 Rotondo arranged for a contractor, Ben Parness, to introduce Hyman to the secretary-treasurer of Local 804, John Long. Hyman told Long that he was a partner with Rotondo and that they had a sure bet investment for his union's funds. He also told him there would be a nice "finder's fee."[34] The scheme involved using union money to illegally lend to several businesses at interest rates of 2 to 4 percent a week over a two-year period. If they didn't pay, the mob henchmen would threaten them. Long would receive a 2 percent kickback on all funds invested.

Later, Long would introduce Hyman to another Teamster, John S. Mahoney, the secretary-treasurer of Local 808.[35] His Local consisted of around 1,500 workers on the Long Island Railroad and Metro-North Railroad. Mahoney also invested his Local's pension funds in several of Hyman's schemes.[36]

Long and Mahoney were indicted on December 14, 1987. It was a sealed indictment. The actual indictment was unsealed on January 13, 1988. Long was charged with receiving kickbacks in 1981 for arranging for Local 804 to invest $150,000 in a company called Penvest; aiding and abetting Mahoney's wrongdoing; assisting Emgee Pharmaceuticals and Bottom Sportswear to avoid unionization; obstructing justice; making false statements; and getting his wife, Olga, a no- show job with the maintenance contractor Parness, whom Long was extorting.[37]

About a month later, on January 4, 1988, Vincent Rotondo was murdered gangland style in Brooklyn. He was found with a bag of squid on his lap signifying that he had double-crossed the mob. Hence the expression, "sleep with the fishes."[38] When the indictments were unsealed and made public, Ron immediately acted to get rid of Long. "When I found out he had been involved with something, he had two choices. He could either retire, or we'd have to move to remove him," declared Ron.[39] Ron had no real power to fire Long; he was elected by the members. But he pressured him out. "That's the difference between Ron and the others," says Ken Paff, a founder of the Teamsters for a Democratic Union (TDU). "When an Old Guard officer gets indicted, they form a defense squad and say it's a government plot. With Ron, he goes up to the guy and says, 'Get out!'" Long decided to "retire."[40]

The trial, which began in late September and lasted twelve weeks, was held before U.S. District Judge David N. Edelstein. Giuliani offered Ron immunity to testify against Long. Ron's lawyer, Fred Hafetz, advised him to accept the immunity. Ron said at the time, "The government will not prosecute me unless I was lying."[41]

During the trial, it was revealed by Hyman and others how Long duped Ron into signing the checks. All union business required a signature from both the president and the secretary-treasurer. Hyman testified:

John [Long] explained to me that whenever he issued or arranged to issue a CD or do anything with those funds that he had, Ron Carey was the co-signature on the checks. So anything John had to do had to be scrutinized or passed by Ron Carey before he would sign it. . . . He said Ron would never go for it, that he would never buy it, and we couldn't do it that way.[42]

Even Long himself testified. He said, "I wrote the check and it was payable to an account number and I put it in front of Carey. He just thought we were moving money to a different union bank account for $100,000."[43] He basically told the jury that until the subpoena arrived in 1983, Ron had no reason to question the investment or to investigate the matter. Long admitted duping Ron into thinking he was signing basic deposits of all dues money into interest-bearing certificates of deposit.

On December 21, 1988, John F. Long and John S. Mahoney were found guilty of numerous charges of participating in and conspiring to participate in racketeering activities in violation of the Racketeer Influenced and Corrupt Organizations Act (RICO) and other crimes. They were sentenced on May 5, 1989. Long was sentenced to twelve years. They both appealed their cases, and in 1990 their convictions were reversed.[44] The Appeals Court stated that "there were multiple errors" by the judge, and "erroneous RICO pattern instructions prevented the jury from determining whether a pattern existed."[45]

All the while, Ron was leading wildcat strikes against UPS and their unjust firings of his members. On September 10, 1982, Local 804 members staged a walkout in the Maspeth facility. It began when a driver who had called in sick on the Friday before and the Tuesday after Labor Day weekend arrived back at work on Wednesday claiming he had a bad back. When management mandated that he be examined by a company doctor, the driver refused. Management then refused to let him work, which led all workers in the Local 804 building to walk out.[46]

By the next day, the entire Local was on strike. It caused many disruptions in service. UPS got a restraining order in Federal District Court in Brooklyn against Local 804 saying that it was violating the no-strike clause in its contract with the company.[47] Ron acknowledged that the walkout was illegal but stated, "UPS has violated the contract and so can we!" He said that this was only the spark rather than the reason for the walkout: "Thirty days ago we wrote the company a letter reminding them of their violations," which included reaching separate agreements with members, reducing salaries, and using supervisors to intimidate and harass members. It was settled the next day.[48]

Two weeks later, on August 25, Ron called a work stoppage in the Melville, Long Island, facility after a driver was suspended for "failing to report an accident." He told the press that there was "major harassment on the job." When the IBT told Ron to send the members back to work, Ron ignored them.[49]

Another time, a Maspeth Business Agent was talking to his members and a supervisor told him to "talk off UPS property." So the BA did just that and walked his members across the street threatening not to come back in.[50] Actions like these were a common occurrence in Local 804.

Tim Sylvester, who started in 1979 with UPS, recalls many work stoppages in the 1980s. "Most of the time it was just Maspeth. He'd pull us on a Thursday then we'd be back to work on Monday. It was kind of routine. The manager would say, 'Here's your paycheck, you're fired, see you Monday'!"[51] Pete Mastrandrea recalled, "We had wildcats all the time back then. They were usually on a Thursday. I would turn the corner and hope that Ron had us out on the street that day."[52]

"We had a certain routine," remembers Gilberg, Local 804's lawyer at the time, "where the UPS lawyers would try to track me down on a Friday and drag me down to court after Ron pulled a wildcat. I'd say 'OK, let me try to find a union officer.' Meanwhile, I knew no one's around. But usually things would be fixed by Monday. We'd agree to kick it into arbitration and then we mention settlement. There were lots of three- or four-day weekends. Things were very hostile."[53]

Ron's shop stewards saw him directly under fire in the trenches taking on UPS management. "Ron knew the contract and his rights. He never walked into a situation that he couldn't control," remembered Sylvester. "When he walked into the office with management, he was always emphatic. He was 'NO, you're not doing that!' One Christmas Eve, the members were told by the Division Manager that we all can go home early if we come in early in the morning and load our trucks.' Well, Ron comes in that morning and asks the drivers, 'What are you doing?' The driver said, 'They said we can start early.' Ron responded with, 'Is that so?' He then went to the DM and said, 'You're paying them overtime for start-ing early, right?' The DM said, 'No, it's Christmas Eve. We all just wanna get home early.' Ron said, 'No way!' He pulled us all out of our trucks immediately."[54] Ron was a no-nonsense type of leader.

According to one of Ron's Maspeth shop stewards, Pete Mastrandrea, "Ron was always there for me. If I had a 72 [the 72 hours from the time a member is made aware of disciplinary charges and the hearing of such charges] and someone was in trouble, Ron always answered his phone. He took our calls no matter where he was. What time of the day or night it was. He always knew the right thing to do. The right way to handle any situation. I always felt he had our backs, the shop stewards, the members."[55]

RON KNEW HOW TO KEEP UPS on its heels. UPS needed predict-ability and continuity. But with Ron in control, management never knew what he or his crew would do next. It kept the company in check. It made them think before taking hostile action against the members. It made his members feel safe and protected. And they admired him for that. If only they had similar leadership at the International level.

After Fitzsimmons died of lung cancer in May 1981, International VP Roy Williams succeeded him as General President. According to a Senate Permanent Subcommittee on Investigations report, Williams had deep ties to the mob. He was described as "an organized crime mole operating at senior levels of the Teamsters Union." [56] He had a long relationship with Nick Civella, the boss of the Kansas City mob. Civella helped Williams's career moving up the IBT hierarchy, and Williams put mob associates in important union positions that helped Civella.[57]

Regardless, the General Executive Board (GEB) unanimously elected Williams General President of the Teamsters. A week later, on May 22, the Justice Department indicted Williams and others on federal charges of conspiring to bribe U.S. Senator Howard Cannon to stop a trucking deregulation bill.[58]

On the opening day of the Teamsters convention on June 1,

1981, then U.S. President Ronald Reagan sent a videotaped message of thanks to "his friends" in the Teamsters.[59] Day one of the convention also included Williams getting officially elected to a five-year term as General President by the delegates to the convention.[60]

The only positive highlight of the 1981 convention was a proposal introduced to the delegates by Canadian Teamster troublemaker and Teamsters for a Democratic Union (TDU) member Diana Kilmury to create an Ethical Practices Committee to investigate corruption and organized crime in the union.[61] Of course, it was ridiculed and voted down.[62]

Ron again decided not to attend the convention that year. He told Ken Crowe: "I'm not really interested in going. I think it is all preplanned, preset. The results are pretty obvious." Ron, with maybe his mind on the future, continued, "I sure would love to have the opportunity to make some changes."[63] But Ron's secretary-treasurer, John Long, attended. He felt comfortable in the presence of the Old Guard IBT hierarchy. Pandering to the Teamster power structure, Long offered a motion at one point to continue a roll call that would have embarrassed a challenger to Williams, Pete Camarata. The convention ended with the corrupt leadership still intact.

But on December 15, 1982, Williams and Allen Dorfman, a mob-affiliated owner of an insurance agency, were convicted of bribery charges.[64] A month later, on January 20, 1983, Dorfman was murdered, gangland-style, to keep him from cooperating with the government.[65]

In April, after Williams, sixty-eight, was sentenced to fifty-five years in prison, he was offered a deal: If he resigned as president of the Teamsters he would remain free on bail pending the outcome of his appeals.[66] Williams accepted and began cooperating with the government. In 1987, Williams testified that "organized crime was filtered into the Teamsters Union a long time before I came here. I was controlled by Nick Civella," no doubt ever since Civella's associates threatened to kill his wife and children.[67]

At the Teamsters' next GEB meeting, Jackie Presser was picked to complete the remaining three years of Williams's term. After the meeting, Presser told reporters he "knew of no organized crime influences on the IBT." Days later, Angelo Lonardo, a Cleveland organized crime boss who was associated with Presser, who was convicted of dealing drugs, also decided to cooperate with the government. Presser was the only leader of a large U.S. labor union to endorse Reagan for reelection in 1984.[68] He also had a hatred for the TDU. Presser created a group of Teamster thugs called BLAST, the Brotherhood of Loyal Americans and Strong Teamsters, who harassed, threatened, and violently attacked all reformers, especially TDU members.[69]

The Labor Department started investigating Presser on allegations that he allowed "ghost employees" on the payroll of his Cleveland Local 507. But the Justice Department got the investigation squashed due to his role as an FBI informant.[70] Nevertheless, Presser was subpoenaed by the President's Commission on Organized Crime (PCOC); he showed up and repeatedly invoked the Fifth Amendment. Stephen Ryan, a deputy counsel of the PCOC, already had testimony from Roy Williams, who had decided to cooperate with the government in 1983.

In March 1986 the President's Commission published its report on the IBT's mob ties. The report said: "The leaders of the nation's largest union, the International Brotherhood of Teamsters (IBT), have been firmly under the influence of organized crime since the 1950s."[71]

The U.S. Attorney for the Southern District of New York, Rudy Giuliani, and his Assistant U.S. Attorney, Randy Mastro, started working on a RICO case against the Teamsters union.[72] They realized that "labor leaders could be held accountable not only for what they do but what they failed to do. Union leaders are considered fiduciaries under federal law, meaning that they have an obligation to protect the membership from organized crime, corruption, and the misuse of union funds."[73] As Ken Crowe wrote at the time, "Obviously, the Teamsters were incapable of reforming themselves, and the union's power was so enormous that the nation's top elected officials were as willing as the delegates to ignore the evidence of corruption."[74]

On May 9, 1986, the Senate Permanent Subcommittee on Investigations issued a report officially confirming the fact that Presser was an informant for the FBI. A week later a federal grand jury in Cleveland indicted Presser and other Teamster officers on embezzlement and racketeering charges.[75]

The following Monday, May 19, the 1986 Teamsters convention convened in Las Vegas. Presser and the Old Guard were not backing down. He opened the convention with fighting words against the TDU, the Department of Justice, and the Department of Labor. He compared it to how authoritarian governments treated unions in other countries.[76]

This GEB election year, Sam Theodus, the principal officer of Cleveland's Local 407, was the reform movement's sacrificial lamb. He ran on the TDU platform on the right to vote for the General Executive Board, salary caps for officers, and larger strike benefits. He lost, 1,729–24.[77] Ron Carey attended the convention but kept a low profile. On the final day, Presser told his cheering delegates, "We attended the funeral of TDU this week." Diana Kilmury, the TDU activist and firebrand, went to a mic with a rebuttal: "Mr. Presser, we never will die. Your funeral is premature!"[78] How right she was.

After some jurisdictional squabbling between the Washington Organized Crime Section and the Southern District of New York, Giuliani's team was awarded the still secret Teamster RICO case on August 19, 1987. Mastro immediately found an ally with AUD (Association for Union Democracy, led by Herman Benson) and TDU, which for years were fighting for reform and pushing for the DOJ to bring a civil RICO suit against the Teamsters and their mob buddies.

Rumors of a possible RICO lawsuit surfaced publicly. The TDU urged the Department of Justice to use democracy and the right to vote to reform the Teamsters instead of a court-appointed trustee.

Ken Paff pointed to the example of the United Mine Workers as a template. Their insurgents won rank-and-file secret ballot elections and oversight.[79]

Presser preemptively counterattacked, claiming that the government was trying to take over a trade union as they do in authoritarian countries. He launched an all-out lobbying campaign to prevent Giuliani from filing the RICO lawsuit. The General President pressured local executive boards to support him. He urged his "friends" in Congress and the White House to kill it. Presser even mended fences with the AFL-CIO and had the Teamsters rejoin the umbrella group in October.[80] He was trying to play the victim.

But on May 4, 1988, the terminally ill Presser took a leave of absence. His secretary-treasurer, Weldon Mathis, took over as acting president and continued the fight against the government.

Despite these efforts, on June 28, 1988, Giuliani and Mastro officially filed the 113-page civil RICO complaint, which supported the allegations against the IBT, its general executive board, one current and eighteen former GEB members, the La Cosa Nostra Commission, and twenty-six alleged LCN members and associates. They presented the complaint, *US vs. IBT*, as an organized crime case.[81] They immediately routed the complaint to Federal District Court Judge David Edelstein, the "government-friendly" judge who presided in the case against John Long and John Mahoney that Giuliani prosecuted. The lawyers for the Teamster hierarchy were not happy. They even tried to get him removed. The trial was set for March 14, 1989.[82]

Eleven days later, Presser died of a heart attack. A power struggle ensued in the GEB between interim president Mathis and International VP William ("Billy") McCarthy. After a long and contentious meeting, the GEB selected McCarthy in a 9-to-8 vote.[83]

Later that year, the IBT general counsel, James Grady, requested settlement talks on behalf of the Teamsters GEB to avoid a costly trial. On March 13, 1989, one day before the trial was supposed to start, the GEB agreed to a settlement with Mastro and the new

U.S. Attorney, Benito Romano, appointed after Giuliani resigned to run for mayor of NYC. That agreement was incorporated into a consent decree approved by Judge Edelstein.[84]

On May 31, 1989, Judge Edelstein named the three court-appointed officers who would oversee the terms of the agreement. He named Judge Frederick Lacey as the Independent Administrator, that is, the highest authority regarding all union activities. Lacey, the former U.S. District Judge in New Jersey, who "sat as the judge without a jury," spent fourteen years as a partner at the prestigious corporate law firm LeBoeuf, Lamb, Leiby and MacRae.[85]

Edelstein picked former Assistant U.S. Attorney in the Southern District of New York Charles Carberry to be the Investigations Officer, the "top cop on the Teamster beat" who was "investigator, grand jury, and prosecutor rolled up into one." [86] He chose Michael Holland, the former United Mine Workers' general counsel, to be the Election Officer who would oversee the upcoming election. The Teamsters were to cover all expenses for the oversight. Lacey charged $340 an hour, Carberry $250 an hour, and Holland $125 an hour.[87]

The Old Guard locals joined the "resistance" against the consent decree. However, in Local 804, Ron saw a golden opportunity. With much national positive notoriety from Steven Brill's book, *The Teamsters*, and traveling the country to speak against the national contracts and the 2/3s Rule, Ron understood this was his moment. The consent decree was to be his vehicle for reforming the Teamsters. He and Gilberg, his lawyer,[88] read through the consent decree with a fine-toothed comb.

Gilberg was not only the lawyer for Local 804, but he was also a huge fan of Ron's type of unionism. "Ron wasn't a radical but when it came to UPS and his members, he was a wildcatter," said Gilberg. "He didn't take any shit. He visited his buildings every morning and he never lost touch." It was just a feeling in his bones as a working-class guy that his members were getting a raw deal and that he could do something better. Gilberg described Ron as a meat-and-potatoes guy who had a "righteous anger about working people not being treated fairly or with respect. He saw UPS raking in huge profits and they were fighting over every nickel in wages and benefits and trying to make you work harder and harder. Ron saw things in a very straightforward way. It's what drove him."[89]

Moreover, Gilberg said, Ron Carey was the most genuine and honest leader he had ever encountered. "One day the Local won a huge appeal on a lawsuit that saved it hundreds of thousands of dollars," remembered Gilberg. "We went out to celebrate. Susan and I took him out to a nice place, a French restaurant. He was happy but he felt out of place. The bill came to a couple of hundred dollars. He's taking out all these small bills and counting them out. It never even entered his mind to have the union pay for it on the union credit card. That was just who Ron Carey was to the core."[90]

Susan Jennik of the Association for Union Democracy recalls that "Ron didn't care much about politics. He was just a local union leader who just focused on running his local and taking care of his members."[91] Ron was a cautious man, but he did believe in fate. He might not have been very political as so many have said, but he did have a philosophy. As it said on the poster he hung behind his desk, "MOMENTUM: Once you are moving in the direction of your goals . . . nothing can stop you." Philosophy: deliver for your members.

Ron and his lawyers saw a path to victory through a rank-and-file election supervised by the government. He understood how out of touch the Teamster hierarchy had become. According to Ken Spillane, Ron had kicked around the idea of possibly running for Joint Council or International Vice President. He told Gilberg: "I've got to do something." When Gilberg asked what position he would run for, Ron responded with "Why not go for the whole magilla?"—the General Presidency.[92] "Let's change this thing from the top!" Ron was all in![93]

After he decided to make a run at the General Presidency, Ron gathered the people around him he most trusted—Gilberg, Davis,

Pagnanella, Spillane, and Redmond—to put together a national campaign organization. It wasn't going to be easy. The first priority was raising money to travel and the second was hiring a campaign manager to run the operation.

As Gilberg recalls, this was going be a grassroots campaign, not your average modern political campaign with big-name campaign managers, pollsters, and public relations people. Ron wanted a campaign that was grassroots based. He was always skeptical of the liberal labor community and was "nervous about opening up to people that he wasn't familiar with."[94]

Ken Paff recalls how it all came about: "Right after the consent decree was signed, I set up a meeting with Carey for April or May. I'm coming to town to ask him to run for president. Not sure how this was gonna go. Turns out he's already thinking about it. So it went fine. We set up a big meeting at Susan Davis's law office in July [Davis worked for Local 804 at the law firm of Cohen, Weiss and Simon] with people I knew like Steve Early, Bob Master, myself, Ron, Gilberg."[95]

They needed to get a picture of what this would involve. They spoke about how this would totally change Ron's life. How demanding the campaign would be, constantly on the road in a national campaign. How much fundraising they'd have to do. They'd have to create an entirely new organizational structure.

The first person Gilberg and Davis came up with for campaign manager was Steve Early, who had some experience with reform movements in the United Mine Workers and the Steel Workers. He was now a union representative and organizer for the Communication Workers of America (CWA) in Boston.[96]

Early came to Queens to meet with Ron on June 13. There was a long discussion on tactics and strategy. Early recalled: "We all spoke about a lot of the challenges we faced; how Ron would juggle his local responsibilities and traveling the country; who would deal with the press; taking advantage of TDU and their preexisting network of activists." But Early could not accept the position as campaign manager. "At the time, I had two small kids; it wasn't a money thing I just couldn't," said Early. "I already had a job as a union rep; it would have been family-wise too much."[97]

A month later, Ron's brain trust of Paff, Gilberg, Davis, Master, and Early met again. Some big-name marketing and public relations firms were approached but were afraid to be associated with an insurgent. But the name Eddie Burke kept coming up. Burke, the Regional Director of the United Mine Workers, was at the time running the Pittston strike in Virginia. Burke had lots of experience in the union, politics, and its reform movement.

By the end of the summer, Ron was beginning to tell people he was close to making a decision about his run for the IBT presidency. At a Labor Day barbeque, Ron let it be known to people there that he was running. "We were all very excited and enthusiastic about the announcement," recalled Tim Sylvester, who was one of Ron's shop stewards and later became close friends with. "He told us he was officially announcing at our next General Membership meeting."[98]

On Sunday, September 17, Ron officially announced his candidacy to a packed union meeting at Washington Irving High School auditorium in Manhattan.[99] Pat Pagnanella noted, "There must have been more than 2,000 members at the announcement. Everyone was so excited. Ronnie, one of us, was running for the Presidency of the IBT!"[100]

Ron laid out why he was running in an interview with *Newsday*. He railed against all the corruption and how the bad publicity hurt the Teamsters' image when trying to organize more members. Ron was sick of the concessionary contracts claiming the leadership was "asleep behind the wheel" and in bed with management. Sounding like some radical, he exclaimed, "If a company makes money, we're entitled to some of it."[101]

With reform in mind, he said he wanted to sell off the Teamster jet planes and eliminate the multiple salaries that went mostly to the few at the top of the hierarchy. While Ron was making about $45,000 a year in 1989 as president of Local 804, Old Guard Teamster officials were raking in over $400,000 a year. "I don't think an official making that much can relate to a guy who drives a truck or even care about him," Ron said.[102] Recalling his record in Local 804, he vowed to always "Put Members First!"

Words like that even impressed left-wing labor writers like Stanley Aronowitz. He wrote that "Ron is extremely sincere. He is very intense and very smart with an impeccable record over the past 20 years. This is unprecedented."[103] In a city of corruption and mob connections, Ron was a "straitlaced leader."

CHAPTER 4

The Insurgent

A few weeks after his announcement that he was running for IBT president, Ron and his eldest son, Ron Jr., traveled to Camp Solidarity, Ed Burke's Virginia base for directing the Pittston strike. Ron was aware that the United Mine Workers were one of the few unions whose officers were directly elected by secret ballots cast by the rank and file. Ron met Burke, but the leader of the massive strike had a lot on his plate. They shook hands and had a few words. Ron was "impressed by what he saw, the solidarity. You know when you talk to somebody and the chemistry is right. I always believed the eyes are the mirrors of the soul. You look into somebody's eyes, you can pretty much tell where they are coming from." Ron had found a man he could trust.[1]

Soon after, Ken Paff arranged for Ron to come to Detroit to attend one of TDU's Steering Committee meetings at a hotel near the airport. "We asked him lots of questions. He did pretty well. At the TDU Convention in Pittsburgh a few weeks later, Carey came to give a rousing speech at the banquet dinner and then took questions from the rank and file. He went home but the next day we took a vote and there were only a few people who were cranky. They asked, 'Why don't we wait.' So I got up there at the mic and said, 'Sure, we can wait or sit it out.' By the end of the meeting 95 percent of rank-and-filers were for endorsing Ron. And that's what we did."[2]

Though Ron accepted TDU's endorsement, he decided to tread carefully. He never joined TDU and publicly kept his distance from the organization. He didn't want to be labeled the "TDU candidate," even though the Old Guard called him that, among other things. "He spoke at the TDU Convention. I was impressed," recalled Susan Jennik, an activist lawyer with AUD. "He was a good public speaker. And his members loved him. But he kept his distance from TDU because he wanted to stay independent, not bound to any group. Ron wasn't comfortable with that group, politically. He was more of a centrist."[3]

After a few tries, Ron finally got in touch with Burke by phone in late November. He told Burke that he "still needed a campaign manager," and he wanted Eddie to be his man. Burke told Ron that in theory he wanted to help but he was still deeply involved in the Pittston strike: "I hope you can appreciate that I can't give any consideration to leaving. My plate's full. I just can't consider anything else at the moment. Why don't you call me in the future."[4]

On January 4, 1990, Ron, unaware that the Pittston strike had been settled four days earlier, called Burke back. He once again reiterated how much he wanted Burke to lead his campaign. This time Burke agreed, but he wanted to come to New York and talk face to face with the candidate. They arranged for Burke to come to New York the following week.[5] Ron said he would pick him up at LaGuardia Airport in Queens.

"I told Ron what color sport coat I was wearing," said Burke. "He told me what kinda car he was driving [a GMC "Jimmy"]. I'm by the curb and Ron pulls up and calls my name. He reached across to shake my hand and I looked at his hand for a pinky ring. He caught me. He said, 'I don't wear 'em.' I said, 'Neither do I' and we laughed." To Burke, wearing a pinky ring meant you were a fat cat, a sell-out union boss. He called them "porkchoppers." "We talked the entire car ride. We bonded. I knew this guy was a different cat," added Burke.[6]

The first stop was Ron's office at 34-21 Review Avenue. Burke smiled when he saw the "Momentum" poster near Ron's modest desk. He got a tour of the health and welfare office upstairs, and Ron introduced him to the rest of his board. Their next stop was the offices of Cohen, Weiss and Simon in Manhattan. They discussed raising money, being an outsider, an insurgent, and the network of TDU. Burke felt comfortable. "The problem in the labor movement is that union people don't know how to be a boss. What impressed me was how he got all his officers to start their days on a worksite with the members," commented Burke. "That swept me off my feet. He had great chemistry with his staff and his members. He was very demanding, but it was always about his members." Burke practically said yes on the spot. "I had to go home and discuss it with my wife. She's had to put up with a lot of craziness over the years," he said. But he accepted the role as campaign manager and would begin on February 1.[7]

The race was on. "I have no doubt in my mind I will win this election," Carey said during an interview in the one-story beige brick headquarters of Teamsters Local 804; he had been its president for the last twenty-two years. "I have unlimited energy and deep convictions. If I can reach the members, I can win their support."[8]

On January 20, 1990, Ron had his first meeting and fundraiser with the rank and file. It was strategically held at the Lincoln Motor Inn in Richfield, Ohio. About 300 Teamsters showed up to hear what Ron had to say that day. It was the official launch of the Carey campaign. "Ron Carey came to the trucking crossroads of America," recalled Rich Devries, who attended the event. "Richfield is the intersection of routes 77, 71, 271, and 80. Ron Carey was already the topic of conversation with the UPS drivers. But to win the Teamsters, Carey had to come to Richfield. To win the Teamsters, Carey had to win freight." Freight was the core of the Teamsters and freight Teamsters vote disproportionally large. "Carey came to Richfield to have the freight members size him up. None of the local Teamster officials showed up. The only officer that was spotted was Sam Theodus, Local 407, from Cleveland."[9]

It wasn't the best organized meeting. Burke was not yet running the campaign. According to some, Ron's speech was not very stirring, but he did speak about ending the corruption and the multiple salaries, better pensions, and making the Teamsters more responsive to the rank and file. Paff thought the meeting went too long, that Ron should have spoken earlier in the day, and the pitch for money and volunteers was way too late. A well-oiled machine it was not.

Burke officially came on board February 1. His game plan emphasized hitting the Teamster worksites, shaking hands, handing out flyers, as well as having rallies and meetings wherever they could be organized. Ron was a natural campaigner. He loved talking to the members. Burke's advice to Ron was "You can't win on weekend meetings. You got to be out there with the people. The votes are at the plant gates and in the warehouses." Ron agreed.[10]

"For the first couple of months, it was just me and Ron going all over the country," Burke recalled. "Every Thursday, Friday, Saturday. Meetings with 10, 50, 100 members, hitting worksites, making calls to people to meet us at the airport or worksite or motel . . . we put about 150,000 miles on an old Dodge Diplomat." Then Ron would return home Sunday evening and be back at work at Local 804 Monday morning. For the next two years, Ron spent every day campaigning for votes all over the country or working as Local 804's president and dealing with UPS.[11]

Their first order of business was to hire Rick Blaylock. Rick had worked with Burke for the previous five years on the Pittston strike. He was the commandant of Camp Solidarity. According to Burke, "Rick caught the union bug. It was hard to go back to the old job; he liked organizing."[12] He was loved by all who met him.

Blaylock served as a campaign aide, but his main job was basically to be Ron's bodyguard, "to keep Ron alive!" He was over 6 feet and 300 pounds. He and Burke didn't really fear Ron being killed while campaigning, but they believed that was a possibility if he won. Blaylock, who is deceased, spoke with Ken Crowe a few years ago about protecting Ron on the campaign trail: "There were a few remarks. Nothing that sent fear through the air. If a real assassin did show up, I figured I'd take the first two but after that he'd be on his own."[13]

Ron had to raise money to pay Rick and set up a campaign headquarters in Charleston, West Virginia, as well as rent an office in Queens as Burke's base in New York. Rick also stayed in New York. Burke would travel to New York every three weeks to review the bills and meet with key people. They ran a mobile, shoestring campaign.

At first, it was a tough juggling act trying to recruit good, clean officers to the slate. "We got TDU involved because we wanted to win, but of course Ron never joined. He stayed independent. He walked that fine line. But he regretted not being able to get more folks like himself on board."[14]

In 1990, there weren't many officers willing to run with a Ron Carey. Some didn't like Ron. Some just thought he was a nut. Others said no out of fear of not having their calls returned from the IBT. Paff describes Ron's mindset on organizing the campaign and building a slate: "Carey was like 'how would we do this? TDU doesn't exactly attract officers.' He stayed away from the Teamster hierarchy. He didn't even go to Joint Council meetings. That's why I liked him." He remembers, "A great thing about Ron was that he knew what he knew. He knew how to run a local, but he was politically savvy. He was always willing to hire and listen to people in other fields and other unions and other political ideologies."[15]

ON APRIL 27, 1990, ELECTION OFFICER Holland issued the election rules governing the 1991 Teamster election. They required every local to hold individual, secret rank-and-file elections to choose delegates to the IBT convention in Orlando. At the convention, the delegates would vote in secret ballots to nominate the GEB candidates: the General President, secretary-treasurer, eleven regional vice presidents, five at-large vice presidents, and three non-voting trustees.[16]

To be nominated, a candidate needed to get the support of

at least 5 percent of the total delegates. These were all expected requirements. But one of the rules allowed candidates who collected the signatures of 2.5 percent of the eligible voters to be declared "accredited candidates." For an outsider like Ron, it meant his campaign was entitled to union membership lists and allowed advertising pages in the International's *Teamster Magazine*. Ron's campaign needed to get around 40,000 valid signatures by the end of the year. This was very doable.

However, another rule appeared quite problematic. Previously, Judge Edelstein had given Holland the power to supervise the elections. But now Holland seemed to be handing that authority back to the untrustworthy locals. Reform groups like AUD (Association for Union Democracy) and TDU were outraged. AUD's executive director, Susan Jennik, erupted, "How the hell can he think these local officers in the most corrupt union in the country would run a fair election? He's still letting the locals run the elections!"[17]

Herman Benson, the founder of AUD, agreed with Jennik's assessment. He added, "The whole point of the RICO suit is these guys are so infiltrated by racketeers that you can't depend on them to run a clean union." They would be in charge of printing the ballots, deciding who can run, running the election, and counting the ballots, and "Without tight supervision of the locals, Carey won't have a chance," concluded Benson.[18]

Jennik wrote up an amicus brief and sent it to Judge Edelstein focusing on the problems of relying on Teamster officials with all their baggage to run honest elections in their locals without proper supervision. Judge Edelstein had never overruled any of his three appointed officers. Even Lacey backed Holland's decision.

It seemed hopeless. But surprisingly, on July 10 the judge ordered Holland to run every aspect of the election process. "[Edelstein] thought I should run all of those elections not just supervise them," recalled Holland.[19] It was a huge win for the Carey campaign.

That summer, the Old Guard started "knifing each other." By the end of August, Billy McCarthy announced that he was not running for the presidency but would continue as Interim President until the 1991 IBT convention. The Old Guard was beginning to split into factions. The majority bloc candidate was led by R. V. Durham, leader of North Carolina Local 391. Durham was a truck driver who rose up through the IBT ranks. He served as President of Joint Council 9, was an International Vice President, and International Trustee, as well as the first Director of the Safety and Health Department. Durham picked Weldon Mathis, the current secretary-treasurer, to continue in that spot on his "Unity Team Slate."[20] Subsequently, Mathis decided to retire and bailed off the slate. Durham took Harold Leu, president of the Ohio Conference and protégé of Jackie Presser, as his running mate.[21] "It was a safe choice. . . . It's the same crowd. It's the Old Guard assembling their forces, wheeling and dealing," commented Ken Paff.[22]

Durham ran as a leader who had already produced positive results on important issues like trucker safety. He also called himself a "reformer" who supported direct rank-and-file elections. Even his opponents thought he was a decent guy. "I liked Durham on a personal level," added Gilberg. "He was a very decent human being. He was not part of the mob wing; he was a nice Southern guy."[23]

The smaller faction was led by the older Walter Shea, an International vice president and executive assistant to the General President. Shea had much experience in the hierarchy of the IBT. He highlighted his thirty years as a researcher, International organizer, executive assistant to four general presidents, and now also an International vice president. His biggest flaw was that he didn't have a political base in a specific local or joint council. Shea had never driven a truck, run a local, or negotiated a contract.[24] He also picked Local 705's secretary-treasurer, Dan Ligurotis, as his running mate, who later shot and killed his son in the basement of Local 705's union hall. Ligurotis was charged with second-degree murder but was later acquitted.[25]

By summer, Ron had been to thirty states, held fifty rallies, and visited hundreds of worksites. By the end of the year, he would hit forty-six states. Ron put Burke in charge of gathering the required signatures to achieve accreditation by the August 31 deadline.

Burke mailed out petitions to 112 volunteers, which soon grew to 600 rank-and-file volunteers. Within weeks they had collected 58,726 signatures, over twenty thousand more than was needed. This entitled Ron to advertise on a full page in the October issue of *Teamster Magazine*. A subsequent accreditation drive that fall allowed the Carey slate to three and a quarter pages in the February 1991 issue.[26]

On November 9, 1990, Ron announced his first four running mates. He managed to balance reformers and activists with the more traditional wing of the Teamsters. He asked Tom Sever, President of Local 30 in Jeannette, Pennsylvania, to run for the secretary-treasurer spot; Mario Perrucci, secretary-treasurer of New Jersey Local 177, for regional VP in the east; Doug Mims, vice president of Local 728 in Atlanta, to run for regional vice president in the Southern Conference; Diana Kilmury, a truck driver out of Local 1555 in Vancouver, Canada, and Chair of the TDU Steering Committee, for vice president-at-large. "We got rejected a lot," offered Burke. "Ron held off on the secretary-treasurer spot and got rejected by four other officers and then he found Tom Sever. Ron originally wanted Chuck Mack from the West Coast on his team. He was Old School, a [expletive]. . . . But that didn't pan out."[27]

The campaign started to get dirty. Ron was out there telling the members that the Old Guard had sold out the Teamsters by allowing the government into the union and "spending $12 million of our money trying to block the members from electing top national officers." One of Ron's ads had three pigs feeding at a trough filled with cash with a headline reading "THEY'RE FEASTING ON YOUR DUES!" Another showed Durham arm-in-arm with a prisoner and a mobster with the caption "TIRED OF 'UNITY' THAT DOES NOT INCLUDE YOU?"[28]

The other side hit back as well. In numerous ads in Teamster Election News, the Old Guard forces accused Ron of accepting sweetheart contracts in Local 804 (all lies), corruption, and mob affiliations (more lies). Durham attacked Ron, labeling him "Mr.

Immunity" for allegedly cutting a deal with the government to testify against John Long.

Later in the campaign, Durham went even dirtier, calling Ron a scab: "Ron Carey scabbed on a UPS strike." Durham's ads wrongly alleged that Ron scabbed in 1962 during a strike against UPS. They said Ron and others leased trucks for Bloomingdale's doing work that would have been done by UPS drivers. In fact, Ron hauled beer for a beer company during that strike.[29]

On the campaign trail, Ron relentlessly put forward his theme of change to the angry rank and file. He promised to "throw the bums out" and stop the corruption at every level of the Teamster hierarchy. Ron's message was taking hold. Ron inspired great enthusiasm for his campaign, and his charisma created an ever-growing army of dedicated volunteers. Rank-and-file dockworkers like Aaron Belk from Local 667 in Memphis was an early supporter. "I was for Ron before I even met him. Just knowing he was running against the other guys was enough for me," said Belk. "I was so impressed by the man. He was a small guy with a big voice who wanted to change the union for the better. I respected his honesty and integrity."[30]

Belk recalled that "Ron stayed at my house while campaigning in the area. He saw a big map on the wall with different colored pegs on the map. Ron asked what they meant. I told him the white pegs mean this guy will make fifty flyers at a worksite, the red ones mean 100 copies, etc. He smiled and said it's a great way to reach so many members. We hit all the barns [buildings or warehouses] in the South." He continued:

> Ron was relentless. He never seemed to eat. No breakfast. He'd just get up and go. We needed to eat. One time campaigning with Rick and Ron we stayed at a place called Grumpie's; we checked in at 3 a.m. Ron says, "We'll meet up here at 6 o'clock in the lobby." Rick's like "Then why the hell are we checking in for?" We all laughed. Then Ron says "Ok, let's just eat a quick breakfast and just take off." He was so full of energy.[31]

But he always had time for the members. "Campaigning in Memphis, at one of the shops, a mechanic from Roadway came out of his truck and shook Ron's hand. At the time, he was supporting RV. Ron told him 'RV would never shake your hand.' The mechanic said said, 'Well, when you're elected, you'll never come here and shake my hand either.'"[32]

Belk continued, "After Ron was elected, one day Ron says to me 'What are you doing today? Remember that guy who said I'd never come back to shake his hand?' I said yep. He said, 'Well, you come pick me up at the airport in Memphis and I'm gonna go and shake his hand.' And he did. It was one of the first things he did when he got to Washington."[33] Ron kept his promises.

Another dedicated volunteer was Dennis Skelton, a long-haul driver for Yellow Freight in St. Louis, a shop steward, and a TDU member. He first met Ron when Ron was speaking in Decatur, Illinois. He too was inspired by Ron's charisma. "He was saying things I've been thinking for years," recalled Skelton. "Afterward, I went up to him and said 'If you ever want to come to St. Louis, here's my name and number, you just call me and I'll pick you up from the airport.' I told him I'm not a goon [Skelton was 6'8" and 325 pounds], but I know my way around. I knew the people he'd be shaking hands with, and I knew he was a contact guy. He liked to look you in the eye and shake your hand. He called later and said, 'I'm thinking of coming to St. Louis. Does your offer stand?' That was it." Skelton continued:

I told Mr. Carey, I always called him Mr. Carey, give me a schedule and I'll give you the most bang for your buck. Any time you're within a 500-mile radius of here, you give me a 48-hour notice and I'll be there to pick you up. I had terminals on seven-minute visits, and I knew when shifts were starting, so we'd get there a few minutes before they started.

He was a natural with the members: "Hey, I'm Ron Carey. This union needs new blood and new ideas." Some at first were a bit suspicious of his New York accent with the whole legacy of the Teamsters being mobbed up on the East Coast. But once he started talking about how those guys gave away our union to the Feds with the consent decree to save their own asses, that was wrong because it affected every one of us and 99 percent had done nothing wrong! That was the ice breaker with guys like me.[34]

Steve MacDonald out of Local 490 in Northern California volunteered as well. He spent six weeks on his own dime on the campaign waking up at 3 or 4 a.m. to hit workplaces. He saw why the members were so attracted to Ron's message: "It was about 11 p.m. when we got to the motel. There were three of us and Ron. The flyers had to be tri-folded. Carey took five hundred and said you guys do the rest. When we woke up at 3 a.m., the entire batch of flyers were all folded. He was a real do-it-yourself kind of guy."[35] It was his own hard work and genuineness that made these members join his army of volunteers.

Burke and Blaylock took Ron to every major city and workplace where Teamsters labored. They went to indoor and outdoor events to meet their volunteers. Burke commented, "There was this chemistry between Ron and the members that showed if you work hard for the member, they will come. They will react. And they put their trust in him."[36]

Burke recalls, "Most of the traveling was Ron and Rick. We split up most of the time, me here, Ron with Rick there. Ron did a lot of the driving. It was a security thing. We seldom met at the airport. We coordinated and kept it real tight between Ron, Rick, and me for Ron's safety. 'Loose lips sink ships!'"[37]

They were on the road for over two years. Ron and his sidekick, whether Burke, Blaylock, Belk, Skelton, or others slept in motels and members' homes. They ate at countless Shoney's restaurants and drove about 110,000 miles in a borrowed Dodge Diplomat. It was a grueling campaign.

ON FEBRUARY 20, 1991, JAMES P. HOFFA, the son of former IBT

General President James R Hoffa (Hoffa, Jr., to distinguish the two), announced his candidacy for General President. He was working as an administrative aide to Larry Brennan, president of the Michigan Teamsters J C 43 and Detroit Local 337. He'd held this job for less than a year. A rank-and-file Teamster in Detroit challenged Hoffa's eligibility to run for the office. He cited an election rule that required candidates for International office to have been "employed at the craft within the jurisdiction of the candidate's local" for twenty-four consecutive months prior to the nomination.[38]

Election Officer Holland ruled Hoffa ineligible, "ruling that his work as an attorney in private practice couldn't be construed as being a working Teamster. . . . The job with Brennan didn't add up to the required twenty-four months of service."[39] Hoffa then endorsed Durham for General President.

While Durham and Shea raised funds from numerous local officers, Ron raised money by appealing to the rank and file. Numerous fundraisers were organized by Burke and Paff throughout the country in halls, barns, and members' backyards. Ron's own Local 804 poured tens of thousands of dollars into his campaign. He also was able to raise campaign funds from liberals in Hollywood such as Kris Kristofferson, Ed Asner, and others.[40] Ron's slate ran a $99 maximum campaign contribution from rank-and-filers. They needed to play by the rules because so many eyes were watching them. There was so much riding on Ron's campaign.[41]

Things were going according to plan until April when a little real life crept into campaigning. Ron's eighty-year-old father, Joseph, suffered a stroke. The Carey brothers and their mother, Loretta, had decided against using extraordinary measures for him.

Several days later, while Ron and Burke were at a candidates' forum in Naples, Florida, Ron received a message from his daughter to come home immediately. For almost three hours they drove across "Alligator Alley" to Miami Airport for a New York flight. This was generally a time before cell phones. At the airport Ron called home and was shocked to hear that his seventy-four-year-old mother had died in her sleep of a heart attack. Ron cried the entire flight back home.[42]

Ron kept the news to himself and a few close friends and family. They buried his mother on a Saturday morning, and that evening Ron and Barbara attended a fundraiser, the Doc Dougherty Scholarship Dinner Dance. "We were all there, about two hundred members and their spouses, and Ron came in with Barbara, and he made all the rounds and stayed awhile," remembered Tim Sylvester. "When they left, Joe Fazio came over to me and said Ron's mother had died."[43]

Several weeks later, Ron's father died. It happened when he was campaigning in Tennessee. Aaron Belk recalls, "Ron was staying at my house when his dad died. He was pacing around all night. Again, Ron was so dedicated to the campaign and his volunteers that he didn't want to disappoint; he still attended his rallies in Memphis and Nashville. Then he jumped on a flight back home to the funeral."[44]

Ron shared with Ken Crowe: "It did blow me out of the water, but they would have wanted me to carry on. My mom and dad were tough folks and very supportive of the campaign."[45] Ron's daughter Sandra remarked that her father was "very close to his mom. He got his strength from her. But he didn't have time to mourn. He was right back on the campaign trail."[46]

At times Ken Crowe met with Ron on the campaign trail. He saw the reactions on the members' faces when Ron mixed it up with the rank and file, face to face. It came easy to him because he never forgot where he came from: he was one of them. Ron was doing what the Pressers and the McCarthys never did. He was making physical contact with the members like Hoffa Sr. used to. And he was winning them over.

According to Rich Gilberg, on June 15, 1991, at a meeting at RV Durham's lawyer's office in Washington, DC, Durham offered Ron a VP spot on his slate. He told Ron, "We've got some things in common. I'd like you to get on board with me." He said he'd be a "one-term president anyway" and indicated that Ron would be his successor. Ron cut him off and said, "Thanks, but I have a different agenda and too many people are depending on me."[47] And that was that. Ken Paff confirmed the story. When RV offered Ron a spot for eastern VP on his slate Ron responded that he had a similar spot for RV. It was a short meeting.[48]

Filling out the rest of the slate was getting difficult, and it was getting close to convention time. Burke explained, "You had Ron breathing down my neck saying, 'I want you to talk to this guy or that guy,' all union officers. I'd call and they'd say, 'I'm honored but I've got a bad ankle or bad back.' Some fuckin' excuse. They just had no balls to say yes. I was just about out of bullshit! We needed to fill out the slate, balance it. It came down to the Convention."[49]

It seems some came to the IBT convention as delegates and left as slate members. Others came as slate members and backed out. Burke recalls how Eugene Bennett, who was originally slated to be a nominee for Eastern Conference VP on Ron's slate, was having second thoughts on the first night of the convention. "It's midnight and the phone rings. I say to him, 'Do you hear that noise? That's a machine making flyers with YOUR name on them! Now you're telling me you're gonna make a decision in the morning?' I said, 'No, it's now or never' and I hung up the phone. We stopped making copies and I called Ron's room."[50]

Ron told Burke that he'd get in touch with Bennett to discuss his issues. He told Burke to make up a second flyer without Bennett's name just in case. The staffers stayed up all night to complete both jobs. By the morning of the nominations, Bennett had dropped out. Ron ran with only two Eastern Conference candidates instead of three.[51]

"Giamcumbo and Aaron were the last to be asked," recalled Skelton. "Burke asked me if I'd be interested in running for VP. I said I never held office before. He said, 'That's not what I said, I said would you be interested in being on the Ron Carey slate.' I told him if Mr. Carey thinks I'm worthy, I'll run. Burke said "I'm on the short list, there's three of ya.' OK, days later I'm out there campaigning, somewhere in Nebraska, in a hotel room. The phone rings. 'Dennis, it's Ron Carey. Welcome aboard!' I was so honored I practically levitated off the bed."[52]

Both Ron and Shea chose not to run any candidates from Canada because the two candidates running on Durham's slate, Charles Thibault and Louis Lacroix, were very popular. "We decided we weren't gonna win in Canada, so we didn't run any Canadian candidates. Kilmury was At-Large and Mims and Shea from Oregon were both TDU guys. Gilmartin from Connecticut. Burke chose some. We chose some. Some at the last minute like Ken Mee and Aaron Belk," added Ken Paff.[53]

On Monday, June 24, the International Brotherhood of Teamsters Convention opened: 1,936 delegates, 1,030 alternate delegates from 615 locals,[54] along with friends, family members, officers, and sergeants-at-arms descended on the Walt Disney Dolphin Hotel and Convention Center in Orlando, Florida.[55] Ken Crowe called it "a theater of democracy in which the central players gathered to cross the threshold from the secretive, authoritarian politics of the old oligarchy to the uncertainty of the secret ballot."[56]

It was all happening under the watchful eye of Michael Holland, the elections officer. He was a constant presence at the Convention: "I was on the podium the entire time. I organized all parts of it that pertained to the CD. We also had about thirty staff people there in Orlando as well as two assistant DAs."[57]

According to the consent decree, the Teamsters were required to amend their constitution to include the provisions for the rank-and-file elections and disciplinary components. "If there were any disputes between the constitutional committees and the government, we had a hook-up with Judge Edelstein by phone and he'd make a ruling. It happened at least once."[58]

Ron's main goal was to get formally nominated, even though Burke had assured him he had enough delegates coming in. His other aim was to help pass reform amendments to the constitution like a salary cap on union executives' pay, a raise in strike pay, and fighting Durham and Shea's attempts to water down any consent decree reforms[59]for rank-and-file elections, the removal of criminal elements, and the creation of a three-person oversight board.

The convention opened with outgoing General President Billy McCarthy getting loudly booed by the large audience. He responded, "I don't know why the hell you boo. I'm getting out anyway!" Which received many laughs. The first order of business was the consent decree amendments. There was a motion to reject the consent decree amendments by Durham's vice president candidate Chuck Mack from California. There was some pushback from reform candidates and delegates but to no avail. As foreseen, a large majority of the delegates voted to reject the reform amendments. But it was all for show. Edelstein's decision and nearby presence demonstrated that the rejection by the delegates had no legal standing.

The second day of the convention mostly dealt with nominations of the candidates for vice presidents. Each candidate was nominated and seconded. Each was greeted with boos and applause. Later that day, the delegates voted via high-speed, hi-tech voting machines implemented by Holland. This was a first for Teamsters. All the candidates of the three slates received enough votes to be certified for the December election. Durham's candidates won 47 percent of the vote, Shea's won 34 percent, and Ron's VPs won 15 percent. [60]

On the third day, the issue of multiple salaries and salary caps arose. Ron supported an amendment banning multiple salaries altogether and limiting the General President to $150,000 a year. What passed was a version limiting the salary to $225,000 and the secretary-treasurer salary to $200,000, with a provision that neither could accept additional Teamster salaries. Later, Durham orchestrated an amendment to return to the Old Guard system of automatically making the Local officers delegates to the convention in order to save money.[61]

The fourth day focused on nominations for General President. Holland allowed for five minutes for the nominating speech followed by two minutes for a second, and then a quick acceptance by the candidates followed by a ten-minute demonstration by their supporters. After Ron's acceptance, his fellow slate members hoisted him up on their shoulders and carried him around the convention room chanting "Carey! Carey! Carey!" When they put him down, "Ron walked to the back of the convention room where we all were, the supporters, the delegates, the family, and friends. He shook everyone's hand. That was pure Ron Carey!" remembered Tim Sylvester, who wasn't a delegate but attended on his own dime.[62]

Ron's supporters were wearing neon-green campaign shirts. Burke remarked, "You should have seen it: 500 neon-shirted supporters strategically placed in the audience. It looked like we owned the fucking place!" But in the delegate votes for General President, Durham received 1,001 votes (53 percent), Shea received 574 votes (30 percent), and Ron received 289 votes (15 percent), a bit more then Burke had predicted.[63]

Next on the agenda was a vote on strike pay. A virtual bidding war began. It jumped from the current $55 a week to $100 a week. Another proposal from the mic upped it to $150 a week and then another to $200. It seemed the Carey forces and the Shea forces were on board for the $200-a-week strike pay. Only Durham refused to stand for the higher benefit.[64] They also voted to grant the rank and file's right to approve all local supplements to national contracts.

The final day of the convention began with another TDU-backed amendment for the International to sell all airplanes. Judge Lacey's report "revealed that the aircraft, a Gulfstream III and a Gulfstream II, serving the General President and the secretary-treasurer, were purchased for about $19 million. The costs of staffing, operating, and storing them amounted to over $3.8 million, from January 1, 1989, through December 31, 1990." It passed easily. In the final hours of the convention, each candidate for General President gave their acceptance speeches. "Shea, an experienced and effective speaker, offered a vision of organizing the unorganized, working to make life better not only for Teamsters but all Americans."[65] He shared the stage and his time with several members of his slate.

Durham gave a fiery speech focusing on his achievements and how his administration would make things better for the union. He did not invite any of his running mates on the stage with him. Ron gave his "Forgotten Teamster" speech: "Today is the beginning of a victory for hundreds of thousands of Teamsters, men and women, part-timers, full-timers, who've lost faith in their union. . . . They are the Forgotten Teamsters, forgotten by the top leaders who travel about this nation and the world in their private jets paid for with your dues money."[66]

BEFORE LONG, RON WAS BACK on the campaign trail. He understood that he would not win the race for delegates at the convention. He knew that he would win the election at the gates, on the campaign trail, with the rank and file. He commented, "This sleeping giant is now becoming awake."[67]

Ken Crowe recalled a moment on the campaign trail when they felt they were going to win the election:

> This was a happier time for Carey. Truck drivers were sounding their horns when they saw him campaigning. Rank and filers were reacting to him at plant gates with a gratifying fervor. At the wheel of his GMC "Jimmy" en route to Boston in mid-August, Carey roused Eddie Burke out of the torpor of a long ride on a summer afternoon by suddenly saying: "I think we're going to win."[68]

Burke replied that he too felt good but scared. He reminded Ron not to "spread that around" because he wanted to keep everybody working hard on the campaign. All three candidates were invited to a lobster and steak bake in Boston. But only Ron and John Morris showed up. They were greeted by a crowd of about 650 Teamsters and their families. Ron received a rock star welcome. The crowd surged toward him as he made his way around the tent.

Morris commented later, "And then Ron Carey comes walking in to the fish fry like Frank Sinatra, stylishly late." To which Burke then laughingly responded, "We weren't late. We was lost!"[69]

The Durham campaign was getting nervous and hitting back with lies. Durham attacked Ron in the September issue of *Teamster* magazine, labeling him "Mr. Immunity" for allegedly cutting a deal with the government to testify against John Long. Ron's campaign responded by flatly calling Durham out for blatant lies.

In the October issue, Burke put out an ad with a Photoshopped picture of Durham arm in arm with gangsters. The Durham campaign hit back in that issue by calling Ron a "scab." He accused Ron of scabbing during the 1962 Local 804 strike against Bloomingdale's. Ron retorted that it never happened. He had proof that he was actually hauling beer for Rheingold Beer Distributers. Numerous people have confirmed Ron's story. Burke had advised Ron to "take a shot at him. Hit 'm, punch 'm."[70]

"Carey's anger boiled over at a candidates' forum at a Western Conference meeting in Palm Springs, California," according to Ken Crowe. "Durham came over to shake Carey's hand. 'How can I shake your hand? You're a bum. You called me a scab!' Ron said."[71] When Durham insisted it was true, Ron disclosed the story of Durham asking Ron to be on his slate right before the convention. The audience booed. Then it was Durham's turn to call Ron a liar. On October 23, Ron filed a $15 million libel suit against Durham for defamation over the bogus scab charge in New York State Supreme Court. Regardless, Durham kept pushing the scab issue against Ron on the campaign trail and the next *Teamster* magazine.

Ron was of, by, and for the members. "This is what this is all about. It's being out there with the members," he once stated. "You'll never serve the members sitting in an office. I see a union as a mechanism to help people."[72] Ken Spillane explained: "He believes in a hard day's work for an honest dollar."[73]

Ron ran to clean up the Teamsters and make it stronger. He believed that if members were more involved and educated, it would better serve their own interests. To Ron, that was real power. Making the members feel proud again in their union was key. He constantly would make it a point to say it's "our" union not "the" union.

Election Officer Holland chose mail balloting for the general election because it increased voter participation from 19 percent to 33 percent. On Tuesday, November 12, 1991, Holland's staff began mailing out 1.56 million ballots to the membership. It was the largest mail ballot election in Teamster history.

The members had to fill in and complete the equal ("=") signs. (They had to fill in or color in between the two lines. No x marks or check marks were allowed.) If they put an "X" or a check mark, the machine would reject it. It would then go to a "re-mark station" with observers around to determine the intent of the voter. When the intention of the voter was determined, the ballot was then re-marked in front of the observers and put back into the count.[74]

The ballots had to be received no later than noon on December 10. As the ballots arrived in Washington, they were stored in a secure room protected by security guards. The security staff were laid-off and vetted union members.[75] There were pickups at the U.S. Post Office twice a day. The ballots were stored in a huge, secured room, open to observers (secure from one side tampering with ballots), with baskets sorted by union local. Mike Holland said, "You could tell which Locals were voting. Then you were able to figure out who was turning out."[76] After each Local was counted, a tally sheet was printed. Each campaign got a copy.[77]

Ken Crowe observed the process and offered his account:

The last mail pickup by Election Officer Michael Holland's staff from the Capitol Heights Post Office was at noon on Tuesday, December 10. The ballots were carried to the eleventh floor of an office building [the Bender Building]. . . . There the final sorting, alphabetizing, and breakdown into locals was taking place. This had been going on for weeks, and the final tally of ballots cast when the counting began at 4:00 PM that day was 424,392. Only 28 percent of the Teamsters had voted![78]

After throwing out ballots that were voided due to voter error and numerous challenged ballots, 396,172 eligible Teamsters had actually voted.[79] As each Local's vote was counted, the results would be announced to the candidate's campaigns.

Things were looking good for the Carey campaign. By 8:30 that evening, twenty-three Locals had been counted: Ron had around 52 percent, Durham 30 percent, and Shea 18 percent. Three hours later, with sixty locals counted Ron had 51 percent, Durham 38 percent, and Shea 11 percent. Ed Burke recalls that moment: "That first day was all pins and needles. We'd know by the end of that day either how bad we were gonna lose by or win by. But by the second day we saw the trend. We were winning in places they should be wiping us out or at least close."[80] Even in Durham's own local, Ron received 33 percent of the vote. Ron won Local 804 with almost 98 percent of the vote.

On Wednesday night, Ron arrived in Washington by train in a celebratory mood. Friends joked that he took the subway to the hotel instead of paying for a taxi. There he enjoyed a few beers in the bar with several of his close friends and associates. The election results were still rolling in, but everyone knew that Ron and his slate had won. Ron declared victory and addressed reporters at the National Press Club on Thursday afternoon:

> I want to welcome all of you to a new Teamsters union. The union that's been won back by its members. The union that's going to work for its members. A union that will not be tolerating corruption. . . . What our members have said today is good-bye to the Mafia, good-bye to concessionary contracts, its good-bye to those who have lined their pockets and put the membership in last place.
>
> This is the new Teamster union, with new ideas, new directions, and a whole new purpose. . . . The Teamster union will not be sitting in the background; we'll be out leading the charge. . . . Starting today, we will start to build this new Teamster union.[81]

He promised to eliminate multiple salaries and multiple pensions for Teamster officials. As president of Local 804, he earned about $45,000 a year in salary. Ron said he would cut his salary as General President from the scheduled $225,000 to $175,000. When Ron was asked about past Teamsters' endorsements of Presidents Reagan and Bush, he said the union members had suffered during their administrations.

Ron also addressed the ongoing government supervision of the Teamsters union. He said he was not happy with the government's role in the union's affairs. Ron asserted that the best way for the Teamsters to end the costly supervision was to "get out there and show them we have the courage and conviction."[82]

In the end, it wasn't even close: Ron's slate received 188,883 votes (48.48 percent), Durham's 129,538 (33.24 percent), and Shea's 71,227 (18.28 percent). The Carey slate beat Durham by almost 3 to 1 in the East and by more than 2 to 1 in the West. Durham only beat Ron in the Canadian locals. Including Ron, all sixteen candidates on his slate won. To round out the incoming GEB, in Canada where Ron didn't file any candidates, two members of Durham's team (Charles Thibault and Louis Lacroix) were elected vice presidents, and in the East, where the Carey campaign ran only two candidates for three vice president spots, John Morris, of Shea's team, was elected.

"The members have spoken, and I wish him [Carey] well," Durham said in a statement. "In spite of the bitterness of this campaign, I urge all Teamsters to do what I plan to do as President of Local 391: put the welfare of Teamsters' families ahead of individual differences."[83]

This proved the reality of rank-and-file power. In the past, most members would follow the advice of their local presidents. But not this year. Not this time. Members were angry and voted on that anger. Local union officers were shocked. It demonstrated just how out of touch these Old Guard leaders were. It showed just how right Ron was in all that he proclaimed.[84]

There was a broad welcoming of the Carey win in the establishment press. In an editorial titled "Can It Be Morning in Teamsterland?" Jonathan Tasini referred to the possible end of Teamster corruption.[85] The *Chicago Tribune* called Ron's win "an earthquake in the US labor movement."[86] The *Boston Globe* proclaimed Ron "a working-class Don Quixote, attacking corruption and entrenched union bosses few thought could be toppled from power."[87]

The win brought with it several firsts. Diana Kilmury became the first woman ever chosen for a position on the GEB. She "captured the title of first vice president—the position formerly held by Joe Trerotola." Leroy Ellis became the Teamsters' first elected African-American vice president, and John Riojas was elected as the union's first Latino-American board member.[88] Seven of Ron's slate members were working Teamsters who had never been elected or unelected union officials.

The following Monday, Ron was back in Queens, visiting his buildings and catering to his Local 804 members' grievances. But he was very much looking forward to the inauguration and getting to work in Washington. But before the inauguration came the transition. Dennis Skelton, who along with Aaron Belk, describes what happened:

> I went up there on December 16. There I met up with Aaron Belk. We were part of the transition in order to keep the creeps from throwing shit out. Me and Aaron developed a good cop, bad cop tactic with the Old Guard bureaucrats in the headquarters. Aaron was the good cop, with the slow drawl and his educated ways, who would try to move them around to where he wanted them to be. I was the bad cop who'd say "I've had enough of your shit, here's where we need to be, or else!"[89]

They found no shenanigans going on. The loss was a complete surprise to the Old Guard. They expected to win and were too busy knifing each other so they didn't sabotage anything. "They split because they all wanted to be king. The building in DC was half Shea, half Durham. Neither side knew what part of the building was Durham or Shea. No side was thinking of Carey, and he went right in between them," added Skelton.[90]

"The transition turned into a grueling experience," recalled Belk, "because the officers that lost the election left many things drifting following the news that the entire Ron Carey slate had won. It took almost six months to untangle what they had left undone. Many left without listing pending litigation, grievances, and other problems."[91]

On January 10, 1992, elections officer Michael Holland certified the 1991 election. It also meant that the new International Review Board was to take over disciplinary duties on October 10 of that year.[92]

CHAPTER 5

The Reformer

On February 1,1992, a beautiful, sunny afternoon, Ron Carey stood atop a makeshift bandstand as he took the oath of office given to him by his second-in-command from Local 804, Pat Pagnanella. He was sworn in before 2,000 people, including Shea, Durham, and AFL-CIO president Lane Kirkland, on the steps of Teamsters Union headquarters, known as the Marble Palace. "I pledge to you today that I will use the full power of this office to rid this union of mob influence and win this battle once and for all!" The phrase "New Teamsters" was every-where you looked. Ron told the crowd:

> Today we begin the work of building the New Teamsters and our mission is to give the union back to our members. We've lived through a period where Teamsters couldn't hold their heads high because of the constant news reports about our corruption, mob influence, and lavish lifestyles of our leaders. . . yes But changing our image will take a lot more than public relations and press releases. Welcome to the New Teamsters union. From the day I walk in the door, the rules are going to change. We are going to clean house and never again have to apologize for being a Teamster.[1]

Ron promised to sell the IBT jets, the condominium in Puerto Rico, and the limousines. He then went on to state his reform agenda to revitalize the Teamsters and the entire labor movement:

> We have the money, the talent, the technology, and the organization to be the strongest voice for working people in the world, and that is just what this union is going to be.
>
> Now is the test. Our mission is to take the enormous resources of this union and give them new direction and new purpose, to win better contracts, to improve pensions, and to organize new workers, to pass a national health insurance system.
>
> Today the eyes of the world are upon us. We have stepped into the history books, and the story is ours to write.[2]

He ended his speech saying, "This building belongs to you. Come on in!" Balloons were released, the Teamsters song "Proud to Be a Teamster" was played, and Ron opened the doors of the Marble Palace and invited all the members and their families inside to walk the halls of the Teamster headquarters. He then went to the president's suite and personally welcomed each guest and posed for pictures.[3] It was truly a populist, for the members, inaugural.

It was a new day for unions. A new day for Teamsters. Excitement and hope were in the air. In a congratulatory message to Ron, Victor Reuther, the co-founder of the United Auto Workers, commented that "not since the 1930s when the CIO was born has there been an event of such profound significance for US labor as your election to the presidency of the Teamsters through rank-and-file membership mobilization."[4] According to Duke Zeller, author of an insider's book on the Teamsters union, *Devil's Pact*, the former president, Billy McCarthy, whispered to Zeller at the inauguration, "I think this guy's going to make it, as long as they don't take him out."[5]

Ron Carey had organized a truly diverse and broad coalition. It consisted of militant TDUers, mainstream reformers, traditional union leaders, and probably a few opportunists. The membership was ready for change and Ron's slate said and promised all the right things. But now, it was time to govern.

Ron was described by the press as a sort of "Mr. Smith Goes to Washington" character. So many articles mentioned how he enjoyed eating tuna fish sandwiches, staying at budget hotels when on the road, and how he carried his own suitcases. They also needed to mention that he still drove his 1989 car, his wife worked at Macy's as a clerk, and they had lived in the same house for over thirty-five years.

Ron was now the president of the Teamsters Union. It was an exciting and promising moment. He had promised a lot and half of the union had voted against him, but obstacles never hindered Ron Carey before. Without delay, Ron moved quickly to implement the reforms he had promised.

He inherited a Marble Palace filled with over three hundred full-time employees who were mostly Old Guard lackeys. So Ron tried to surround himself in Washington with many of the reformers who guided him during the campaign. He kept Burke on as his special assistant, Rick Gilberg as his general counsel, and Aaron Belk as his executive assistant. Ron wanted people he truly trusted close to him.

"As soon as we got in Ron had to deal with uncovering apartments the union owned, the selling of the jets," remarked Burke. "He had major contracts to deal with. Carhaul was already in high-level talks. We needed lots of help. We needed professionals."[6] Ron brought in several top-notch non-Teamsters for key jobs in his administration. Many were recommended by either Ed Burke or Ken Paff. People were imported from the Mine Workers and other unions, like Judy Scott, very powerful in the Legal Department, who also helped hire most of the key people in strategic places, and Matt Witt, in the communications department, while organizers like Bob Muehlenkamp, a special assistant to Ron, were brought over from SEIU. They were scrambling to get good-quality, competent people to help run the organization.

"When you got lots of rank-and-filers in a room, you're gonna need some help running the thing," recalled Ken Paff.[7] So they went outside the Teamsters to get that help. They got some of the best people in the labor movement to be a part of history.

As his chief of staff, Ron brought in David Mitchell, who was for years at the UAW and specialized in labor law and communications. He was asked to come in for a few months to help put things in order and get a budget drawn up. "It was exciting to see the Teamsters be more a force for good," said Mitchell. "I met with Ron and Eddie Burke—Burke had been interim Chief of Staff until he went on the IRB [Independent Review Board]—and I accepted immediately. It was a great opportunity to help get the labor movement going in a new direction. Ron's management style was not easy or fun to deal with. He was very demanding. He wanted strict budgets for every department and agency even the cafeteria."[8]

"Mitchell was brought in. He was a real Washington guy," remembered Muehlenkamp. "For him, Ron was not just a hero like he was to us. Mitchell welcomed him as a humongous breath of fresh air coming to Washington. He wanted Ron to become a player in DC, meet with senators, the President, and accept invitations to speak and become a leader in a broader sense than just the Teamsters. He wanted Ron as the leader of the movement, a spokesman for labor. But Ron could give a shit less. He really didn't care at all about that. He was just dedicated to the union and his members."[9]

Burke worked closely with Paff and TDU to fill positions and hand out power. Some of the paid campaign consultants tried to get in the game. Martin Davis's company, the November Group, tried to take over the *Teamster* magazine. Ron rejected that. He wanted committed labor journalists and organizers like Matt Witt, not political hustlers, in control of the magazine. In the end, Davis and the professional consultants were allowed to run the political wing.

At the first General Executive Board meeting, Ron pushed to cut his own salary by $75,000 and new officers and staff salaries by 14 percent. The GEB ended perks at the Marble Palace like unlimited sick leave and free lunch for all staff; they ended a special pension fund that paid twenty-two former officers more than $5 million; they sold off the union's private jets, the limousine, and the condo in Puerto Rico; they implemented new organizing programs for members and a Field Services Department to organize rallies and workplace actions.[10]

Most of these new board members barely knew each other. They each campaigned in their own region with Ron, Blaylock, and Burke. They all gathered at the convention the previous year, but they were basically separate entities. Some TDU members knew each other or at least knew of each other. Regardless, this was a group of strangers with only Ron as the center of that wheel.

The first few GEB meetings were very dense and at times lively. "You vote on all these things: Local X wants to go on strike, do they get strike money?" recalled Kilmury. "There were also copious amounts of daily TITANs [Teamsters Information Terminal Accounting Network, the communications system between the Locals and the International] on authorizations, appointments, etc. on every issue that was in the GEB authority to approve or disapprove." They would also receive large amounts of correspondence and financial reports from employers like UPS that they had to sort through and strategize about.[11]

Kilmury spoke of the complexities of running such an organization as the IBT. "The fight to prevail on any contentious issue is generally carried out prior to a decision taken behind the scenes and often involves only certain people. By the time an action or decision is put before the GEB for ratification it is a fait accompli."[12]

Vice President Skelton added to the description of the early meetings: "Mr. Carey was of course always running the meetings. We did have people like Johnny Morris from Philly who was friends with RV Durham. So, yeah, the first couple of meetings were a little salty. Morris ran the state of Pennsylvania and was used to getting his way. But once he figured out what Ron was all about," Skelton continued, "and that he wasn't going to attack the state of Pennsylvania and bust up the way he did business, everything was cool."[13] Morris wound up being one of Ron's best allies. He never refused Ron or anyone on the GEB the use of his huge fleet of trucks.

According to Kilmury, at first she was "underwhelmed by his [Morris's] reputation that preceded him." She was aware of his "abusive, autocratic regime in his Local since it was TDU members who bore the brunt." Kilmury challenged Morris's "Old Guard misogynistic viewpoints." Ron allowed his board members to freely engage and challenge one another.[14]

At one meeting, while Morris was rambling on about how powerful he was, Kilmury went off on him: "Give us a break. The only reason you got elected was because one of OUR candidates for Eastern VP backed out at the last minute. We could have run Mickey Mouse and beaten you!" Morris didn't necessarily like the comment. Ron was seen trying to disguise his laughter. Eventually, they learned to get along and achieved a grudging mutual respect for each other.[15]

Bob Muehlenkamp was at first hired to be the organizing director. At the time, Vicky Saporta was the incoming director and Ron didn't feel comfortable firing a woman, so Bob became a close assistant to Ron. He observed the early GEB meetings. He didn't see much infighting. He happily observed that the Canadian guys on the GEB who ran with the Old Guard slate unopposed "were much more trade unionists than most of the Old Guard. They weren't mobsters at all." As for Johnny Morris, he was "a mixed bag. Johnny insisted on being heard in the building. He'd try to get through to Ron almost every day with a complaint or a suggestion. Ron had no time for it, so he assigned me to him for a few months as a buffer."[16]

Under the leadership of Ron Carey, the "wise guy" culture was no longer the style of the Teamsters. Ron brought with him a Put Members First agenda that solely focused on rank-and-file issues, as well as programs to better organize the already organized. The "New Teamsters" fostered a culture of solidarity and rank-and-file democracy.

Ron was now living in the Washington area. His average day began with a breakfast of a muffin and a cup of coffee in his Washington office by 7 a.m. He worked straight through to meetings after dinner. His day ended around 8 p.m. Most days he was on the road traveling, meeting members and hearing their problems. When he was in Washington, there were meetings and more meetings.[17]

His board and staff worked hard, long hours. Several key players remarked: "You never go home by 5 p.m.," "It was impossible to be a dedicated officer and have a good home life," and "The work never stopped." Everyone observed how hard Ron worked and the fourteen-hour days he put in, so they didn't want to either disappoint or displease him.

"Ron was a trusting person," said Burke. "He understood he inherited. He purposefully wanted people to get their feet wet and run things themselves. So Ron delegated. He made appointments that were at times trainings in progress. He took people who had never done this thing before, it was a big responsibility. Lots needed grooming."[18] Muehlenkamp agreed: "Absolutely. Ron assigned me to meet with the new VPs who were fresh off the trucks, etc. To help them with the things they didn't know, like labor law, how the constitution worked, how to bargain a contract. Some never handled a grievance."[19] But certain activists like Diana Kilmury didn't need much training. "Being involved with TDU for years, I knew the constitution," recalled Kilmury. "I knew what to do on day one. I was ready. But some needed schooling."[20]

Mitchell's office was right across from Ron's. When Ron was in his office, which was rare for he traveled much of the week visiting barns and meeting members, and he had many visitors. "He was always busy," said Mitchell. "There were politicians, GEB members, different Teamster directors but he especially enjoyed when rank-and-file members visited."[21]

One visit in particular was recounted by Tim Sylvester. Tim had taken a trip with his family to DC and he stopped in to visit Ron. "I called in to say hi and see if I could get tickets to the White House.

His secretary says he 'wants to see you and bring the wife and kids.'
So we did. He comes out of his office all smiles, invites us in. He
gives me the tickets and says, 'Come here, sit in my chair.' I did.
He put his arm around me and said, 'I want you to know everyone
who has ever sat in this chair has either been murdered or gone to
jail.' I said thanks a lot, and laughed."[22]

From the first day, there were so many things going on at once:
Carhaul negotiations, Northwest Airlines flight attendants who
wanted to leave the Teamsters, GEB meetings, filling positions,
dealing with his old Local in Queens. Plus he had to deal with
the Old Guard that remained infested throughout the bureaucracy looking to undermine him at every turn. He also had some
internal conflicts within his own administration: bringing in "outsiders" from other unions pissed off "real Teamsters." Old Guard
bureaucrats battled with Reformers, and TDU fought everyone.

But his first priority was Northwest Airlines. "Eighty-five hundred flight attendants were scattered among six Teamster local
offices nationwide. In each local they were a minority, competing
with members from other industries [Freight and UPS] whose
interests often clashed with theirs."[23] Over 80 percent of the flight
attendants were women who worked irregular hours and needed
day care for their children.

The previous leadership had failed to address their concerns.
"There was no support from the Teamsters," said Patricia Reller,
from Local 732 in New York and a leader of the rebellious flight
attendants. "We would never get anything we asked for. The company would violate the contract and the Teamsters did nothing."
They gathered over 5,400 signatures, 68 percent of the membership, on a petition that called for a vote to decide whether to join
the Association of Flight Attendants. In early January, before his
inauguration, Ron invited Reller to his transition office at the
Marble Palace.[24]

The attendants, led by Reller, came to Washington a bit skeptical. They told Ron they wanted their own local. Ron agreed. He
then traveled around the country to several airports, including

New York, Boston, Los Angeles, Detroit, Minneapolis, Seattle, and Memphis. Ron said to them: "You are looking for a new union? Well, the Teamsters ARE a new union!" A vote was taken and on March 12, 1992, almost 90 percent of the membership voted; 4,667 votes were to stay in the New Teamsters and 2,830 votes were to leave. Ron immediately changed the person in charge of the Airlines Division and created the new Local 2000.[25]

Ron also needed expertise in certain fields, as well as people who knew how to negotiate contracts with employers and run a meeting. There were not enough qualified people to keep things running.

In response, he practiced what people called Ron's "Olive Branch" strategy. He reached out to the opposition for directors for their knowledge and experience. They generally turned him down. According to Aaron Belk, "As strong as the Teamsters were, we were still a divided union. We often fought with one hand tied behind our backs and that arm was usually punching as hard as they could."[26]

Steve Early described some of the headwinds Ron had to fight against:

> There was lots of hostility in the headquarters. Ron and the new board weren't exactly welcomed with open arms. Many feared some sort of purge. They suddenly needed job security so the staff immediately organized an OPEIU [Office and Professional Employees International Union] bargaining unit. Of course, Ron wasn't going to be a union buster, so they negotiated a first contract. It was funny and ironic that the Old Guard had kept the union out all those years until now. Ron's Local 804 staff was also unionized.[27]

It seems Ron bent over backwards to give everyone a chance, but he expected performance. "He didn't just fire someone because they supported Durham or Shea but before you knew it, most showed their true colors and tried to do things that blocked what Ron was doing," said Gene Moriarity, an International Rep and later a close friend of Ron's.[28] Herman Benson, long time director of the Association for Union Democracy, commented, "The Old Guard could make Carey's life absolutely miserable; he needs them; the Teamsters as a union can't fight UPS or any big company without these local leaders."[29]

Hence, Ron didn't do a broad-brush firing of the old regime. He kept on the secretaries and people in the Education Department. "They wanted to keep their jobs so they were nice to Ron's face, but the Old Guard was getting a lot of inside information to undermine Ron," said Doreen Gasman, an International Rep and close friend of Ron's later in life.[30]

"It was challenging," described Skelton, who took over as freight director as they took office. "My secretary was hired by Hoffa, Sr., and she had worked for Durham when he was freight director. I knew she was loyal to RV but I went in there and said, 'Your training and knowledge are important to the Freight members of this union so as long as you do your job I don't have a problem with you. I know where your loyalty is and that is OK. But if I catch you outside the box, providing stuff to outsiders, trying to undermine our intentions or progress, it will be met with the proper response.'"[31]

By July, Ron had removed twenty-seven of sixty high-level International reps. His method of removing undeserving bureaucrats was asking each of them for reports explaining their responsibilities as International reps. Some refused, and some sent him brief, dismissive remarks. "We sent them 'Thank you, God bless you, good-bye' letters," Ron told a reporter.[32]

Ron put out that "olive branch" to Chuck Mack. In California, Safeway was planning on transferring its warehouse work (Teamster jobs) to another, non-union company. Chuck Mack, the West Coast Teamster leader who ran with Durham in 1991, organized a boycott of Safeway in the region. Ron reached out to Mack and sent them $30,000. "I spoke with Carey throughout," mentioned Mack. Ron promised Mack that he had the entire Teamsters union behind them.[33]

Safeway immediately gave in, opening the warehouse with Teamster jobs with good benefits and wages. Mack appreciated the importance of the support. He recognized that the Old Guard would not have gone all in for them like Ron had. He commented that Ron "knew that if we lost what is probably the largest distribution warehouse in the West, we would take a beating everywhere."[34] Ron was expanding his coalition.

Also within his first 100 days, Ron had to deal with the 16,000 member Carhaulers contract. The Carhaulers, who transport cars from factories and ports to the car dealerships, had been working without a contract since May 1991. The previous regime had negotiated two agreements that were both rejected by the Carhaulers, the last in December, by over 74 percent.

Those contracts were negotiated with the Old Guard director of Carhaul, Ernie Tasino, still in charge. Over time, Ron eased Tasino out. Sadly, he then became lead negotiator for the car companies.[35] The biggest issue was "double-breasting," the method by which companies would form non-union subsidiaries to carry cars for less than their Teamster-contracted drivers. It was a backdoor way to cut wages. The Old Guard refused to take on the issue. They feared it might lead to a long strike.[36] Ron wasn't afraid.

After twelve years of Reagan/Bush policies eviscerating workers' protections and encouraging employers to destroy unions, Ron called for a corporate campaign against big employers. Ron wanted to start a Corporate Campaign Office, so he hired Ron Carver, one of the foremost corporate campaign people in the country. Carver became the Teamsters' first Director of the Office of Strategic Campaigns.[37]

Carver had a long and distinguished career fighting for the underdog in many social justice fights. In the 1960s, he joined SNCC (Student Nonviolent Coordinating Committee) and fought for civil rights. In the 1970s, he supported the anti-Vietnam War movement. Since the 1980s, he was a crusader against corporate greed and a master of the "guerilla advertisement," which usually attacked greedy companies in contract negotiations with its union workforce. "These companies are spending tens of millions of dollars creating good will," said Carver. "We want to expose the companies for the mean-spirited treatment of their employees."[38]

The Carver strategy was to first research the facts of who were the actual owners of some of these corporations, find the weak points, and then devise a strategy to go after those weak points. At first, it seemed foreign to Ron Carey, but after hearing Carver's presentation, he was all in. "The first campaign we did was Carhaul," explained Muehlenkamp. "We did our research and built our campaign around the facts. Since Ryder has 45 percent of the car hauling nationwide, we decided to break Ryder then get the rest in line." He continued:

> There was the annual Ryder National Golf Tournament in Miami. So we hired a plane with a large banner behind to fly low over the golf course every day. Ryder was huge at the time. Lots of consumer outlets, truck rental places. Ryder got an injunction from some asshole judge prohibiting us from flying over. So we got a counter injunction. Now it's in the press.
>
> We then went mobile all over the country. Every Saturday we had Teamsters standing outside Ryder commercial outlets with leaflets and picket signs. It destroyed their fucking weekend business and they finally caved and we got the best contract ever. We then expanded that department.[39]

It was a really smart move. The Teamsters were directly telling consumers to stop renting Ryder trucks for their moving needs. They were using the same Saul Alinsky methods used by Martin Luther King Jr. and Cesar Chavez during their movements for social and economic justice.

Delivering on his promise to take action against the big companies, Ron and his team organized rallies throughout the country. At one of the rallies, Ron said, "This is your fight! It's your contract. We need your help. Get involved. This belongs to all of us!" They distributed leaflets proclaiming that Ryder "creates hardships and suffering" for the drivers because Ryder's non-Teamster drivers were being paid a far lower wage.[40]

Some Old Guard local officers wouldn't cooperate, but Ron went around them to appeal directly to the rank and file. Ultimately, the local officers saw the light. According to one of Ron's vice presidents, Tom Gilmartin, "We were leafleting more than six hundred locations."[41]

The Teamster's Corporate Campaign included a media campaign as well. Ron invited Wall Street trucking industry analysts and the press to a breakfast briefing session where he presented a clear description of the campaign. The campaign also reached out to religious groups and community organizations like Jobs with Justice to attend the rallies.[42]

By May, Ryder had given in. The new agreement called for a preservation agreement of work performed by Teamster members, prohibiting further double-breasting: "They were not allowed to subcontract to non-union subsidiaries," recalled Fred Zuckerman. "All the work done by the parent company had to be given to the union division of their companies. That was outside the box thinking. Never done before. It was fucking brilliant!"[43]

Besides protecting work performed traditionally by Teamsters members and a prohibition against any future double breasting, the new agreement called for a limit on the number of employees who now work for double-breasted subsidiaries that are not represented by a union; a prohibition by parent companies and subsidiaries of any attempt to evade traditional Teamsters work; and expedited grievance procedures for double-breasting disputes, including a sixty-day arbitration procedure and the right to strike to enforce an arbitrator's award. It was the best Carhaul contract negotiated in decades. [44]

RON AND HIS TEAM NOT only had to deal with the Old Guard trying to undermine him at every turn, but the federal government was there from Day One as well. "It was very unpleasant. They treated us all as though we were all crooks," remembered David

Mitchell. "They were in the building all the time. And when they interviewed people, it was like, 'Who the hell are you and what are you doing?' They didn't give anyone the benefit of the doubt."[45]

The consent decree mandated that the new administration work with the new Independent Review Board. Starting in October of 1992, the IRB was to take over disciplinary cases. The deal was that the IRB would work on investigations and oversight, while the IBT would charge, adjudicate, and impose sanctions:

> The consent decree provided that DOJ would appoint one IRB member and the IBT would appoint another, and those two appointees would choose the third member. In March, DOJ appointed Independent Administrator Frederick Lacey, and the IBT appointed Eddie Burke.[46]

Ron was never a fan of government involvement in the union. He understood that there was a need for the government's presence during the election process. Though he opposed the power grab of the incoming IRB, Ron and his board generally cooperated with the government. In March the Bush administration's Department of Justice appointed Independent Administrator Frederick Lacey to the IRB. Lacey was no friend of unions.

On January 6, 1980, Judge Lacey ruled against striking members of Local 177. UPS had fired three workers on Leave of Absence (LOA) who were serving as Business Agents who organized brief work stoppages while BAs.[47] Ron had picked his former campaign manager and current special assistant, Eddie Burke, as the IBT's appointee. Both Lacey and Burke were then to agree on a neutral third appointee.

"We were thinking of someone like former Labor Secretaries Ray Marshall or Bill Usury, a labor statesman," remembered Burke. "But Lacey wanted more cops, more FBI types. It became a pissing contest." Lacey wanted someone with an investigative and prosecutory background, and Ron wanted someone who understood labor relations and labor unions.[48]

Ron directed Burke to object to all of their choices, including Lacey's favorite, William Webster, former director of the FBI and the CIA. That particular choice angered Ron. He was aware of Webster's other background as a member of the corporate board of Anheuser-Busch, which so happened to be a Teamster employer, and a board member of Pinkerton Security and Investment Services, which had a long history of violently breaking union strikes.[49]

An incensed Judge Edelstein called both parties to Washington for a status report. "He called me out. I thought he was gonna cuff me right there," Burke said, laughing. "He gave us seventy-two hours to come up with a name." Edelstein urged Burke to accept Webster. "He said, 'Clean up needed law enforcement experience.'"[50] Ron wouldn't budge. Days later, Edelstein declared that "the impasse is hopelessly irreconcilable" and appointed Webster himself as the "neutral" IRB member. He stated that "the IRB will serve as a perpetual agent of reform."[51]

Angered by Lacey's power grab appointing Webster, Ron accused the government of breaking their own rules set out by the consent decree. By imposing its own choice to the IRB for the neutral member, Lacey was "making a mockery of the idea that a third member will be neutral." Ron also was outraged over the rules and the exuberant costs that the Teamsters Union had to pay. He criticized the $385/hour fees paid to Lacey over the past three years; it cost the Teamsters over $85,000 a month. This was money Ron would have loved to use on organizing.[52]

Ron was always looking out for the members' money and best interests. During the campaign, he had promised to establish an Ethical Practices Committee to deal with union corruption, to prove that the IRB was unnecessary. At their first General Executive Board meeting, Ron introduced a resolution stating that "the General President and the GEB are firmly committed to ending Government supervision of the affairs of the IBT and substituting an effective and vigorous Ethical Practices Committee (EPC) to ensure that this Union operates democratically and is free from corruption at all levels."[53] He established his own disciplinary apparatus to demonstrate to the Bush Department of Justice that the IRB was unnecessary.

Ron appointed fifteen EPC members: five regional vice presidents, five local union officers, and five rank-and-file members. The committee was divided into three-person regional hearing panels. He appointed Aaron Belk, a close adviser whom he trusted, as the EPC's administrator.[54]

By October 30, the Ethical Practices Committee was in operation. The committee's job was to review and investigate all complaints of wrongdoing and corruption by Teamster officials at every level. The EPC invited rank-and-file Teamsters to submit complaints, and Belk and his staff would decide whether the complaint warranted an investigation. If Belk decided that a certain complaint needed to be investigated further, he assigned the case to one of his EPC members to conduct a more extensive investigation which meant questioning union officers about the allegations. The EPC did not investigate organized crime. That issue was dealt with by the IRB.[55]

Ron gave Belk the authority to bring disciplinary charges against the accused. Then Belk would channel the charges to the specific regional EPC panel to convene a hearing. After presentations and witnesses by both sides, the panel would then recommend charges for Ron to decide. He would also use this evidence to impose trusteeships on locals and joint councils.[56] It was not used for political retaliations against the Old Guard. Even local officers that supported Ron were charged and removed. They hired a private detective, Jack Paladino, to conduct investigations.

RON WAS NOW HOLDING DOWN two full-time jobs himself. He was still the president of Local 804. Over his tenure in Washington, Ron missed maybe one General Membership Meeting in New York. Ron bought a condo in Arlington, Virginia, 2100 Lee Highway. He tried balancing his travels around the country meeting members with time in Washington making decisions and negotiating and getting home on the weekends. It was a hefty balancing act. Of course, he always flew coach.

Gene Moriarity, a rank-and-filer and International Rep, told a story about taking a plane ride home with Ron:

> We were flying back to DC from LaGuardia a few years in. He liked US Airways the best. Now he did away with officers using First Class, so we were in coach. But the flight attendant always would reserve the emergency exit row for him and put him in the middle seat and not put anybody on either side of him. She was a union worker.
>
> I get on the plane, he sees me and says "Sit here." A guy gets up from his seat and starts to walk by us and he looks down and says "Holy shit! You're Ron Carey; I voted for you twice. I worked on your campaign. Can I sit there?" Ron said "Sure." The guy said "I'll be right back." He turned around and said, "I really can't believe this, you're like a hero to me. If this plane crashes I will die a happy man having died with you!"
>
> He walks away laughing to the bathroom. A few minutes later, Ron turns to me and says, "Gene, don't you think you might want to go back there and see what that crazy fucker is doing in the bathroom?" We had a good laugh.[57]

In his first 100 days, Ron had kept Northwest Airlines flight attendants in the Teamsters union, won against Safeway, and personally negotiated a historic Carhaulers contract. Ron had his Teamsters acting like a powerful union once again. He was truly in command. But he didn't like DC much. Remembered Belk: "He never liked being in the DC office, in that building, meetings. He enjoyed being in the field with the members. He got energy from that. That's where he got his information for what needed to be done."[58]

In Washington, he felt out of place. He felt Washington was a place of phonies. Ron appreciated straight talk to blather and people kissing up to him. "At times, Ron would come into my office to bounce ideas off me," continued Belk. "I was of course flattered. Since I never was an officer in my local, he said he valued my rank-and-file common sense. He thought the Marble Palace lacked that."[59]

Ron feared losing touch right from the beginning. At first, he wanted to read and answer every letter that arrived from the rank and file. His executive staff members told him that there were way too many for one man to read. "We carried in to his office all the boxes of mail and said 'Here it is!' Burke started pouring them out onto his desk. There were thousands. Finally, he realized he had to delegate some stuff. It was too much. So I read and answered the letters for Ron. But he signed them all himself."[60]

Ron also traveled home to Queens nearly every weekend. He never gave up his first love, so he was in New York a lot taking care of Local union business there. According to Tim Sylvester, Ron missed maybe one General Membership meeting during his time in DC. Pat Pagnanella, Local 804's secretary-treasurer, ran the day-to-day business of the Local while Ron was in Washington, and Ron fully trusted him. He was never concerned about Local 804 in Pat's hands.[61]

"I had a tiny 'office,' a small desk, in Ron's office in Local 804," said Muehlenkamp. "We would commute to New York a lot. He always came back on Thursday nights, so he could be in the Local on Fridays." Being home recharged Ron. He would attend his home Local's union meetings and shop stewards' meetings. He also got to see his family and friends. "Ron was comfortable with the guys, his members, in his office dealing with Local 804 issues," continued Muehlenkamp. "Back in Queens, the issues were so simple, and he saw immediate results. And people weren't lying to him all the time. In Washington, he never knew who to trust. He needed a place like that because the Marble Palace was just a nightmare for him."[62]

Though he genuinely loved being General President and shaking hands with rank-and-filers, Ron dreaded being cooped up in the office or in meetings. "He hated meetings," remarked Belk.

"He'd ask me to go to these meetings up the hall with him and take notes. He would never start off a meeting and say, 'This is what I want you to do.' No, Ron would ask everyone's opinion and at the end of the meeting, he would sum up everything from my notes and put it into a package and then say, 'This is what we're doing' and put it out for everyone to run through."[63]

"Ron hated politicians," said Dave Eckstein. "He used to send me to meetings and stuff that he preferred not to go to, the finger-food occasions. He always made others go for him. I had to take a shower when I got home."[64] Ron would not be wasting time with politicians at receptions or fundraisers.

"Ron's day was a constant barrage," recalled Muehlenkamp. "It was constant incoming. It was a massive operation filled with complications. He had to deal with all the Divisions and the Departments. It was really those guys with constant problems. A lot of his time was spent on internal Teamster issues, the Constitution, the Bylaws, the dues increase, the IRB. Plus the issues in the Divisions that came up, negotiations, and the constant demands on him. These guys would all want meetings with Ron. Everyone wanted a piece of his time."[65]

For his rank-and-file members, Ron had all the patience in the world, but he had a short fuse with the Old Guard, especially the mobster characters. "One day Ron slams the door shut," recalled Muehlenkamp. "Then he goes, 'The problem with these fuckin' dagos is that they all come to me and they all want something but they never come and offer to help out.' Ron had no patience for these guys who were so out for themselves." Ron was a product of his early environment. At times, he spoke in terms of stereotypes using offensive words like "dagos" or referring to the women in the office in Local 804 as "the girls."[66]

Though Ron didn't have many hobbies, he did find time to relax. Sometimes it was doing home improvements back in Queens. Other times it was sneaking a smoke. "I never did see him drink much but he did like to smoke," remembered Sylvester. "But he was like a kid; he wouldn't smoke in front of people. One day he came up to me at the local barbeque at the union hall. I had a cigarette in my hand, and he put his hand next to mine and took my cigarette, turned around, bent over, took a drag out of it and put it back and walked away without anyone noticing. Another time, a driver from Boston parked a tractor trailer in front of Review Avenue. Ron says, 'I never been in a cab of one of those things' to the drivers, so he climbs there, into the cab and he has a cigarette, right there,'" Sylvester recalled, laughing.[67]

Sylvester had many interesting stories about Ron and smoking. "I was in his office in DC during the re election campaign in 1996, and he says, 'Close the door.' He had a sign on his desk that said 'No Smoking.' He picked it up and threw it in his drawer. I said to him, 'Are you serious?' And he said, 'Ya got any?' That was his favorite line."[68]

Though Ron was not much of a drinker or partier, he would go out for meal with some board members he felt close to. "Once in a while we would grab him and go to Western Sizzler Steaks in Alexandria," recalled Skelton. "It was a place where no one knew us. Me and Mr. Carey, Blaylock, Belk. We'd have frogs' legs and fried chicken and have bones stacked up like cord of wood. We'd all be cutting up, especially him and Blaylock. Mr. Carey would say, 'Hey, Peewee. Do you think you're the only big ugly goon I could hire?' They would go back and forth. We'd talk a little sports and just stuff in general. Maybe Mr. Carey would have a beer or a glass of wine. But he was not a big drinker. I never saw the man get inebriated or even tipsy. He always wanted to stay in control and not get tripped up or embarrass the union."[69]

"He never relaxed," added Muehlenkamp. "Ron didn't drink, but he'd sneak a smoke occasionally. If he read, he read work stuff. What he enjoyed was doing handiork in his brothers' or kids' homes on weekends. And he had a wicked sense of humor, evil sense of humor. He'd laugh at the hypocrisy of the Teamster warlords he had to deal with and their stupidity. He'd take you on the side after a meeting with some of these guys and he'd say, 'And that fucker over there with his two mistresses, that phony.' He knew everything about these guys. The lies, the hypocrisy, the selfishness. And Ron hated the ass-kissers who said what he wanted to hear. He just wanted the truth."[70] Moriarity supported that notion: "He felt more comfortable with the International reps than the officers. But he really didn't like it when he entered a room and a rep would come over and kiss his ass."[71]

Ron was of, by, and for the members. "This is what this is about. It's being out there with the members," he once stated. "You'll never serve the members sitting in an office. I see a union as a mechanism to help people." Ken Spillane explained: "He believes in a hard day's work for an honest dollar."[72] Ron was in touch with the members. He spoke their language and even sounded like them. He listened to them, took them seriously, and he didn't act like a big shot. That's why so many loved and admired the man.

He ran to clean up the Teamsters and make it stronger. Ron believed that if members were more involved and educated, it would better serve their own interests. To Ron, that was real power. Making the members feel proud again in the union they belonged to was key. He constantly would say it's "our union" not "the union."

"He showed the members that they did have strength in numbers," recalled David Eckstein, "that they could move things that they thought they couldn't move. Some said, 'You'll get them so high, we won't know how to get them down.' Ron said, 'We'll deal with that problem when we get to it. We need to get them up!'"[73]

Ron knew the membership; he was of them. And he knew how they thought and what they wanted to see. He knew they wanted more than fancy words and a handshake. They wanted a leader who looked you in the eyes and listened intently to their grievances. Ron did that in a genuine retail politics kind of way.

"Whether Mr. Carey was speaking to rank-and-filers, politicians, or company owners, he was always himself," recalled Skelton. "He was no phony," continued Skelton.

When he spoke with a dock worker, he would talk their language, hear their problems and then tell them to write their name and phone number on a 2-by-3 index card along with a brief description of the issue. He would go out all the time with a bunch of empty 2-by-3 cards in his left suit pocket. He'd return to the office with all of them in his right suit pocket and then separate the Small Package questions, Freight questions, etc., and send those in an envelope to the Division Directors, like myself, and say, "Get back to this guy in 24 hours and let me know what the next course of action is."

If it was a grievance that hadn't been handled or missing, he'd tell me, "Look, I know it's gonna cost you a few bucks but you fax me those or make copies, mark 'em and send them to me personally." You had to do that. That was the accountability factor he was striving for. To Mr. Carey, all members, even the assholes, were members too.[74]

Ron's style was genuine and to the point. Dave Eckstein remembers, "Carey was a hands-on guy. He had regular meetings with all his staff. On any issue, he only wanted to know how it was going to benefit the members."[75] But he was also not the most open kind of person. "He kept his cards to his chest," recalled Rand Wilson. "He was an experienced leader but not the most affable, friendly guy. You really needed to get to the point. His knees were always bothering him. He was in lots of pain which made him crabby. So it wasn't easy working for the man. He required a lot from you. Just do your job, no playing around. He was a very serious guy."[76]

They still had to deal with a divided union. Staff needed to be aware of who were friendly and who was not. "We rated unions on how much they supported Ron," recalled Gene Moriarity:

We had our little book of every local union in it. We had a rating system of 1 through 4. A one was very supportive and a four was an enemy of Ron. We kept this pretty quiet for obvious reasons. One local in Pittsburgh, Jerry Lee was the PO and I was working with him on some stuff. I got the Communications Department to do a flyer for him.

He calls the Communications Department and the guy on the phone says, "Oh, OK you're a '2.'" Jerry calls me. He says, "You fuckin' guys are rating us?!" The guy from Communications says, "I don't know why I did it but I figured he'd be happy to know he was a '2'! Well, I think he just went to a 3![77]

In August 1992, Ron's father's UPS stock was sold. Under federal law, officers were to report ownership or interest in any stock directly or indirectly in companies that they represent. It had to be shown in Form LM-30.[78] Ron had never owned any of the stock, nor did he know his father had this stock in UPS. Ron's brother was the executor of their dad's estate. The $2.1 million estate was split six ways between the brothers. Ron received $350,000 before taxes.

TRAVELING THE COUNTRY IN A beat-up old car, Ron had made a connection to the rank and file. He seemed to get an awareness that he never had. He presented himself as the reformer, the underdog, fighting for the little guy. He ran on changing how the Teamsters were perceived by others. But he also seemed to change himself. According to those he campaigned with as well as people he knew for years, Ron was beginning to see things differently. He saw lots of things and heard from lots of people about their livelihoods and lives. It made Ron see the world from a little different perspective.

Once he was in Washington, all the politicians courted Ron. The year 1992 was a presidential election year. But Ron was smart and a strategic thinker. He was looking at what some of these politicians could do for the working families, his members, if he endorsed them. Though Ron was rightly described by Steve Brill in his 1978 book *The Teamsters* as a "conservative Republican," by 1992 it was obvious to anyone who knew Ron that he had moved away from that perspective. On cultural and social issues, Ron was still quite conservative but on economic issues, he was definitely more progressive.

"The more Mr. Carey watched the big picture of what the Republicans were now about," Dennis Skelton said, "the more he moved toward the Democratic side. I mean, he came from a military background and all that, but when it came to what was right for his members, he put their interests above all."[79] Steve Early agrees with that description. He was inspired by Ron's dedication to his work ethic and his capacity for growth. Early admired that growth:

> Being focused on a single local all his life might be a little parochial had he not had so much contact with other parts of the labor movement. He got out there for two years and traveled the country, met lots of people, stayed in their houses, heard their stories. It opened his eyes to a broader world. He saw the need to have community allies of different kinds of labor struggles. Not many people are capable of broadening their outlook. Ron did, to his credit.[80]

On September 23, 1992, Ron was invited to speak at the National Press Club in Washington.[81] Speaking for about an hour, he hit on many themes including how his "New Teamsters" were in the process of cleaning up the union. Ron mentioned that he installed an Ethical Practices Committee, removed dozens of officers receiving high salaries, and implemented strict budget and spending controls.

Promising that it was "just the beginning," Ron trumpeted all the Locals his administration had put under trusteeship. He also spoke about the costly impact of not just stolen monies but the "members' money" and fixing the dreadful image of the Teamsters.

He railed against "Corporate America's number one value: Greed!" Ron asked his audience, some very important and influential people, "what kind of country do we want to be?" He also went on a tear against "the so-called Free Trade policies of George Bush and NAFTA" that the establishment all supported and that hurt working people.

He described a litany of early successes in his administration: the Pittsburgh Press strike, a Carhaulers contract, a successful leafleting that brought Anheuser-Busch and its distributers to its knees, the Diamond Walnut Strike, reaching out to unions in other countries, etc.

Angered at the Bush administration's attack on the Teamsters, Ron stated that the "government was breaking the consent decree" in trying to expand its power and that it was draining Teamster resources he wanted to use for organizing members. He was angry over the government imposing its own pick, William Webster, as the neutral, third seat on the IRB. He also said that government oversight has cost the Teamsters over $3 million over the past three years, reminding the room that Judge Lacey charges the IBT $385 per hour.

While reminding everyone that since 1968 the corrupt Teamsters hierarchy had endorsed every Republican presidential candidate from Nixon to Bush, he then announced that the Teamsters under his leadership would endorse the Democratic candidacy of then governor Bill Clinton. "In my perspective," Ron proclaimed, "the last Republican turned his back on working people," which was "why we are working to elect Bill Clinton and I'm darn proud to wear this button!" It was a Clinton-Gore '92 button.

He declared that "unions have been taking it on the chin for twelve years. After a dozen years of Reagan/Bush, the Reagan Democrats are coming home" to vote for Bill Clinton. He admitted that "Clinton is no saint or savior but look at the past twelve years, we believe Bill Clinton is someone we can talk to and get this country moving again." Ron said they did a poll of the rank and file and "Bill Clinton got the most votes." He added that Perot came in second and Bush third mostly because "the Republicans were pushing worker replacement legislation."

When asked why the Teamsters supported the anti-union Ronald Reagan in 1980 and 1984, Ron believed that it was "an insurance policy" that the leadership sold to the union in the hope that it would spare them from prosecution. (It was later found that the Teamsters falsified a membership mail poll to justify endorsing Reagan in 1984.) The Old Guard leadership supported Republicans and "sold out the rank-and-file members for political favors against the members' interests" and "Republicans have no concern for working people in this country."[82]

On health care policy, Ron contended that "the American Dream was slipping away, with 37 million people without health care. Using an example from his home Local 804, he maintained that employers like UPS do not want to continue to pay for those who have no insurance, what he referred to as "cost shifting." He said that "Americans are entitled to health care!" This was no "Conservative Republican" speaking that day. He promised to "work toward creating National Health Insurance."[83] (At a February 1992 press conference, Ron spoke of health care reform leading to a "single-payer approach" to cover the other 37 million Americans not covered by insurance because "we are already paying for them.")

Ron ended his speech criticizing "the growth of billionaires." He denounced "corporate greed and how it destroys futures." He asserted these greedy billionaires needed to "pay their fair share" and "stop putting greed and profit over jobs and the community." He sounded more like Bernie Sanders than Sarah Sanders.

Under Ron's leadership, the Teamsters stopped giving political contributions to the GOP. The history of the Teamsters and the GOP went back to the 1960s. Robert Kennedy, JFK's attorney general, went after corruption in unions, especially the Teamsters. He famously confronted Jimmy Hoffa at a hearing. Then in 1971, the Teamsters under Fitzsimmons agreed to support Nixon's reelection in 1972. It was a quid pro quo deal that continued through the Reagan-Bush years. It ended when Ron was elected. He endorsed Bill Clinton and he campaigned for Clinton and the Democrats.[84]

Early on, Ron started preparing for next year's national negotiations with UPS. At his September news conference, he mentioned how they had sent out surveys to the members. It was the first ever national survey of UPSers to prepare for negotiations. They released the results of the survey in the April–May issue of the

Teamsters Magazine, which was edited by Matt Witt. It showed that a majority of UPS workers had workplace health issues, and a top priority was creating full-time jobs for part-timers.

They also released a study by the Illinois Health Hazard Evaluation Program at the University of Illinois that showed that there was a "high-stress atmosphere" at UPS, that required its drivers to meet rigid, precisely calibrated pickup and delivery schedules. The report found UPS drivers' stress levels were higher than 91 percent of all U.S. workers. Ron promised to draft language relating to this stress and harassment on the job.[85]

Mario Perrucci, the Local 177 secretary-treasurer who was elected on Ron's slate as Eastern Vice President, was picked as director of the Small Package Division. He stated that there was "an underlying issue of UPS's policy of 'putting packages before people.'" These negotiations were going to change that. Ron shook things up in negotiations. For the first time, rank-and-file UPS workers, such as drivers, clerks, and loaders, were on the Teamster negotiating committee. Dave Murray, UPS's chief negotiator, was not happy. But Ron wanted the people on the front lines, who drove the trucks, who loaded the trucks, who observed on a daily basis what UPS did. It also demonstrated a part of that new direction Ron promised: transparency.[86]

Ron agreed to extend the contract past the July 31 deadline. The UPS negotiators offered a weak wage proposal of 35 cents an hour each year over the six years of the proposed contract. The Teamster negotiating committee rejected that unserious offer. Ron said the offer was "insulting and ridiculous" and called for a strike vote. He told the media, "UPS is faced with a union leadership that's not going to operate in the interests of Corporate America."[87]

The rank-and-file membership voted 94 percent in favor of strike authorization. The vote—63,883 to 4,079—authorized the Teamsters' national negotiating committee "to take all action needed to win a fair contract, up to and including a strike action, if necessary."[88] Labor writer Dan La Botz commented: "UPS finally got serious only when the membership voted to give the union the authorization to strike and the Teamsters stopped extending the contract."[89]

On September 28, the Teamsters and UPS settled on a new four-year agreement, which averted a strike. In the new contract, the hourly wage increases were 60 cents in the first year and 55 cents in each of the next three years. In addition, the company agreed to pay an additional $1.80 an hour over the life of the agreement for health, welfare, and pension plans for its union members.[90] They also won important language that for the first time added the phrase "innocent until proven guilty."[91] Such a clause allowed members who were discharged or suspended to stay on the job until an arbitrator ruled for or against them.

In truth, the Teamsters were in no position to afford a prolonged national strike. Strike pay had been increased to $200 per week at the 1991 convention, but it was passed without any additional revenue stream to support it. In December, Ron made it known that he wanted a dues increase. The Teamsters hadn't raised the per capita union dues in ten years. Currently, there was around $18 million in the fund. Distributing $2.6 million per month in strike pay around the country was unsustainable. secretary-treasurer Tom Sever predicted that the union's strike fund would be depleted by June of 1994.[92]

The proposal would have the average Teamster see their monthly union dues rise from $25 a month to $31.25 a month. It would go from the current formula of two times a worker's hourly rate to 2.5 times. It seemed a sensible and reasonable proposal to maintain strike benefits and finance the International union and Local unions' programs to win good contracts and organize new members.[93]

When Ron mentioned an increase, the Old Guard was outraged. After years of mismanagement in the Marble Palace and allowing the dues per capita to fall sadly behind, they feigned "shock and alarm" over the IBT finances and especially the strike fund. They recommended Ron "go directly to the members" to get approval for any dues increase.

Believing that it was a good way to get around the Old Guard, Ron proposed a referendum. When Old Guard leaders like RV Durham realized Ron had called their bluff, they reacted by calling for a special convention to deal with a specific dues increase. A special convention was rejected, because it would have meant that delegates to the last regular convention in 1991, where 85 percent opposed Ron, would again go against him. That would be a prelude to failure.

Old-time reformers like Herman Benson of AUD agreed that going directly to the members was a lot better than making a deal with all the Old Guard powerbrokers. GEB members like John Morris, who was a vocal advocate of the $200 per week benefit at the 1991 convention, remarked that "some of the Old Guard would oppose Carey if it were a 3 cent an hour increase."[94]

Moreover, a win would give Ron both greater leverage and a huge war chest as he was entering the final week before the expiration of the National Master Freight Agreement with "Less-Than-Load" trucking companies. Those Old Guard local union officers pushed for a no vote. And they got what they wanted. The ballots were counted on March 21. The referendum was rejected by a 3–1 margin: 383,222 votes to 121,925.[95]

But money was still desperately needed: 70,000 truckers had already voted to authorize a strike if negotiations failed on March 31. Ron called a special GEB meeting to deal with the crisis, which boiled down to simply paying the bills. On May 17, the GEB met and voted to impose a temporary emergency dues assessment. The meeting was contentious but not out of control. "People would make their points," reflected Kilmury, who pushed for the assessment, "and other members would refute them. But everyone knew that a dues increase was necessary." It would bring in $17 million a year and be temporary unless the strike fund got below $25 million again. It also called for slashing spending.[96]

Ron was methodical. "He was psychological in all of his movements in order to keep the bad guys guessing," remarked Dennis Skelton, adding:

One day Mr. Carey calls me into his office and he asks about three guys in the Central Region, vintage assholes, which I was taking off of the grievance committee and national negotiating committee. I told him "Because they were assholes. Purely Old Guard, never will be anything but Old Guard." Mr. Carey leaned back in his chair and says, "Do you gamble?" I said, "Yep." He says, "When you play Five-Card Stud, you get that one card down. Do you have them deal all your cards up?" I said, "No, 'cause then everyone would know what I have in the hole." He said, "Exactly. There's 10,000 people in this room and 10,000 people would know how you feel about them three guys. But only one person would know how I feel about those guys." The point was well taken. Then as I'm walking out the door with my tail between my legs, he says, "Dennis, you're right. They are all cocksuckers!"[97]

Though Ron was "not very political," he certainly had his own point of view on certain issues of the day. But he transcended politics. He was just for the members. In everything he did as Teamsters General President, he would ask first: How will this affect my members? Is this in the best interests of my members? Whether it was NAFTA, worker replacement, minimum wage, etc.—Ron put members first. He wasn't left or right; he wasn't conservative or liberal; he was for what was in the best interests of his members. As Muehlenkamp noted:

He just wasn't interested in politics if it was outside the union. That was his life. He was great. Ron was never intimidated by big names or politicians. Being around them didn't affect his behavior.

One day he said to me, "Bob, I'm not going back there anymore with those guys." He was referring to the White House. At times he would go to the White House with the top leaders of the unions to talk about their issues. They would all meet beforehand and plan on what they were going to say, the talking points and who would say what. Then they would get in there with Clinton or whoever, and Ron said to me, "None of them would speak up. I'm the only one who talks up. Those big shots were so in awe." But not Ron.[98]

But he did reveal something during a talk with reporters. When Ron was asked if he was considering endorsing hard-right Republican Pat Buchanan for president in 1992, he responded that he "wouldn't be looking in that direction." He continued, "I've heard people say 'I'm a conservative Republican, etc.' and then when you start talking about the issues that have effect upon their lives and it's not there. It's about family, kids going to school, and health care. The whole quality of life issues, pension programs and when you start explaining these things to them, I think what happens is most members will say. 'That is an interesting point that I never thought about.'"[99]

NAFTA was a very big issue at the time. During the 1992 presidential election, George Bush and the Republicans had become the Free Trade party; Bush backed NAFTA 100 percent. Bill Clinton was a free-trader, but his Democratic Party had long championed workers' rights and the environment. Clinton supported NAFTA but wanted to add some protections for labor and the environment. But most of labor continued to be against it.

NAFTA, the North American Free Trade Agreement between the United States, Canada, and Mexico, was a treaty that aimed to eliminate all tariffs on imports and exports between the three nations. It was proposed by President Ronald Reagan to the Mexican government in the 1980s. It was a bipartisan affair that was supported by most Republicans and some moderate to conservative Democrats. Reagan launched the neoliberal idea of NAFTA, Bush negotiated the actual treaty and signed it, and Clinton pushed it through a Democratic Congress mostly with Republican votes. It was ratified in December 1993 and most of it went into effect on January 1, 1994.

It was promised that if NAFTA passed, it would create jobs and bring new markets for American-made goods. Jobs that were lost to cheaper competition would be balanced by growth in high-wage jobs in the import and export industries. The problem was that it was not geographically balanced: the West and East Coast saw some growth, while the South and Midwest did not.

Ron was an avid opponent of the agreement. He trusted that Clinton, when elected, would either renegotiate it or add protections for labor and the environment. In the end, protections were added, but they were not enough to satisfy most unions. To the unions it was about the possible loss of many good union factory jobs.

To Ron and his Teamsters, it was about trucking jobs and safety. If NAFTA was fully implemented, eventually Mexican truckers would be allowed to cross over and drive on U.S. roads. U.S. highways would become fully accessible to vehicles of trucking companies based in any NAFTA nation.[100]

As the leader of the Teamsters, Ron wrote letters, attended rallies, and appeared before Congress numerous times. He wrote a letter to then Senate Minority Leader Bob Dole asking him to oppose NAFTA, stating that "NAFTA is bad for working people on both sides of the border and poses a threat to highway safety." Nevertheless, Dole voted for NAFTA. Ron also urged Clinton to renegotiate NAFTA to include trucking safety rules, a North American minimum wage, and other provisions to protect workers in all three countries. He stated that "in the current NAFTA agreement, there are over 2,000 pages protecting corporations but not one mentions workers and how to protect them." He continued that Mexican workers in these factories made only $4 a day, which is not enough to purchase products made in the United States.[101]

At a rally outside the White House with Ralph Nader and Jesse Jackson, Ron exclaimed, "We are sick and tired of trade agreements that benefit big corporations instead of working families!" The speakers vowed to help lead a major political realignment. Ron alluded to possibly supporting a third party: "The White House thinks we have no place to go than the Democratic Party. That's just not so. We have to look for alternatives because the President of the United States has turned his back on the people who got him elected!"[102]

Days earlier, he stood on the steps of Congress with Democratic leaders Richard Gephardt and David Bonoir, as well as AFL-CIO secretary-treasurer Thomas Donahue to decry NAFTA. Ron announced that over 250,000 "Teamster-grams" were sent to Congress from Teamster members wanting NAFTA ended or renegotiated. He said that the treaty must "stand for fairness and human rights and raise the wages on both sides of the border and lift standards for the environment."[103] Regardless, NAFTA passed and was now the law of the land.

After the enactment of NAFTA, Ron's relationship with Clinton changed for the worse. Though the anti-union Republican Party was still the enemy and the Democrats were solid on most union issues, Ron hated Clinton by now. He felt cheated and betrayed by NAFTA. Ron rejected several invitations to come by the White House for a breakfast. According to Paff, "When a President calls a union president, it's a big deal, you cream in your pants. It means you're really important. But by now Carey didn't like Clinton. One time, Carey got off the phone with Clinton and started doing a very condescending impression of the President, 'I've got you covered, Ron' with that Queens accent."[104]

Ron hated the attention from politicians and their underlings. "That is what was so great about Ron Carey," recalled Paff. "He wasn't into that bullshit, the schmoozing . He wasn't into meeting important people and being patted on the back and stroked while something is being rammed up the members' asses." Furthermore, Paff continued:

Carey never endorsed Clinton in 1996. Instead, he put his energy and money into member mobilization and voter turn-out. Of course, it all fed eventually into Clinton, but he couldn't publicly endorse him after NAFTA. Ironically, this is what gave Martin Davis the opening for the swap in through the back door, because Carey was giving money to these grassroots groups instead of directly to the politician.[105]

Though NAFTA was now reality, the trucking part of the agreement was supposed to start on January 1, 1995. Trucking companies were seeking further deregulation and lower wages for their workers. There were many safety problems with the Mexican trucks and their driver's licenses: permitting eighteen-year-olds to drive tractor trailers, no medical exams or drug testing, no insurance, or no hours of service on the road.

"We went down to the border, Mr. Carey and myself," recalled Skelton. "We crossed over and went to the point of entry where those Mexican trucks would be coming in and doing an inspection. It was scary how bad a shape those trucks were in. I said, 'Look at those brakes, no grease. Do you want those things driving on our roads?' When we got back to DC, Mr. Carey told Clinton about what we observed. Clinton said, 'I need your support' and Mr. Carey said, 'How am I gonna tell my members and show them how this benefits them?' He handled it as good as he could."[106]

When fully implemented, U.S., Canadian, and Mexican truckers were to have full and easy access to the roads of each other's countries instead of being allowed to drive only within a twenty-mile corridor in the United States. Although it was scheduled to start on January 1, 1995, the Teamsters under Ron pressured Clinton to postpone that part for "safety reasons." Clinton was up for reelection in 1996 and, of course, he needed Teamster contributions and votes. "The administration's decision is a temporary victory for highway safety," Ron explained. "The real solution is to have American trucking done by American workers with American safety standards and American wages."[107]

Behind the scenes, Ron's political director, Bill Hamilton, was speaking with Clinton's deputy chief of staff, Harold Ickes, to smooth things over and make people happy. According to Ickes, "Carey was not a schmoozer. He wanted results on issues he cared about like the Diamond Walnut strike and organizing Pony Express." The White House assisted by getting U.S. Trade Representative Mickey Kantor to talk to the CEO of Diamond Walnuts to settle the dispute with the Teamsters. Hamilton said:

> Every day we got help in small ways from Bill Clinton; he makes a phone call, he makes a veto threat, he makes an appointment. He did stop the NAFTA border crossings and told his negotiators to open up Japanese airports not only to FEDEX but also UPS. He was against OSHA cuts and the TEAM Act and appointed pro-union NLRB picks.[108]

However, Hamilton believed that Ron spent a lot of his political capital fighting NAFTA. "I think we spent too much time fighting NAFTA and not nearly enough time fighting the World Trade Organization (WTO), the global body that tramples over labor and human rights," said Hamilton. "We did make NAFTA workable by screwing up the crossing of trucks into the U.S.; instead of just fighting it, we could have fought for better standards in NAFTA, be a part of making it work with stronger standards."[109]

CHAPTER 6

The Incumbent

I n late January 1994, in the midst of the dues issue, UPS unilaterally announced that starting on February 7 it was raising the weight of its packages from 70 to 150 pounds in order to "make the company more competitive." This was despite just settling a contract with the Teamsters in late September. If they wanted this change, Ron believed, they needed to bargain for it.

After negotiations went nowhere, Ron set February 7 as the strike date. On Friday, February 4, a federal judge issued a temporary restraining order blocking the Teamsters from striking until at least Wednesday, February 9.[1] Nevertheless, Ron ordered a strike to begin at 8 a.m. Monday morning. "We immediately drafted a TITAN on Sunday that we were going on strike to all the locals," recalled Aaron Belk.[2] At 8 a.m., Ron defied the judge's injunction and had his members walk.

Even though the contract had not expired, he believed that UPS's unilateral change in operations "violated human decency." "If Kent Nelson, the Chairman of UPS, had to spend this week lifting 150-pound packages, UPS would quickly decide to negotiate a settlement," Ron stated that morning.[3] A spokesman for the Teamsters, Matt Witt, maintained that "Federal labor law and

OSHA rules allow employees to refuse to work in situations of 'imminent danger' and anyone with common sense realizes lifting a 150-pound package exposes a worker to imminent danger of permanent back injury."[4]

While both sides negotiated by phone on Monday, "We got information that Yellow Freight was gonna haul some UPS trailers to the rails," remembered Belk. "Dennis Skelton, the Freight Director, called Yellow and said that if they pulled one trailer outside any terminal, we were gonna strike nationwide. Pull one out and see!"[5] Skelton recalled that "we had a little bit of influence there. I was there for forty-four years. I knew who to go to, who would listen. I got a hold of this guy whom I generally trusted, and I said, 'If you guys want to get in this I have ways of causing you grief, maybe nationwide, who knows.' Regardless, no trailers left any terminal!"[6]

Anywhere from 70,000 to 95,000 Teamsters joined the strike out of 165,000. Some big cities and key choke points joined in the strike: the NYC area, Boston, Pittsburgh, Atlanta, Seattle, most of West Virginia, parts of Florida.[7] "A lot of the Old Guard that didn't support Ron didn't want to go along with it," observed Gene Moriarity. "Of those who would have gone along with it found some reason not to when UPS got a court order."[8] Tom Leedham commented, "Two-thirds of union officers told their members to scab. It was a turning point."[9]

Some local leaders accused Ron of playing politics to "consolidate power" and "win some votes for his dues increase." RV Durham supported taking on the issue but couldn't "in good conscience take his people in the street" calling it "irresponsible."[10] But Ron knew UPS well. He had sat across the table from this outfit for a long time. He knew this was a huge safety issue and knew he had to protect his members at all costs. UPS unilaterally doubling the weight of a package was a bridge too far.

This move by Ron forced the company to compromise. But Ron gave the credit to the rank-and-filers. "The courage of Teamster members won this agreement. No corporation has the right to break workers' backs just to make another buck." Under the new agreement, drivers were not required to handle packages over 70 pounds without help from another Teamster. Safety equipment like better hand trucks and procedural training on handling "over 70s," as well as properly labeling by customers, was also part of the deal. UPS agreed not to discipline the strikers and to drop its effort to have the Teamsters union fined and Ron held in contempt for violating the federal court order.[11]

THOUGH RON WAS IN CHARGE of the Marble Palace, there were hundreds of Little Marble Palaces throughout the country. Even with Ron at the helm, the Old Guard still retained control of the middle-level Teamster leadership: the fifty Joint Councils and the four Regional Conferences. It was here that most grievances got settled. It was also the place where the union got most of its money and power for collective bargaining. With the rebellion about the dues increase from local leaders it was obvious that the "olive branch" strategy was not working. "I've walked around with an olive branch in my hand and I'm tired of having it shoved up my ass!" remarked Ron.

So he went after a source of their power: the Area/Regional Conferences. Ron heard there was to be a meeting to take place with four heads of the U.S. Area Conferences in Chicago. No one spoke with Ron about it. He threatened to discipline them if they met without his authorization. The meeting never took place. On March 21, 1994, Ron made his move on the Area Conferences. He asked his General Executive Board to remove the charters of all four U.S. Area Conferences; the Canadian Conference was left untouched. Gene Moriarity tells the story:

> It was amazing to watch Ron in action, to see how firm he was, and these guys didn't get it. He called them for a meeting in DC and he met them in one of the huge conference rooms. When he took the podium he just had a couple of pieces of paper with him and he started telling them what we can achieve together and then one of them would get up and start screaming at him, "This

is bullshit! You're not gonna get away with this!" Ron would calmly just move on to the next guy and get the same response.

At the very end, he just shuffled his papers, folded them up and said, "Thanks a lot for coming, guys" and walked out the conference room door. These guys just all stood around looking at each other in disbelief and said, "What the fuck is going on? Is he coming back?"

I think it was Aaron Belk who stayed in the room afterward and told them, "No, he isn't going to be coming back." They storm out of the room into the lobby, and you can hear all their cell phones going off at about the same time. Their Conferences had all been taken over.[12]

It was meticulously carried out. Ron sent people like Ken Hall to the Eastern Conference, Tom Leedham to the Western Conference, Bob Knox to the Central, John Wayne Garrett to the South, all at exactly the same time. Each leader went with a few other reps and a lawyer assigned to each. According to Bob Hauptman, himself an integral part of this action, each team did audits of each conference and tried to decipher what the books said and the contract that had to be dealt with, as well as watch over their bank accounts and financial records.[13]

This reform would save about $15 million a year for the Teamsters. It also displayed democratic accountability and stopped the "sweetheart deals" with employers. Ron called the Area Conferences "fertile ground for corruption and mob influence" that were "outmoded, undemocratic, and wasteful." The Area Conferences had become an "out-of-control monster" run by the Old Guard that colluded together in order to stop Ron's policies and reforms.[14] Going forward, dues would come to Washington and be spent on the members instead of redundant services and bloated salaries.

On March 23, the IBT filed internal charges against the Eastern Area Conference office and filed an injunction in the Southern District of New York to enforce the invocations. A few weeks later,

Ron made his proposal to his GEB. While it revoked the charters of the Area Conferences, it kept in place the forty-three Joint Councils that worked closely with the local unions on strikes and contracts.

Both sides made their case for and against revoking the charters. Tom Leedham made the case to revoke them. "The opposition was determined to see Ron fail," stated Leedham. "He sent me into the fight over the Area Conferences, a true fight, and chose me to make the case against the conference at the meeting before the GEB meeting." Leedham continued:

> In the Western Conference, few rank-and-filers ever saw the inside of that place, with its beautiful view. After we took them over, we invited the rank-and-filers, who were protesting outside the Area Conference office, inside. We were stunned to discover how their dues money was being spent. It put us in a better position to deal with national employers in a unified way.[15]

On Thursday, June 9, by a vote of 14–3, the GEB officially gave Ron the constitutional right to close the conferences down. The Old Guard went to court to stop the closings. But the following day, Judge Edelstein of the Federal District Court of Manhattan, who oversaw the Teamsters under the consent decree, denied their request.[16]

Reformers like Ken Paff welcomed the changes as "long overdue." Of course, the Old Guard thought it was unnecessary. Some like RV Durham called it "anarchy" and accused Ron of "retaliation" against them for fighting him on the dues increase. Former reformers like GEB member Sam Theodis turned on Ron and reform, calling the move "revenge." Theodis split from being pro-reform and pro-Ron to considering challenging Ron in 1996. On the other hand, Ron made a powerful ally in John Metz, a Durham supporter in 1991, who observed Ron walking the picket line with the members at his St. Louis local. Metz commented, "I never saw an International President on the picket line."

Even the FBI had an opinion on the reform, which revealed just how anti-union and out of touch they were. In Ron's FBI files were several newspaper articles about the issue as well as interviews with Ron's political enemies describing Ron's actions as "authoritarian" and "political retaliation." They wrongly surmised that his purpose was to "consolidate power and centralize power" similar to how the more militant and radical United Mine Workers did in the 1980s. They saw Ron as allied with radicals (TDU), and the FBI hated and feared radicals.[17]

A few weeks later, hundreds of Old Guard officers from around the country, along with Jimmy Hoffa, Jr., marched on the Marble Palace. They pounded on the doors of Teamster headquarters shouting for Ron's removal. Some in the crowd shouted, "Storm the building!" while others yelled "Get a rope!" Their grievance was not for better contracts for the rank and file or for better reforms. They had traveled hundreds of miles to protest Ron's removing their fat cat Area Conference jobs and perks.[18] But it was all just a political show. Many protesters were wearing black and yellow Hoffa hats. This was basically the kick-off of Jimmy Hoffa, Jr.'s (the son of the infamous Jimmy Hoffa) 1996 campaign for General President.

All this was happening while 80,000 Teamster truckers, warehousemen, dockworkers, and mechanics were out on strike against major trucking companies, operating under an umbrella group, Trucking Management.The strike, which was called at 12:01 a.m. on April 6, was the first nationwide strike by Teamsters since the nine-day walkout in 1979, right after the federal government began to implement its neoliberal deregulation of the trucking industry.

"Picket lines went up at some trucking terminals early this morning as the Teamsters union went on strike against 22 major trucking companies that move about 15% of the nation's dry freight," began the coverage in the *New York Times*.[19] Among the 22 companies was Yellow Freight, Consolidated Freightways, Roadway Express, etc. Carolina Freight was not struck because it did not insist that Trucking Management's final offer be accepted.

The main issues were the expanding use of part-time workers during peak periods and an increase in the use of "intermodal" (rail transport) from 10 percent to 35 percent. "Trucking Management wants to shift to using part-time workers with low wages and little or no benefits," said Ron at a news conference. "This is wrong for workers and their families. It is wrong for our communities. And it is wrong for America."[20]

Ron was fighting a two-front battle. On the one hand, he was dealing with the company and the issues of job security, intermodal language, and part-timers. On the other, he had Old Guard local leaders refusing to distribute any information on the issues and the strike, which Ron's people were sending out in daily bulletins.

Those Old Guard officers told freight director Dennis Skelton, "You can't directly communicate with our members unless you ask us first." Ron sent Skelton back there and said to them, "Wrong, they are all Teamster members and are covered under this International union. If you don't want to work and help the members, we will!"[21] And that's just what Ron and his freight director did. They went around the Old Guard officers and made contact with lots of workers creating rank-and-file networks.

They told the chief negotiator for the companies, Art Bunte, that the part-time issue was a strike issue. "I will bankrupt this union before you get part-timers!" exclaimed Skelton. He learned a lot from Ron's style. During negotiations, Skelton and Ron watched as some of the Old Guard on the negotiation committee sat and ate lunch with management. "Mr. Carey said to me, 'That shows where their bread is buttered. They told you something without even opening their mouths. Just catalogue that,'" recalled Skelton.[22]

On April 28, both sides came to an agreement. Compromise was the word of the day. On the positive side, the agreement blocked Trucking Management from introducing part-time workers. "We won on the key issues by not letting them change good, full-time jobs to low-wage part-time jobs, said Ron. "We drew the line not just for Teamster members but for all American workers."[23]

On the negative side, it allowed more goods to be shipped via rail: from 10 to 28 percent. Some union officers described the added use of the railway system as a concession. Durham called it "concessionary" and would not recommend his members to vote for it. Regardless, on June 5, the Teamster rank and file overwhelmingly approved the tentative agreement with 81 percent of the vote.[24]

WHEN REFORM DIDN'T MATERIALIZE overnight, some in the corporate media started to turn on Ron. They received numerous calls from certain of Ron's political enemies and wrote articles criticizing Ron's administration. At first, it was about how "passive" Ron appeared about reforms and then how "slow" reform was going in the Teamsters. But Ron responded to the criticism and defended his record and the enormous task before him. "You're dealing with a monumental union. How long does it take me to change what has been fundamentally wrong for eighty-eight years?"[25]

It was not "passive"; it was not "slow." Ron's strategy was methodical and pragmatic. Yes, he went after corrupt officials and locals. He also tried to work with some of the Old Guard at key times to get things done and make progress. Ron's job was not only to clean up the Teamsters union. It also included running a huge bureaucratic organization that had to deal with contracts, strikes, employers, pensions, health care funds, organizing, and educating the members.

Nevertheless, they criticized the Ethical Practices Committee as being a political weapon used by Ron to attack his enemies or a "halfhearted" effort. Nothing could have been further from the truth. The EPC brought charges against Teamster officials who were pro-Carey and anti-Carey. They brought charges against Ron's own GEB member, Gene Giamcumbo. The case was given to the Independent Review Board, which removed him from office for placing friends on voting rolls of his home Local, accepting a monthly car allowance, among other things. Giacumbo charged that Ron was "trying to defame" him over his opposition to the dues referendum. But actually, the charges were made by members of Giacumbo's own Local 843 a year earlier.[26]

Ron also had to remove another GEB member, Mario Perrucci, after an investigation found that Perrucci had taken gifts, including a boat, from employers he dealt with in New Jersey.[27] Ron's first director of Carhaul, Ron Owens, from Detroit Local 299, was investigated for allegations of favoritism and improperly helping friends and relatives get jobs at the Local. Ron asked Owens to take a leave of absence until the investigation was done. At first, Ron seemed to defend Owens but then distanced himself and suspended him. He even accused him of choosing an organized crime associate to oversee the corrupt Local 295 in Queens, New York.

On the day before Ron was sworn into office, U.S. District Court Judge Eugene Nickerson approved the trusteeship of Local 295, which represented about a thousand truck drivers and warehouse workers for airfreight companies at Kennedy Airport and the other airports in the region. The government said that by controlling the Local for forty years, mobsters had extorted millions of dollars from companies at the airports.[28]

Ron gave the assignment to appoint a trustee to Ed Burke, who recommended William Genoese, the principle officer of Local 732 and former International Teamster director of the airlines division until 1991. It had been rumored that Ron picked this Old Guard officer as part of his "olive branch" strategy to unite the union. He needed experienced officers in charge of certain things. Others thought that to ease tensions after the brutal election, Barry Feinstein, the powerful Old Guard New York Teamster, asked to have Genoese for the Local 295 trustee spot. Regardless, Burke said he "saw no harm in trying to ease political tension in the union."[29]

However, Burke and Ron were unaware of Genoese's affiliations with the Lucchese crime family. According to FBI files, on March 5, the day after he was appointed, Genoese was spotted at dinner with a reputed Lucchese family member. When Independent Administrator Lacey found out about Genoese, he immediately rejected the appointment and sent a letter to Ron's general counsel, Rick Gilberg, saying the appointment would "further an act of racketeering activity" within the Teamsters and that Genoese was unfit to be trustee of that Local due to his lack of crime-fighting experience. He said Genoese had "a sad record of inaction in the face of a long history of corruption at JFK airport."[30]

Burke later recalled, "I recommended Genoese. Lacey overrode it. I relied on others' information on the situation. It was my mistake."[31] It seems it was an honest mistake. Ron called it a mistake himself and offered that "it comes back to haunt me."[32]

On April 29, Judge Nickerson appointed Thomas Puccio, a New York lawyer who prosecuted corrupt Congress members in the ABSCAM bribery scandal in the early 1980s, to be the trustee in charge of Local 295. Interestingly, Puccio had no experience in investigating unions and was the defense attorney for Claus von Bulow who in 1985 was tried for murdering his wife. He basically "defended corporations and rapists" and was part of the old boy network of ex-prosecutors and judges who were paid a lot of money to oversee crime-infested unions.[33]

Since he lacked experience dealing with unions, Puccio picked former Labor Department investigator Michael Moroney as his special assistant. Moroney quit the Labor Department after a memo he had written was blocked from being disseminated for recommending policy action instead of just turning in facts. Many of Moroney's statements are very biased and tainted. He's been described as a conspiracy theorist.

In June 1993, Puccio and Moroney filed a motion with Nickerson asking to extend their trusteeship to include Local 851, the sister local of Local 295, which represented the airfreight clerks. Some have claimed that this was a power grab by Puccio. Taking over Local 851 would put him in charge of $250 million in pension funds, and there would be many lucrative perks from picking stockbrokers and people owing favors. They claimed Local 851 was moving work away from Local 295. When Ron refused at first to expand their trusteeship, they tried to pressure him.[34] Others have claimed that after years of their high-salaried trusteeship with no charges against anyone, they were not doing their jobs but wanted to expand into Local 851 to keep their lucrative positions.

The duo contacted Teamster attorney Charles Ruff and threatened to turn over "evidence" linking Ron Carey to mobsters. The so-called evidence was hearsay from an interview Mike Moroney did with reputed mob boss Alphonse D'Arco. It was later discovered that D'Arco never even met or knew Ron Carey but heard "what two other mobsters had told him" about Ron. Frankly, the "evidence" was not very credible.[35]

Ruff sent a letter to Judge Lacey about the threat. Lacey then wrote a letter to Puccio which was, of course, leaked to Ron's political enemies. The confidential letter was exposed in a May 1995 *Time* magazine article by Richard Behar. In the letter, Lacey objected to Puccio's litigation tactics, releasing unproven allegations publicly for the purpose of blackmail. Puccio backed down and Moroney resigned after reports of his "autocratic and intimidating attitude."[36]

Instead of agreeing to allow Puccio and Moroney to extend their trusteeship to Local 851, Ron appointed Curt Ostrander from Local 25 to be the Emergency Trustee of Local 851. Ron also removed Genoese as principal officer of Local 732 after an investigation found a "pattern of malfeasance" in the use of members' dues and other improper conduct. He appointed a trustee, Tom Sever, to run this Local.[37] Ostrander meticulously went about his business, quietly seeking damages from a company that paid Local officers $500,000 to dismiss two-dozen clerks and saw the Local's principal officer, Anthony Razza, sentenced after pleading guilty to criminal racketeering charges related to the dismissals.[38]

On the other hand, Puccio, after two years, didn't have much to show for his huge salary. Averaging only around ten hours a week (Ron Carey made $150,000 and worked seventy- to eighty-hour workweeks) for a massive $250,000 a year part-time job (Ostrander made $62,500 a year), Puccio couldn't even claim new shop steward elections in Local 295. The team of Puccio and Moroney were accused of overspending: dues coming in to Local 295 brought in $1.3 million a year, while Puccio/Moroney spent $2 million.[39]

Former head of the Intelligence Division for the New York State Organized Crime Task Force, Joseph Coffey, disagreed with Moroney's allegations and smears. Coffey described Ron as "the best around." Furthermore, Puccio and Moroney did not seem to be people who could be trusted to conduct a fair investigation. According to Susan Jennik of the Association for Union Democracy, "Moroney was on a quest to show that Ron was corrupt."[40] She was right. Moroney and Hoffa surrogates George Geller and Richard Leebove solicited reporters to write attack articles on Ron. The noted labor reporter for the *New York Times* William Serrin called them the "three mysterious enemies of Carey" who fed clueless reporters false or misleading stories about Ron.

While being the deputy trustee in Local 295, Moroney was running a campaign against Ron. He "used phones, office space, etc. to communicate with political foes of Ron Carey."[41] Later, Ron described him as a "disappointed job seeker," believing that Moroney wanted to be an investigator on the IRB but was turned down for the job.

Richard Leebove and George Geller were both backers and close supporters of the American Fascist Lyndon LaRouche and his so-called Labor Party. LaRouche was ultimately convicted of credit card fraud. He also supported mob elements in the Teamsters and conspiracy theories about communists. Leebove was a propaganda specialist who put out false claims that communists were taking over the labor movement. He also worked as a propagandist for the anti-reform group of thugs, BLAST (Brotherhood of Loyal Americans and Strong Teamsters), who threatened and beat up reform Teamsters across the country. In the 1990s, Leebove worked for Detroit Local 337's Larry Brennan, who was a political enemy of Ron and was currently working for Hoffa, Jr.[42] He also was a supporter of Local 282's president John Cody, who was a reputed mob associate. Geller was a Detroit lawyer who represented Hoffa, Jr. in election matters and public relations. They worked to weaken or hurt Ron before the 1996 IBT election, spreading lies and smears about Ron to gullible and uninformed writers and columnists at the *Wall Street Journal, New York Times,* AP, *Washington Times, Time,* and *Fortune.*

All of a sudden, stories about Ron's father's stock holdings were in the news. Ron's father, who had died in 1991, had bought eight shares of UPS stock in 1935 for $320. Back then, drivers were allowed to buy UPS stock. Over the years, the investment had grown to 112,000 shares worth $1.9 million. A year later, the stock was sold back to the company, and the money was dispersed to Ron and his five brothers. As we have seen, each received around $350,000 before taxes.

In August 1993, a *Newsday* story came out attacking Ron for "not disclosing" that he inherited money from the estate sale of his father's holdings in UPS stock. Under federal law, the Labor-Management Reporting and Disclosure Act (LMRDA), union officers are required to report ownership or interest in any stock directly or indirectly in companies that they represent by filing a LM-30 form. But Ron never owned any stock in UPS and therefore had no connection to it.[43] The Department of Labor agreed that the stock was inherited, therefore Ron was not required to disclose it.

In the next wave, negative articles about Ron's real estate holdings were written in the corporate press. They accused him of being a phony "man of the people" who lived it up in his numerous real estate investments. Ron's detractors like Gene Giamcumbo called Ron "our land baron." But as Ken Paff stated at the time, "I don't care what Ron Carey does with his money as long as it's legal." And it was. Some people invest their savings in stocks and bonds. Others like Ron invested in property.[44]

His first land purchase was the two-family house he bought with his father in 1958. By 1973, Ron had paid off that mortgage. He lived frugally. He had no major expenses: his kids who decided to go to college paid their own way, he charged them rent, Local 804 afforded him a car, he paid his credit card bills every month, his wife worked at Macy's and brought home $14,000 a year, and he took tuna fish sandwiches to work. Vacations with the family meant a few days in Ron's father's bungalow in New Jersey.[45]

In 1979, Ron bought a duplex in Queens. He fixed it up and rented it out. A few years later, he invested in two more rental properties in Florida and a condo in Arizona. One of the Florida condos he bought on behalf of one of his daughters, Barbara, who couldn't get a mortgage herself. She paid all the monthly costs of the property. The second Florida property was a condo in the Keys he purchased along with his mortgage company manager, who put up half the money. The Arizona property was a condo for his wife, whose sister lived in Scottsdale.[46]

Two years later, Ron purchased a home for his son, Ron, Jr., in Rockland County, New York. Ron called it a "handyman's special." He was a good carpenter; he did all the work himself along with his son. A year later the property was sold for a nice profit. Ron then bought a second property, an oceanfront retirement home in the Florida Keys and sold the other condo to his son. Since becoming the president of the Teamsters, he had bought a condo in Arlington, Virginia, for when he was in Washington.[47]

William Serrin wrote an article discussing the disinformation campaign against Ron. He wrote, "Lacking a sense of the issues, the personalities, the history of labor, even good reporters get suckered by bad stories." He goes on: "The press today is cynical and quick to condemn, and many reporters are as ambitious and career-minded as bankers or politicians."[48] TDU's Ken Paff remarked that "Moroney never saw a conspiracy he didn't believe; they are saying Carey is a 'Mafia guy' and a government guy. What a joke."[49]

On July 11, 1994, the anticipated IRB report was released. The 85-page report extensively investigated all the allegations made against Ron over the previous few years concerning ties to the mob, corruption, and his real estate ventures. Ron had met with the chief investigator, Charles Carberry, twice and turned over documents and records. He was vindicated on all the allegations. The report found that most of the allegations against Ron "came from or were stimulated by, Carey's political opposition within the IBT."[50]

In allegation after allegation made against Ron for wrongful association with organized crime members or associates, the IRB report concluded that "the evidence does not support recommending a charge." They found that most of the allegations were raised by Alphonse D'Arco, the former acting boss of the Lucchese crime family in NYC. It was revealed that D'Arco never met Ron but heard what "two other mobsters had said about Carey," which is pure hearsay.[51] Longtime reporter on union affairs Ken Crowe stated, "I knew the organized crime shit was baloney. They hated Carey because he wouldn't go along with them!"[52]

One allegation was that Joe Trerotola (Joe T) told Ron to have his members not cross a picket line. Well, that was a joke. Ron didn't have to be told not to cross any picket line. No one controlled Ron Carey. Moreover, D'Arco falsely alleged that Ron and Joe T were close and that Ron followed his orders. The evidence showed no such relationship; Ron kept Joe T at a distance but had to deal with him since Trerotola was head of JC 16.[53]

The IRB also looked into Ron's real estate holdings. Their report stated that there was no evidence that he financed his real estate investments with illegal payments from mobsters or kickbacks. The only thing they criticized him for was a forged signature of Ron's wife, Barbara, on an affidavit. It asserted that Ron had his Local 804 office manager in 1992 sign a form as a witness to Barbara signing the form that Ron had signed himself with his wife's permission. It was over real estate documents. Ron lived in DC while his wife still lived in Queens.[54] The report labeled it "improper conduct," but since it was not dealing with Teamster union business, he did not violate any IBT rules.

Ron responded to the IRB Report, saying, "I've been facing a smear campaign from opponents of reform inside the union management and the mob." In an interview with the *Christian Science Monitor*, Ron said, "It certainly had an effect on my family. So yes I am relieved."[55] George Geller, the Hoffa lawyer, called it a "disgraceful cover-up" and asked Senator Nunn who headed up the Senate Committee on Investigations to hold hearings on this.

BY 1996, THE CAREY ADMINISTRATION had trusteed over sixty
Teamster locals. Ron would have his International Reps go around
the country doing "Article 19" hearings where charges would
be referred against Local union officers and he would name the
panel. According to Richard Hurd, the director of Labor Studies
at Cornell University, "The trusteeships are a very legitimate
role to make sure there is no illegal activity or corruption."[56] Ron
would take control of the Local by temporarily appointing his own
trusted people to manage its day-to-day affairs with auditors and
investigators until new elections could be held.

In Chicago, Ron sent his trusted aide Eddie Burke into Local
705 to prove he was serious about the Teamsters' image and corruption. In Local 714, he picked onetime opponent John Metz, St.
Louis Teamster leader, as a trustee to investigate Bill Hogan and
nepotism. Hogan railed that it was retaliation for running with
Hoffa, Jr. in the upcoming election. Ron remarked on the trusteeship of Local 714: "Those who scream the loudest about retaliation
are the ones with their fingers deepest in the cookie jar."[57]

In the New York City area, Locals 282, 272, 966, 817, 807, 851,
295, and many others were put under trusteeship. The Javitz
Center in Manhattan, Local 807, was notorious for mobsters and
corruption. It was being run for the benefit of a select few officers,
mobsters, and convicted felons—not the members. "Corruption at
JC 16 and Local 807 is robbing this city," said Ron. "It robs good
jobs from hardworking people, robs hundreds of thousands of dollars by driving convention business away." Ron put in a person he
trusted from his home Local 804, Johnnie Brown, saying there was
"no one more honest and harder working guy than John Brown."[58]

Ron then put Pete Mastrandrea, another Local 804 member
and respected shop steward, in charge of Local 282. Mastrandrea,
who had just finished successfully trusteeing Queens Local 363,
recounted, "There was no training. We were thrown right into the
fire. He trusted us from what he knew of us, our skills. It was a big
step, but we had help from lawyers and actuaries. When things got
intense, we just called Ron."[59]

An International Rep Ron truly trusted and respected was Gene Moriarity. Gene recalls a trusteeship he presided over in Mulden, Massachusetts:

> They were Hertz workers and they had just voted to strike at midnight. Ron called and asked how things were going. He said, "You sound distracted." I told him, "This thing is a fucking mess. I just took a strike vote, and these members are going out at midnight and during that vote I looked out on those four hundred or so faces knowing they are not going to have a paycheck tomorrow. I am but they're not. My knees are knocking together." Ron said, "You know, if you ever call a strike of that magnitude again and your knees AREN'T knocking, then there is something wrong. You should be scared! Now just go out there and win the God damned thing!" It was very inspiring.[60]

However, not all trusteeships were inspiring or cheerful. Many trusteeships were dangerous ordeals. Mastrandrea said that Local 282 was the scariest one he ever went into. Gene recalls a frightening story while he was trusteeing Local 966 in New York City:

> There were lots of threats directed at those of us who did trusteeships. I got to my apartment at the end of a day, and my phone rings. A stranger says, "Is this Gene Moriarity? You don't need to fuckin' know who this is because you ain't asking no fuckin' questions. You just listen because you are gonna go down and I'm the one who's gonna do you. I could have done you today. I walked you right the fuck home asshole from your office to the shuttle to the 6 train and right to your front door and the day will come where I do you!" I was rattled. I called DC and they got a former cop to watch out for me.[61]

Ron was able to get close to some of the reps. They weren't officers so he felt he could trust them. "Ron felt more comfortable with some reps than with others," recalled Gene. "He didn't like it when he entered a room, and a rep would come over and kiss his ass." Ron also expected his rules to be followed by his reps. As Gene recalls:

> All 26 reps were told to contact the travel office. We were all going out to California for a week of just getting everything together to hear a presentation about the upcoming UPS negotiations. We all knew that there was travel rule: if you are traveling more than three hours you can fly First Class. But that was not a Carey rule. That was an Old Guard rule. No one dared do it under Ron except for one rebel rep from New Jersey. A guy named Bill. When Ron got out there, he was livid. When Bill went to shake Ron's hand, Ron refused and told the rep, "As soon as the meeting is over I want to talk to you." The guy was reprimanded and from that day on, he was known as Dollar Bill.[62]

Robert Sampson from Local 743, an International Trustee who ran with Durham and won in 1991, was banned after he was found guilty of allowing his predecessor, Donald Peters, who was barred in 1989 from holding office for having mob ties, to continue to influence his members.[63]

The Carey administration even investigated Ron's own secretary-treasurer, Tom Sever. He was eventually cleared of vote rigging in his Local 30 in Jeannette, Pennsylvania. Independent Investigator Carberry found that Sever did not retaliate against Thomas Felice for political reasons. And the director of the Small Package Division, Mario Perrucci, was banned for taking a gift from an employer. Ed Burke was Ron's messenger. He had to inform Perrucci that "the gig is up. You took a fuckin' boat!"[64]

The corrupt Old Guard sicced its bought politicians on Ron and his team. Local 714's Hogan challenged the anti-union Republican Congress to investigate Ron, particularly Illinois Congressman Henry Hyde. After the Republicans took over Congress in January 1995, after a historic "Red Wave" in the 1994 midterm elections, the new Speaker of the House, Newt Gingrich, appointed the right-wing, anti-union Congressman Pete Hoekstra to be chairman of the House Committee on Education and Workforce.[65] Gingrich and his crew were upset over losing one of their big cash cows, who were now funding the Democratic Party.

Some went directly after the NLRB. The Gingrich Republicans lobbied on behalf of the trucking company, Overnite Transportation, arguing that the NLRB should side with the company in its handling of Teamster complaints of unfair labor practices. The Teamsters were at the time trying to organize Overnite. When the NLRB voted to force Overnite to halt its unfair practice, the Republican-controlled Appropriations Committee introduced an amendment to double the $26 million cut in the NLRB's 1996 budget.[66]

Hoekstra embarked on a crusade against the entire labor movement and especially the Teamsters. He wanted to "alter the basic labor movement and laws that governed working conditions in the country." Ron's warehouse director, Tom Leedham, said that Hoekstra wanted to "eliminate the forty-hour workweek, gut overtime and job safety laws." He was especially close to the trucking industry and was willing to use his power and position to protect his corporate masters.[67]

On September 5, 1995, Ron took 5,000 Teamster carhaulers who worked for Ryder Trucks out on strike. He chose to target Ryder, the largest carhauler, because GM was its largest customer, and it wouldn't hurt the smaller companies. By focusing on key industry participants that depend on unionized labor Ron was able to guarantee that companies could not use replacement workers.[68]

Moreover, Ron strategically chose September to strike because he knew the car dealers were desperate for the delivery of the new models for 1996. He implemented this strategy knowing it would be like going out on strike against UPS in December.[69] "Carey was very hands on," recalled Fred Zuckerman, who was appointed chairman of the Central Southern Region for Carhaul. "He attended rallies, mobilized the members, and kept them informed. The members knew everything we knew."[70]

The Teamsters contended that the companies had refused to

provide economic and operations information it needed to evalu-
ate their proposals. But on October 8, after a full month of weak
September car and light truck sales by the Big Three, Ryder gave in.
A month later, the new Master Contract was approved by 70 percent
of the strikers, guaranteeing them higher pensions, higher employer
health care contributions, and tough new job security protections. [71]

As only Ron Carey would, he proclaimed, "Our members
deserve the credit for this victory by gearing up early and using
smart strategies that made it possible for us to win the best agreement at the bargaining table." But it was a bit of modesty on Ron's
part, for he implemented these smart strategies.

However, that smart strategy, that corporate campaign, made
Corporate America take notice. Corporate America recognized a
threat to their power in the workplace. They recognized unions
were finally waking up from their twenty-year snooze. They
immediately got their congressional puppets to help them out.
The United States Chamber of Commerce called for immediate
congressional hearings on the Teamsters. The Hoekstra committee
went about looking to damage the Carey image. The "Get Carey
Campaign" had begun.

Along with the American Trucking Association, these business
groups launched a campaign of their own to stop unions from
engaging in corporate campaigns that seek to influence corporate behavior by pressuring investors, customers, and institutional
shareholders.[72]

THE YEAR 1996 WAS GOING TO be a big year, with Ron's reelection
campaign and mobilizing for contract negotiations with UPS. It
would be a difficult two-front war. But people like Rand Wilson
saw it as a good thing:

> Ron was seen by the membership as a leader who was once a
> driver who identified closely with the rank and file. And now
> this leader is running as a leader during contract negotiations
> was the best way to get re-elected. Members certainly don't want

to change horses midstream. It was very compelling. He would be the general out front with the members. It was a perfect storm of union politics and bargaining come together.[73]

Ron announced in the summer of 1995 that he was running for reelection. But according to Paff, Ron originally didn't want to run again:

He felt burned out. All the shit of calling him a "scab," etc. He dealt with it, but it wore on him. Plus, his knees. I remember one time he was speaking at a TDU convention. He spoke at every TDU convention but one during his tenure. As he's walking up the riser to give his speech, he takes two steps and hesitates. He was in a lot of pain. He said to me that he "hoped he didn't look weak." He was aware that Hoffa was out there campaigning. And TDU wanted Carey out there campaigning, doing the one-on-ones. He said, "I really don't want to run, but this is gonna be my last term."[74]

It was going to be another Teamster election supervised by the federal government. Judge Edelstein appointed Barbara Zack Quindel as the new Elections Officer and Kenneth Conboy as Elections Appeals Master (EAM). It was not going to be an easy reelection. Since the Old Guard was no longer split as it was in 1991, Ron felt compelled to make some changes.[75] He felt he had to broaden his appeal, so he added new faces to his team, like Carroll Haynes, president of Local 237 in NYC, George Cashman, president of Local 25 in Boston, Lon Fields, president of Local 89, and Tom Leedham, secretary-treasurer of Local 206.

It seemed Ron was moving to the center with his reelection slate. "He had left the 'New Teamsters' label behind by now," explained Muehlenkamp. "He wanted to make it more 'The Teamsters.'"

Ron was never comfortable with the name New Teamsters, but he went along with it. Ron thought it was too polarizing of the majority against us. Was there anything wrong with being an Old Teamster? I mean, only a handful of Teamsters were the bad guys. Everyone else were proud Teamsters.

Anyway, Ron needed help from guys who could get things done, who understood how to negotiate with employers. More middle-of-the-road Old Teamsters. He was coalition building so he broadened his slate.[76]

Instead of using Burke again as his campaign manager, Ron hired Jere Nash to run his campaign and Martin Davis as a campaign consultant. Nash threw out the grassroots-focused winning playbook of 1991 and implemented a top-down campaign strategy that relied on outside consultants, raising questionable funds from questionable contributors, and using focus groups. Nash had just finished a winning campaign getting a Democrat elected governor in Mississippi. So he sold himself as someone who could get anyone elected.

Paff described Nash as "a smart guy but a sleazeball. A real insider, arrogant asshole."[77] Martin Davis was a political operative who worked in Democratic campaigns as well. He was known as "a man who could get anything done." Davis was cofounder of the November Group, a direct-mail company but was also known as "a savvy middleman who could make deals happen."[78]

Ron ran on his record of reform and keeping his promises. He boasted about selling the jets, the condo in Puerto Rico, the limousines, and ending the bloated and multiple salaries. He also ran on his record of removing corrupt union officials and trusteeing sixty-seven corrupt locals, along with striking employers and delivering strong contracts for the members by using aggressive corporate campaigns. But he was hindered at numerous points by an angry and passionate Old Guard.

The Old Guard wanted revenge. They even got to pick their own Old Guard horse in the race. On August 30, James P. Hoffa, Jr., announced on *The Larry King Show* that he was challenging Ron Carey for the presidency of the Teamsters union. Unlike his father, who worked his way up the Teamster hierarchy, Hoffa, Jr. was a labor lawyer who worked in the Detroit area. He had no experience running a Local, or anything for that matter. He had been hired a few years back as administrative assistant to Michigan's Joint Council 43 under the watchful eye of Larry Brennan.

Hoffa ran as an "outsider" on the platform that Ron Carey was "bankrupting the Teamsters." Whether Hoffa was aware of it or not, the financial problems predated Ron's administration. Ron also used the strike fund as a potent weapon to attain strong contracts. Hoffa thought that Ron was "over his head" and that he "lacked star quality." He also criticized Ron for hiring so many "non-Teamsters" in his administration. The campaign was a choice between going forward with reform and going back to the bad old days.

President Bill Clinton was also up for reelection that year. So was the Republican Congress. Ron had a close relationship by now with the Democratic hierarchy. "Carey didn't want to endorse Clinton because of NAFTA, but he didn't want to tell people not to vote for him either. So, we did voter registration rallies in big cities," said Dave Eckstein.[79] Hoffa was wooed by the congressional Republicans, although it was more a relationship of convenience. Both the Republicans and Hoffa hated Ron. Upon taking office, Ron had stopped funding the Republican Party, which infuriated the party bigwigs. In turn, they colluded with Hoffa, who promised to "restore the power," to return the Teamsters once again into a piggy bank for the Republicans. A weaker Teamster union meant a stronger GOP. Hoffa took help from whomever would help him "Make the Teamsters Great Again" and return the union to the past when mobsters ran the show, before the deregulation of the trucking industry.

But Hoffa had a long and questionable record. He was a onetime business partner of Allen Dorfman, who was the conduit for loans for the mob and was later convicted of conspiring to bribe a U.S. senator. Hoffa, Jr., was also legal counsel for Local 283 in Michigan, whose president, George Vitale, took kickbacks and embezzled funds. Moreover, Hoffa, Jr., traveled to Long Island to serve as legal counsel for a local associated with Nicky "Black" Grancio, who was a captain in the Columbo crime family. Hoffa used his name to endorse incumbents who refused to leave office after being voted out. In this instance, even Judge Edelstein was compelled to comment that Hoffa's behavior was "irresponsible and thoughtless."[80]

But now Hoffa was working for the Michigan Conference of Teamsters' Health and Welfare Fund. It was controlled by Larry Brennan, and its director was convicted of taking illegal kickbacks. Hoffa's sons were given jobs at the fund as well.[81] It was a nice little patronage system with a slush fund for the Hoffa family and his political allies. The Old Guard groomed Hoffa, Jr. They gave him jobs,income, and a platform to make sure he would be eligible this time.

Ron called Hoffa "an empty suit, a front man for the mob. If he didn't have that last name, he wouldn't have a chance."[82] "When you look at the people who his father left behind, his associations with the mob. I've had to make some tough decisions about . . . putting members first," Ron stated in an interview. "There are lots of people out there who are not happy about that."[83]

DAVE ECKSTEIN RAN THE FIELD Office for Ron's 1996 reelection campaign. The campaign was run out of a two-bedroom apartment on D Street near the Marble Palace. Eckstein recalled:

> By the convention I saw things I wasn't happy with, namely Nash and Davis. Right before the convention I said to Ron, "I got a bad feeling about these guys. They never come over to the office and they are doing stuff from the November Group offices in Davis's firm." Ron said, "It's too late to change things up now."
>
> Nash and Davis didn't seem to have Ron's best interests in mind. They ran the operation as though we were not under a consent decree. This wasn't the DNC. But Ron unfortunately trusted these guys.[84]

On Monday, July 15, Teamsters convened for the 1996 Teamsters' convention in Philadelphia. Though Ron chaired the convention, he struggled to control the agenda. Hoffa's plan was to disrupt Ron's command and control of the convention and the agenda. They were prepared and organized. All the Hoffa supporters dressed in matching red vests. Some observers believed it might get violent. It was reported that at a Sunday evening rally, Hoffa told his supporters "Don't bring your spouses and children because it's going to get rough. By Wednesday, we are going to force Ron Carey to shut this convention down!"[85]

Hoffa's supporters were able to stop proceedings numerous times. Hoffa's floor whips in headsets directed the action from the floor. They outshouted and outvoted Ron's supporters at key moments. They even heckled during the moment of silence for Teamsters who had died over the past year.[86]

When Ron gave his opening address to the delegates, he was met with a "wall of noise." Aaron Belk called the disruptions "the mouse that roared. The last gasp of corruption."[87] Ron angered the supporters of Hoffa with his attempt to have tighter control over the convention and votes on constitutional amendments.

When Hoffa made a motion to prohibit voting by eighty "super-delegates" who were either appointed by joint councils or automatically selected (each JC is entitled to appoint a super-delegate; GEB members, International Reps, and International trustees also enjoyed "super-delegate" status). Ron declared the motion defeated by a voice vote.[88] This infuriated Hoffa supporters. They began shouting at Ron.

When the respected keynote speaker at the convention, pro-union Republican Senator Arlen Spector, attempted to give his speech to the delegates, the booing "grew to a roar" and drowned him out. Spector stopped speaking and denounced the extremely rude delegates at one point. He called their behavior "a black mark on the Teamsters and a black mark on the American labor movement."[89]

Eventually, Ron was forced to temporarily shut down the convention until order was restored. "I'm asking all the guests to kindly leave the hall," he announced. The Hoffa supporters continued to protest. The police were called. But the Hoffa forces left the convention hall without the police directly forcing them out.[90]

By the end of the day, order had been restored after a three-hour recess. It seems a deal was made between the two factions allowing a more open debate and a "division of the house," meaning that delegates would stand to be counted on votes instead of Ron declaring the winner on a vague voice vote, especially in such an evenly divided convention hall.[91] The remainder of the convention was mired in procedural debate and delays. Ron used parliamentary tactics to outmaneuver Hoffa supporters, ruling opposition speakers out of order and stretching out debates. At one point, Ron proposed that candidates for International office must be IBT local officers or have worked at least two years for Teamsters' employers. That particular requirement would have disqualified Hoffa, who was never a union officer. Hoffa barely won that vote, 784 to 745.[92]

The final days became a nominating contest. In his acceptance speech, Ron defended his administration's record of strong contracts and fighting corruption. He proclaimed his "administration will never, never apologize for stamping out corruption. We are working every day to protect our members against corruption."[93] Hoffa countered, speaking about how "Carey failed miserably for the last five years and now has the guts to ask for five more."[94]

On the last day of the convention, a straw poll was taken of the delegates. Ron received 775 votes to Hoffa's 954.[95] The poll highlighted that this race was going to be close. As one delegate said, "Don't be fooled. The convention outcome only means we are in for a bare knuckles campaign like none we have ever seen before. This race is wide open."[96]

After the convention, the Carey campaign acknowledged the closeness of the race by sending out letters to supporters, calling it a "wake-up call" for all reformers and activists. Ron then embarked on a "caravan" across the United States and Canada. He campaigned on ousting corrupt officials, reversing a membership decline, stronger contracts, rank-and-file involvement, and a balanced budget.

Hoffa was traversing the country as well, looking for votes. He campaigned on vague slogans like "Restore the Power" and "Bring Back the Teamsters' Glory," whatever that meant. Hoffa enjoyed being the "outsider," yet criticized Ron for hiring numerous people from outside the Teamsters. He was using his famous name to draw crowds.

It was a nasty campaign. Ron and his supporters called Hoffa a "flunky of the old guard, the same old mobbed-up, on-the-take Teamster his daddy was!" The Hoffa side called Ron a "chicken" for refusing to debate Hoffa, and labeled him a "failed leader who resorts to power grabs."[97]

Both campaigns ran into each other at times on the campaign trail. International Representative Gene Moriarity recalled such an encounter:

We were campaigning in the Carolinas. Hoffa shows up and we are already at this UPS facility. Hoffa is standing across the street from us. Every tractor trailer that went by he would signal with his arm, you know, to blow their horn. So they would blow their horns. But what he didn't understand is that those were non-union truckers that went by.

It's getting late and the guys start coming into the gate and Hoffa walks across the street saying, "I'm Hoffa, I'm Hoffa!" Me and Gilmartin are handing out our flyers and the drivers are listening to us and Hoffa but very soon they had to go and punch in. Hoffa isn't aware of what time they start. So we let him go on and on.

Then I felt it was time to get the last word in right before they went in so I yelled, "Look, that guy wants to be your General President because his daddy was. Well when I was a little boy my father was a fireman and I wanted to be one too but I couldn't because I didn't know the job and my feet wouldn't reach the peddles, and that's his problem."

Hoffa just stumbled back and all he had was "He's Carey's buddy!" The drivers all laughed. Gilmartin calls out, "Hey Junior, you want to debate Ron but you can't even debate Gene!" The drivers then went into the building.[98]

On November 12, ballots went out to 1.4 million Teamsters. On December 10, Elections Officer Barbara Zach Quindel and her staff began opening, sorting, and counting the almost 500,000 mail ballots. The count was held at the National 4-H Center in Chevy Chase, Maryland. Both campaigns had thirty-six observers at the count.

By Sunday, December 15, the EO proclaimed Ron the winner by around 15,000 votes: 52 to 48 percent. However, Hoffa and his five vice presidents on the Hoffa slate won the Midwest. That meant that Ron's second-term GEB would have five members who actively campaigned against him and his board.[99]

At a news conference at Teamsters headquarters, Ron stated, "This victory sends a message to every mob boss in America: our treasury, our pension funds will never, ever again be used by organized crime in the form of a piggy bank." It was an extremely close race. According to labor reporter Steven Greenhouse, it was so close because "like so many revolutionaries, he faced a counter-revolution, one plotted by hundreds of Local union officials, many of them eager for revenge because he had hacked away at their power, prestige and perks."

Ken Paff asked, "Why is it that in countries that are new to democracy, dictators always try to make a comeback? The people in the counterrevolution don't like someone trying to take away their power. They control armies; they control people and pensions. They mustered a lot of power and resources to defeat Carey."[100]

CHAPTER 7

The UPS Strike

"First, you have to get organized. You have to have something that brings you together. When you are organized, you then create the leverage you need," Ron stated.[1] Those words were the battle cry that kick-started the huge national contract campaign against UPS.

Ron ran in 1991 and for reelection in 1996 on stronger contracts with UPS. Upon taking office in 1992, he created the Field Services Department to organize contract campaigns and run strikes against Teamster employers. He put Dave Eckstein in charge of it. Together with Matt Witt as the director of Teamster communications and Rand Wilson coordinator for the UPS contract campaign, this was Ron's Army and Air Force for taking on Big Brown in 1997. The array of ground troops and air cover grew to forty full-time field reps, who were taken from their buildings, from trucks, clerk stations, tractors, and loading docks. They were put on a leave-of-absence and trained to work on the UPS contract campaign to organize worksites, set up networks, and encourage work actions.[2]

Before the 1996 Teamster convention, Ron and his team, which now included Ken Hall, who was then the small package director.

Ron's first director of the small package division, Mario Perrucci, was barred from holding office after it was found that he accepted a boat as a gift from an employer of Local 177 members. Hall started putting together a survey of the membership to find out the rank and file's priorities.

The experience and division that occurred during the one-day strike against UPS in 1994 was on all their minds. Ron certainly did not want a replay of that time. He was a meticulous person who liked to plan ahead and get everything right. "He wanted a strategy that brought the union together for this contract by any means necessary," recalled Rand Wilson. "He wanted everyone moving in the same direction and not have UPS divide us like they did in 1994."[3]

Ron and his crew methodically planned the lead-up to the July 31, 1997, strike deadline. Each month or so they rolled out a different tactic to educate, organize, and mobilize the rank-and-file membership and keep UPS on their heels and on the defensive. They adopted the contract campaigns that they used in earlier contract disputes, only this time on steroids.

In 1995, UPS rolled out its "Team Concept Program" to weaken the union by getting the workers to supervise each other. Ron's Teamsters rejected Team Concept. "We got into the 'Team Concept' fight with the company which built support and sent a message to management that we were not gonna be split by any management schemes," said Wilson.[4]

At the 1996 convention, Ron had Wilson "buttonholing dozens of UPS shop stewards and stuffing their pockets with a booklet called 'Countdown to the Contract.' It contained a month-by-month calendar until the July 31 strike deadline." It was a playbook on how to escalate pressure on UPS and build a communications network that kept workers informed.[5]

After the convention, the surveys went out to 185,000 UPS Teamsters. The surveys asked the members what their key priorities were: full-time jobs, wages, benefits, pensions, subcontracting, etc. The questions were carefully crafted so as not to divide part-timers from full-timers or region from region. When those surveys were returned and analyzed, the union got more than 100,000 Teamsters to sign a petition demanding UPS stop increasing the number of part-timers. "He got the Research Department to get at that issue, the growth of part-time jobs—underpaid and overworked," said Wilson. "How full-time work and jobs were being split apart. How the full-timers, they hated *their* work being shifted to part timers and losing full-time jobs. That pissed people off and united full-time and part-time workers."[6]

The results of the survey allowed Ron and his team to attain key information about which Locals were able to get their members to fill out and return their surveys; this was called "organizing capacity." It also showed which Locals were not willing to fully participate in the campaign.

A directive was sent to all Teamster Locals to establish member-to-member networks in which each shop steward was responsible for communicating with about twenty workers. The International union deployed educational staff and field reps to help Locals get their networks established. "We did Town Hall meetings with UPS members at their union halls and built up a network of key people to distribute information," remembered Eckstein. "We had people in each Local in each shift."[7]

On one level it seemed all Locals and officers were on board. But there was minor resistance from some Old Guard–led locals close to Hoffa, Jr. "A little later, he had our two-person meetings. We set it up in Chicago," said Eckstein, continuing:

> Some of the locals were really nasty to him. But Ron was very blunt. He told them, "We are putting together a plan that we want you all to endorse it and then discuss with your members. Plan A is we provide all the information and services that you need to move this campaign and give the members what they deserve. Plan B is where we run this campaign around you through the TDU networks and do it without you. And if any of you get in the way, you're putting your Local in jeopardy of

being trusteed for impeding a national campaign." Most of them endorsed it, even if they didn't like him.[8]

Back at Teamster headquarters on the eighth floor, regular meetings were held. "Ron expected you to come and ask important questions and offer ideas," recalled Eckstein. "When someone brought up an idea, he would always respond with: How does that benefit the members? Ron was a hands-on leader. He reviewed all the plans and strategies. We never moved without his approval."[9]

Rand Wilson agreed. "Everything we did or wanted had to be approved by Ron. He wanted to know when and what and how much. His signature was gonna be on those expenses, and some things were not cheap. Mailings for videos, leaflets, tens of thousands of whistles."[10]

Ron had faith in the people he put in key positions. "At times he would think some of our ideas were either 'childish' like blowing the whistles [a tactic where members would blow a whistle every time they saw management violating the contract] or 'wouldn't work,' like doing safety checks, at first," continued Eckstein. "Then me and Rand would say, 'But it will get the members involved.' A little while later he would call us into his office and say, 'If you really believe this will work and is a good strategy ... you guys have done the right thing so far, let's do this!'"[11]

He knew UPS from sitting across the table from them in local negotiations and going toe-to-toe with management daily over workplace issues. He had learned valuable lessons from the one-day strike against UPS in 1994. "Ron was hopeful going in that a good contract would be reached without a strike," remembered Wilson. "But he wanted to go into negotiations from a position of strength. He knew what happened when we got divided in 1994. He hated UPS, but he understood the company and respected their phenomenal power of management. But he was not pollyanish on what we were taking on. He was very sober. He knew he had to deliver big."[12]

It was Ron's idea to bring rank-and-filers into the negotiations directly on the National Negotiating Committee. The committee was a group of around fifty rank-and-filers representing every craft and shift, full-timer and part-timer, at UPS. It included reformers as well as Old Guard members/officers. Of course, UPS was not very happy with the rank-and-filers in the room. They would be used to give real-time expertise to Ken Hall, whom Ron put in charge of the day-to-day negotiations with UPS.

But it was Ron who made the big decisions and was always several steps ahead of the company. "Ron was a great psychologist," recalled Aaron Belk. "He anticipated every one of UPS's decisions and responses. And he knew Ken Hall was up to the task."[13] Rick Gilberg added, "Ken was very talented and smart, even though he came from a local with few UPS members; he was plenty skillful at the bargaining table."[14] Hall was brought on board by Ed Burke. "Back then Hall was a million-dollar diamond in the rough. Ron had confidence in Ken to do the right thing and was impressed with his skill sets."[15]

ON MARCH 7, RON MET in Chicago with the two top officials in all 206 UPS locals, followed by a huge rally. Days later there were rallies held in Atlanta, Dallas, Los Angeles, New York City, Philadelphia, and Seattle. The rallies gave the rank and file the confidence that their Teamster union was behind them and that their demands and grievances were being heard by the leadership.

On March 11, contract proposals were exchanged between the two parties. The UPS team was led by Dave Murray, UPS's top labor manager and lead negotiator, a known commodity to Ron. Ron was also familiar with the company's new CEO, Jim Kelly (longtime CEO Oz Nelson retired in December 1996). Kelly had been UPS's Northeast Director of Human Resources.

UPS was looking for concessions. They offered slight wage increases, no guarantee of new full-time jobs, more subcontracting, and a pension grab. UPS wanted the right to set up its own company pension plan and leave the twenty-one multi-employer plans managed by the union. It was their big opportunity to skim the extra investment income and use it for things like executive bonuses. Ron knew it was a way to weaken unions and hurt retirees and pensions in other companies. He called it a deal breaker.

On the pension issue, it seems UPS did some research. A few years earlier, some workers became dissatisfied with their pensions and wanted to withdraw from their multi-employer plans. They hoped to create their own independent plans. Management assumed there was an opportunity for the company here.

On the other hand, Ron's Teamsters were in no mood for concessions. The union's demands were higher pay increases, a three-year contract, less subcontracting of union work, 10,000 new full-time jobs, and, of course, maintaining control over the pension. Stronger and better pensions controlled by the union were the linchpin to all the other goodies the Teamsters were gunning for. Better pensions lead to more retirements by full-time drivers and feeders, which, in turn, lead to more full-time jobs opening up to part-timers. The same with subcontracting. If allowed to grow, subcontracting meant fewer package drivers going to feeder, which meant fewer driver jobs opening up for part-timers. The issues were all connected.

"The real deal was the pension," remarked Eckstein. "We didn't publicize it too much because the average American didn't give a crap about that too much but we finally hit on 'Part-Time America Won't Work.' Everybody had full-time bills, so a part-time job was unfair. That really hit home with lots of people. And the media ate it up."[16]

That was all part of the plan. The union spoon fed the media by putting out packets highlighting their demands and grievances. The media learned that the research had found that about 10,000 part-timers actually worked more than thirty-five hours a week. In other words, the union worked the refs, in this case the media.

In April, the Teamsters introduced the campaign to document unsafe working conditions. Dave Eckstein explains: "Per our contract, there is language that provides members the right to stop if there was a safety issue. Whether in their package cars on their routes, in their feeders, or while loading trucks, if a worker noticed a possible safety issue with the equipment, that member had the right to stop and check it out. So we had everyone doing safety check all at once."[17]

UPS immediately sent a letter and called Ron and said that if anybody did this work stoppage, they would be disciplined. "Ron said 'Fine, I'll take you on on that because it's gonna happen and I challenge you to fire our members!'" recalled Eckstein. "The public was already on our side." The workers stopped and documented all their safety issues on a massive scale. There was no discipline filed against any Teamster. "That was when we knew that the rank and file was ready for this fight!"[18]

Every month there was a new tactic. In their "Blow the Whistle" campaign, the Teamsters bought 140,000 whistles and distributed them to the members. If a member saw a UPS supervisor doing bargaining work, they would blow their whistles and fill out a grievance form. It supplemented the point on creating full-time jobs: if supervisors weren't doing so much bargaining work, management could create more jobs.

"I'd be out in the parking lot, and you could hear the whistles out there," recalled Tim Buban, a UPS driver who was sent to organize in the upper Midwest. "You thought it was a fire station, there were so many whistles going off."[19]

They held rallies in front of buildings, like the "Don't Break Our Backs" rally where the union handed out shirts and stickers stating "It's Our Contract. We'll Fight For It!" They even went out and got over 100,000 signatures on a petition to demand UPS create 10,000 new full-time jobs.

On May 7, more than 97 percent of UPS pilots voted to give their union, the Independent Pilots Association of UPS, the authorization to strike if an agreement on its wages was not reached with the company. The pilots' contract is under the Railway Labor Act not Taft-Hartley as the Teamsters are.[20]

The methods Ron implemented in this particular campaign were definitely making an impact. The rallies, the mobilizing of the workers, and especially having rank-and-filers in the room at the negotiating table threw UPS off their game. UPS negotiators were not used to the transparency and the openness. They were accustomed to backroom deals and concessions by the Old Guard leadership at contract time. The Old Guard would never hold rallies to energize the rank and file. When UPS complained about the rallies, Ron responded with more rallies.

There was an ebb and flow to the bargaining that included both genuine negotiating and some theatrics. Ron internationalized the fight too. He got the International Transport Workers Federation (ITF) to organize a World Council of UPS Trade Unions, "whose international activities threatened UPS operations in competitive overseas markets."[21] On May 22, they organized 150 job actions and demonstrations at UPS buildings around the globe.

At one point, Ron invited forty representatives of the World Council of UPS Trade Unions to Washington to observe the ongoing contract talks with UPS. Naturally, UPS was not pleased and objected to their presence. "UPS was gonna walk out," remembered Eckstein. "Ron said, 'Go ahead. You are not gonna tell us who to bring!' Management did not want others to see what a bunch of jackasses they were."[22]

The talks were held at the Hyatt Regency, a union hotel in Washington, in their huge ballroom. They divided up the ballroom with the international negotiations in one part of the room and Local supplements in another. "We had like thirty or forty people on our side and almost as many on UPS's side," recalled Wilson. "There were lots of tables and subcommittees and supplements going on but the main table had a huge group of our rank and file. They were very helpful but largely more theatrical." He continued:

> Both sides put on presentations on full-time jobs, over 70s [packages weighing more than seventy pounds], subcontracting, etc. Proposals went back and forth. But I think a lot of the real bargaining took place away from the table. Murray and Hall had regular phone calls and discussions: "Hey, Dave, do you think

we can make progress on this issue?" Ron, on the other hand, did not like Murray. They didn't have a good relationship.[23]

Negotiations were suspended on April 22 when Ron saw the talks with UPS as "stuck." The rallies continued as planned. On May 13, talks resumed. The next day, upon hearing of some Locals' non-compliance, Ron sent a blistering letter stating, "Some Local unions are not complying with the negotiating committee policy and strategy." He instructed all UPS Locals to "implement and carry forward all policy and plans, with an emphasis on membership involvement and participation."[24]

On May 15, once again Ron suspended the talks claiming that "UPS still wants concessions." A week later, they implemented the "Blow the Whistle" action. On that day, May 22, Ron was in New York City at the 43rd Street UPS Facility in Manhattan to rally the troops: "This billion dollar company must be living on another planet to waste our time with proposals like these. These negotiations are only about one thing—making improvements that will give our members the security, opportunities, safety, and standard of living that they deserve."[25]

In June, the Teamsters made their focus full-time jobs. Their Research Department released the report "Half a Job Is Not Enough!" They found that since 1993, the part-time workforce at UPS had grown 43 percent while the full-time workforce grew only by 10 percent. Moreover, 83 percent of the new jobs created by management over that time span were part-time jobs, allowing UPS to make over $4 billion in profits. Over 90 percent of part-timers chose creating full-time jobs as their number one priority in the upcoming contract negotiations.[26] All shop stewards received a seven-minute video about contract negotiations as well as stickers to hand out to their members.

Days later, both sides were back at the table. On June 28, a Saturday, Ron called on the rank and file to take a strike authorization vote in order to give the negotiators more leverage. "UPS is a rich company that can afford to provide good, full-time jobs, but they refuse to negotiate seriously," Ron declared at a rally in Louisville, Kentucky. "We don't want to strike for a good contract, but we will if we have to!" [27] Within weeks, UPS Teamster rank and file voted 95 percent to authorize their leadership to call a strike if warranted.

By now, the rank and file were mobilized into a well-oiled machine that was radicalized. In Jonesboro, Arkansas, "members came to work wearing contract campaign stickers; their supervisor fired the union shop steward and told the other workers to take their stickers off or leave; they left to talk to a local TV station and later that night management apologized and assured the workers that if they came back to work they would be fully paid for the time they missed."[28]

Actions like these frustrated UPS and its negotiators. Their lead negotiator, Dave Murray, was heard and taped saying that he believed $8 an hour was not only adequate for part-timers but that it was a "fine full-time wage." An audiotape, "From the Horse's Mouth," was put out which angered members even more. Murray sent a "cease and desist" letter to the Teamsters to stop the further distribution of that tape. Ron ignored the letter.[29]

Nine days before the strike deadline, UPS issued its notorious "Last, Best, and Final Offer" to the Teamsters. It called for a lower wage increase than in 1993, creating only 200 full-time jobs, more subcontracting, and the demand to take over control of the full-time pension fund. UPS claimed that they needed "flexibility" to compete with FedEx and that "many only wanted to work part-time."

UPS demanded that the Teamsters accept the offer and agree to an extension while they worked out the details. Ron immediately rejected it, calling it an "insult." Management wanted him to allow the members to vote on the offer. Ron said there will be a vote but only after the rank-and-file negotiating committee negotiated an agreement that met the needs of the members. UPS requested a ten-day notification period before any strike action. That too was rejected.[30]

The "last, best, and final offer" was meant to be provocative. UPS was assuming that either Ron would back down or, if a strike did occur, it would be short-lived because of a "divided" union. UPS wrongly believed that part-timers and full-timers wouldn't agree on what was in their own best interests. They wrongly believed that nine months after a close election, the Teamsters would still be divided between the Old Guard and Reformers.

"Management assumed that full-timers wouldn't fight for more full-time opportunities and better pay for part-time workers, while the younger part-time workforce wouldn't fight for better pensions or reduced subcontracting," Rand Wilson and Matt Witt wrote retrospectively.[31] Well, they certainly underestimated the resolve of both Ron Carey and his rank and file. I'm sure they thought that the UPS Teamsters would be more loyal to their center management team than to some vague union leadership in Washington.

But Ron and his team had groomed the membership into a force to be reckoned with. The company seemed oblivious that its own workers absolutely hated management for all the mistreatment and harassment over the years. Those whose labor fattened UPS's bottom line saw Ron as the White Knight hearing their grievances, feeling their anger, and acting on them. Furthermore, Ron had a decades-long history dealing with UPS management. He was able to funnel that rank-and-file anger in the fight against the company.

"One night Ron comes to the campaign headquarters and calls me into his office," recalls Eckstein. "He said, 'Do you think we are ready for this strike?' I said, 'I can tell you we are stronger than we've ever been in any other campaign we've ever done. I believe if you don't strike 'em you're gonna have problems with the membership.'"[32] Ron feared that if they lost the strike it would hurt his members.

With the Thursday, July 31, deadline looming, UPS tried to go directly to the workers. They offered a signing bonus of $3,060 for full-timers and $1,530 for part-timers if they agreed to their "last, best, and final offer." UPS CEO Jim Kelly threatened layoffs if there was a strike and talked about using replacement workers during the strike. Nothing worked. An angry Ron told the press that they were being misled by UPS and their PR people. "The company wants to get its hands on the members' investment money," he lectured the media. "And put it into their pocket through a multi-billion pension grab."[33]

Meanwhile, management was making unforced errors. UPS negotiator E. Linhart, frustrated over the rejection of their "last, best, and final offer," was overheard calling UPS Teamsters "little nobodies." It went viral and actually strengthened the rank and file's resolve. It was more direct evidence of why UPS Teamsters hated their mean and cruel management teams.

The talks were getting nasty, and a strike appeared imminent. The White House feared a strike. "I was in Detroit dealing with Caterpillar negotiations when I got the call from White House adviser Bruce Lindsey," recalled John Calhoun Wells. "He said there might be a strike and you might need to get involved."[34] Wells was the director of the Federal Mediation and Conciliation Service (FMCS). There already was a monitor on site, but they were only observing and not active in the talks.

Wells jumped on a flight and by 6 p.m. he was meeting with both parties. "I went to a hotel not far from the Capitol," said Wells. "I met with Ron Carey and the Teamsters committee for a few hours. Then I met with UPS and their people." Wells then invited both chief negotiators to meet him in his office on E Street for "off the record" discussions. His job was to narrow the differences. "I asked Ron for a postponement in order to give me some time," recalled Wells. Ron agreed to "postpone until further notice." By now the talks were held exclusively at the offices of the FMCS.[35]

Both sides continued to talk on Friday, August 1. But later in the day, Ron broke off the talks in order to consult with his larger bargaining committee. Ron communicated that he was "discouraged, but that there had been some interest but not an agreement."[36]

The following day UPS sweetened its "last, best, and final offer," but, according to Ron, the sticking points were still full-time jobs and subcontracting. The Teamsters also updated their proposals to UPS, but they were not interested. Regardless, Ron set a new deadline of August 4 at 12:01 a.m. and warned: "The brown trucks won't be rolling unless this company agrees to provide the good jobs that American families need."[37]

Wells had worked with Ron over the years during earlier Teamster strikes and negotiations and knew Ron as a person. He commented, "President Carey at my personal request didn't go on strike last Thursday night. I think it's highly unlikely that that will occur again. He told me unequivocally 'This is a drop-dead deadline. I did it once because you asked me, John. It's not going to happen again. We need a deal.'"[38]

On Sunday, August 3, both sides met at Wells's office again to try to avert a strike. "We were at the mediator's office all day," remembered Wilson. "There was some optimism to reach a deal. Then it just didn't come together. UPS wanted some concessions, but Ron was not in a concessionary mood."[39]

Two hours before the deadline, Ron walked out of the talks and met with his staff. He once again asked, "Are we ready? OK. Then we are going!" Ron announced around 10 p.m. that "we went the extra mile from Thursday to Sunday. We have exhausted every possible approach to try to resolve the problem. At this point, it's just a waste of time."[40] At 12:01, Monday, August 4, the Teamsters struck UPS. It was on!

Thousands walked off the job that night joining the pickets that went up at every UPS facility nationwide. Union officials passed out signs reading: "United We Stand, Divided We Beg," "Full-Time Jobs Not Full-Page Lies," "Part-Time America Won't Work," "On Strike Against Unfair Labor Practices!" Regular members who never went to a union meeting, never submitted a grievance, became radicalized overnight.

Moreover, 2,000 Independent Pilots Association pilots announced that they would recognize the Teamsters' pickets and refused to cross the picket lines. They were shortly joined by the unionized mechanics at UPS as well.[41] No work was moving in or out of the facilities. The Teamsters stopped 12 million packages in their tracks. They shut down Big Brown!

Compliance was high. In certain regions of the country, a handful of Teamsters crossed the picket lines. Members were already quite aware of what they were fighting for. They had saved their money for this contingency. They were all in. There were a few exceptions. "Ron had called me and said he was told from the Legal Department that Mario Farinac, the PO of Local 385 in Orlando, was not going to take his people out," recalled Gene Moriarity. He went on:

> I said that doesn't make sense since he was a big supporter of Ron, but Farinac was a phony. When I called him he told me, "I can't do it here in Orlando because we have a city ordinance that you need a permit thirty days in advance if more than twelve people are going to assemble." Farinac said he requested the permit so we'll have it in thirty days. Then he'll be able to take them out.
>
> So I said, "OK, Mario, I will relay that message to Ron but I pretty much know what his response is going to be. And within twenty-four hours, I am going to be heading down to you and you're either going to be taking them out or we'll be taking you out of office! You are not going to defy this strike or your General President!" I went down there and he was ready to go. He found Jesus![42]

Management delivered whatever packages that were left in the buildings. Some drivers followed them on their routes and harassed them. They were also informing their old customers not to use UPS for the duration of the strike.

In general, it was a peaceful strike. Violence on the picket lines was minimal, though over time tensions did flare. In Somerville, Massachusetts, twenty-three Teamsters were arrested for blocking trucks coming and going. In Minnesota, a judge issued a temporary restraining order limiting the number of pickets outside each entrance of a Minnesota facility to three. In Florida, a judge issued an order prohibiting strikers picketing in groups of six or more from interfering with UPS managers making deliveries.[43] In my Local 804, we had a skirmish at the Foster Avenue building where a clueless FedEx driver attempted to cross our picket line. He was allowed to cross, but when he was leaving the facility, words were spoken and someone jumped the driver. The police broke it up and took the picketer to the precinct. No one attempted to cross our picket line after that incident.

For Ron Carey, this was a strike for which he had been preparing for the last thirty years. Back in the 1970s and '80s, he took on UPS, an "ancient enemy," at the local level to gain stronger pensions, higher wages, and fewer part-timers. Now Ron was using that experience to fight on a larger scale. He was ready and his membership was ready due to his hard work and planning.[44]

Commentators and intellectuals believed this was a make-or-break moment for the labor movement. "If the Teamsters win," commented Stanley Aronowitz, professor of sociology and labor scholar, "it will send a signal to restart the labor movement. It will say you can succeed fighting for better wages and part-time workers."[45]

There had not been a nationwide strike in the United States since the PATCO strike in 1981. This strike was capturing the interest of both the media and the public. It was about full-time jobs and how companies purposefully break up a full-time shift into three-hour increments. It was about companies, in general, abandoning their commitment to their workers and creating these "throwaway" jobs, as Ron described them.

Ron had forcefully drawn a line in the sand over the part-time issue. He knew that, as Professor of Industrial Studies Harley Shaiken said, "Part-time work is a way of life at UPS. It is a hidden downsizing" method of maximizing profit over people. Ron not only went toe-to-toe with UPS but with the beast that was Corporate America.[46]

The strike was very popular with the American people. Many

Americans had their sons and daughters working part-time shifts or their brothers and friends as UPS drivers. They were regular faces on America's Main Streets, in businesses, diners, and coffee shops. Polling showed the public siding with the Teamster workers 55 to 27 percent. During the PATCO strike, Americans supported the government by 52 to 29 percent over the workers.[47] People, strangers, dropped off food and drinks at picket sites. They drove past the picket lines and demonstrated their support of the union cause by beeping their horns in solidarity.

Ron appreciated the additional funds and the support but insisted, "This strike won't be decided by the strike funds. This is a strike about the future . . . about good jobs, about our children, our grandchildren." Of course, UPS complained about the strike and its possible impact on profits and customers leaving. Losing around $40 million a day, management threatened layoffs if the strike persisted, even though it "had a $4.5 billion bank line and a fair amount of cash."[48]

UPS's strategy consisted of a top-down model of fear, intimidation, and lobbying of powerful entities. They once again threatened to use replacement workers and implement layoffs in an attempt to shift the narrative away from part-time jobs and fairness. Ron responded, "UPS doesn't have to replace its workers. It needs to replace its strategy of low-wage part-time jobs!"[49]

At one point, UPS negotiators tried to blame the strike on Ron, wanting to distract attention from the 1996 campaign scandal that was still swirling around. "That's all bull being spun out by the company and by my opponents," responded Ron.[50] It didn't work. Even the factions that came out of last year's close Teamster election put their many differences on hold in a huge show of union solidarity. Chuck Mack, leader of Local 70 in California, who ran with the Old Guard Hoffa, Jr., slate only a few months earlier, announced, "I agree totally with the stand Carey has taken. Politics is a luxury when we've got the future of our members at stake."[51] Tony Magrene, who worked with Ron in the 1960s and was then on Local 804's Executive Board, commented, "Ron Carey would not keep people recklessly on the street. He knows it's the last card you play. He knows that strikes are very hard."[52]

UPS, Big Business, and its corporate allies in the Republican-controlled Congress as well as Republican governors, lobbied President Clinton to intervene and invoke Taft-Hartley. In 1935, the Democratic Congress passed and the Democratic president, FDR, signed the Wagner Act. It gave private sector employees the right to organize and created the National Labor Relations Board (NLRB) to enforce workers' rights on the job.

In the 1930s and 1940s, there were numerous large national strikes against big and powerful industries. Labor commanded the high ground. But Big Business was able to claw back some power when the Republicans won the 1946 midterm elections taking both the House and the Senate.

Anti-labor forces in business and right-wing politicians now in control of Congress succeeded in 1947 with passage over President Truman's veto of the radically anti-union Taft-Hartley law, which is still firmly in effect. This law rejected much of the thrust of the Wagner Act, restricting the ability of unions to strike, to picket, and to boycott employers. Most kinds of "sympathy" actions, that is, support by one group of workers for another group of employees on strike, are illegal and subject to immediate court injunctions. In addition, the U.S. president can declare a strike a national emergency and force an end to it. Congress can even impose the terms of a new bargaining agreement. Under Taft-Hartley, individual states are free to enact a law that prohibits unions from negotiating certain kinds of union security. For example, in such a state, a provision compelling an employee to join a union within a certain number of days after beginning to work for a unionized employee would be illegal. Such states are called right-to-work states, a misnomer since there is no right to work in the United States.[53]

President Truman labeled Taft-Hartley the "slave-labor bill." But this didn't stop him from using its national emergency provision.[54] President Clinton also directly intervened in strikes. He informally meddled in a five-day strike by American Airlines flight attendants in Florida. He pushed them into binding arbitration. Clinton once again intervened in February 1997 to end a strike by American Airlines pilots ninety-seven minutes after they walked out. Clinton suspended that strike by invoking emergency powers under another labor law, the Railway Labor Act.[55]

The Railway Labor Act has a lower threshold for federal government intervention in a strike than does Taft-Hartley. However, the president can invoke Taft-Hartley by ordering the attorney general to issue an injunction to halt any strike the president believes "imperiled the national health or safety." UPS was claiming that the Teamsters' strike against it was causing severe economic consequences. But President Clinton refused to invoke Taft-Hartley. Even though he was getting thoroughly pressured by Big Business, Wall Street, and right-wing politicians, Clinton refused to turn his back on labor. He had already angered unions and especially Ron Carey in 1993 by signing NAFTA and welfare reform. He scared unions when he stated, "The era of Big Government is over." Labor unions needed Big Government to protect workers from Corporate America. So Clinton knew he needed to give some support to the unions this time even though he didn't speak out against UPS's policy of using part-timers or their pension grab.

Moreover, Clinton's vice president, Al Gore, would be on the top of the ticket in 2000, and part of Clinton's legacy would be to get Gore elected. Angering unions would only make that task more difficult. It didn't hurt that the Teamsters gave $160,000 to the Democrats and zero to the GOP in this cycle. UPS gave $150,000 to the GOP and zero to the Democrats. Clinton weighed a strike affecting the economy versus the issue of union rights. He chose to let the collective bargaining process play out. Though Clinton was not a huge friend of labor, he at least was not an enemy of unions like the GOP.

In addition, Clinton was a keen observer and follower of polls. He knew that 75 percent of Americans did not want him to intervene in this strike. He also knew that the strike was popular.[56] "The biggest reason that the public supported the strike," said Matt Witt, "was that the workers rather than the union officials did so much talking . . . standing up for working people generally and not just themselves."[57]

"We didn't want the local leadership in the press conferences," stated Eckstein. "Maybe just in the background. We wanted the members to speak, and we prepared them and schooled them on how to speak and basically what to say to the media. Though many spoke of their own experiences and really didn't need us."[58]

By not invoking Taft-Hartley, Clinton indirectly legitimized the strike in many people's minds. It was a delicate balancing act, but by the very act of not acting was a big win for the union's right to strike. He wanted both sides to settle the strike on their own. Meanwhile, Speaker Newt Gingrich was urging Clinton to force the Teamsters to put the "last, best and final" offer to a vote of the members. Ron angrily responded that Congress should keep out of the strike, while insisting that it was management that needed to come to the bargaining table and to end their "diversionary tactics" and their "misleading information."[59]

Instead, Clinton called in his newly confirmed secretary of labor, Alexis Herman, to mediate the talks. "We were told UPS and the Teamsters knew each other. We didn't believe it would come to a strike," said Secretary Herman. Even Clinton's senior adviser on economic policy, Gene Sperling, who was keeping an eye on the talks in June and July, was shocked. The Secretary was in Chicago giving a speech when she got the call to come back to Washington. They monitored the situation. At first, she just "let it play out a bit." On August 6, at Ron's request, secretary Herman called UPS president Kelly, asking him to resume talks. Both sides agreed to meeting again on Friday, August 8.[60]

On August 5, Ron was at a rally at a UPS facility in Burtonsville, Maryland. He told the massive collection of Teamsters: "The fact of the matter is this company is shut down!"—insinuating that it was too early to even start talking about going back to the table. The Reverend Jesse Jackson joined Ron and the Teamsters at the rally. He led chants on the picket line: "We'll march one day longer! We will not surrender!"[61]

On the following day, Ron attended a huge rally in Chicago. He insisted that UPS should be "negotiating, not dictating, not intimidating or threatening" as they spoke about using replacement workers. Ron rallied the troops as only Ron Carey could: "We are really fighting for America's future! Working people have been taking it on the chin long enough. It's a crime that they have forced our members into a strike!" He continued:

> It's about corporate greed, a company that has made $1 billion in profit. A company that has over 10,000 part-time workers who work 35 hours a week on part-time, low wages. That's wrong. This is really a fight about good jobs. This is not just a fight about Teamsters and their families, it is about working people in this country. You have big companies shifting to part-time, low-wage, throwaway disposable jobs, subcontracting the work out. Enough is enough! Where is America going?
> It's about American families. And about what's right in this country? It's about decency. . . . There are no part-time mortgages, no part-time car payments. . . . We need to stand up to corporate greed...workers are on the move again![62]

This was some radical stuff for a onetime Nixon Republican. It was rhetoric like this that once again put the fear of God into Corporate America and Wall Street. Rick Gilberg, who worked with Ron for years as his Local 804 lawyer, called Ron a "labor nationalist." According to Deepa Kumar, assistant professor in the Department of Journalism and Media Studies at Rutgers and author of *Outside the Box: Corporate Media, Globalization, and the UPS Strike*, Ron's anti-corporate rhetoric was very much in the realm of "labor nationalism" because "it inverts the logic of corporate nationalism by making labor the most important member of the nation."[63]

Furthermore, Kumar explained, "The key arguments of labor

nationalism are presenting the progress of workers as essential for national progress and demonstrating that the interests of labor are really the interests of the nation." With Ron denouncing "greedy corporations," he was stating that "the strike against UPS was for all workers, redefining Americans as workers rather than as consumers."[64] That was a radical idea for 1997.

But it was the part-time issue that really made Ron passionate. He had been crusading against the use of part-timers for a long time. It was an issue "troubling me since 1968. This country needs to do something about it."[65] In 1962, his notorious predecessor, Jimmy Hoffa, Sr., allowed UPS to use part-time workers for the first time. By 1982, the Old Guard let UPS cut the starting wage for part-timers down to $8 an hour. Previously, part-timers made the same hourly wage as full-timers. Now, in 1997, drivers made three times the hourly rate of a new part-timer.[66]

They wound up fighting over the issue of Part-Time America, as defined by the union. The Teamsters set the narrative, to which UPS could only react. This time it was the union that was on the offensive. It was the members directly on the picket lines that were making their own case to the public and the media. It was a brilliant strategy.

Talks resumed on Friday, August 8, but there was lots of skepticism. As Ron entered the building, he threatened to walk out of the new talks if he saw no progress but "if we're making progress, I'll stay till the weekend. If it's just a smokescreen, though, we are out of here."[67]

On Saturday, negotiations between the parties broke off indefinitely after only two hours at the table. Kelly blamed the Teamsters for being "unrealistic" and warned that 15,000 jobs could be lost if the strike lasted two weeks. Ron contended, "At this point it appears it's just senseless to continue any discussions. It's time for us to start digging in."[68]

Ron continued his push to increase public support. But as he'd told David Eckstein earlier, he believed that they "weren't going to win this strike at a fire barrel."[69] They coordinated several tactics.

One method had Teamsters distributing leaflets at baseball stadiums to thousands of people describing how they were fighting for full-time jobs for all Americans. The leaflets had score cards on the other side.

That Saturday, Secretary Herman and John Calhoun Wells met at the White House with Deputy Chief of Staff John Podesta. The plan was to move Secretary Herman to center stage. On Monday, August 11, one week after the start of the strike, Secretary Herman called Ron and "invited him to come over to my condo. We had a beer together. No lawyers or assistants. Just one on one. I wanted to hear it directly from Ron, the issues broken down by him."[70] She also called Jim Kelly and invited him over as well, in a domestic example of shuttle diplomacy. Herman decided to stay at the Hyatt, rather than at her condo, to make sure she was readily available to both sides if they needed her.

"I thought I had enough of a framework to get them both back to the table," she recalled. "But I had to get them to trust me. Eventually they did. I trusted them too."[71] The parties met later that day.

When Ron emerged from that Monday meeting with Herman and the UPS officials, he reiterated what the union wanted the company to address: full-time jobs, subcontracting, the pension, and increased wages. He noted, "The company has got to get the message that the government is not going to intervene on their behalf. They've been playing games and haven't been serious."[72] They were still talking about taking over the pension system.

When the UPS negotiator Dave Murray insisted once again that the Teamsters leadership put their "last, best, and final" offer out for a vote, Ron responded that the workers "have voted on it. They are voting today by walking the pavement, by letting the company know that they are not about to have any contract jammed down their throat." He reminded them that "this is the New Teamsters. We do not operate as was done in the past."[73]

Years later, Ron spoke at length about this moment in an interview with writer Deepa Kumar:

The company gave us what they claimed was a final offer, and I felt that their strategy was to keep us confused, fearful, and I was not going to let that happen. They were playing the bluff game, and I knew it. Given what was contained in the company's "drop dead" offer, I knew a strike was inevitable, but it was not going to be on their terms. It was going to be after we had exhausted every possible remedy.

I knew that we had to stand firm and think out what the company expected us to do, while having all our preparations in place; otherwise a strike against this giant could be a disaster. We had to be able to take on this one, for the whole Teamsters movement. So I played it on my terms.[74]

UPS went about spending over $1 million on ads in newspapers to make their case. The Teamsters didn't have to spend money to get their word out. They were getting free media at the rallies and on the picket lines. At one of Ron's daily press conferences, he brought out a part-timer, Laurie Pisciotti, who worked at a Chicago UPS facility. She spoke to the media about working only twenty-five hours a week and not being able to pay her bills. Pisciotti added passionately and powerfully about wanting "a full-time job with full-time wages and full-time benefits."[75]

Democratic politicians took advantage of the positive polls and publicly supported the striking Teamsters. Politicians like Senators Paul Wellstone (MN) and Ted Kennedy (MA), Congressman Ed Markey (MA), civil rights leaders like Jessie Jackson, the Reverend Al Sharpton, and the Reverend Joseph Lowery joined striking UPS workers on their picket lines throughout the country in solidarity.[76] Republican politicians mostly sided with UPS and pushed Clinton to invoke Taft-Hartley.

UPS accused Ron of always wanting this strike. They accused him of using this strike to distract from the ongoing investigation into his 1996 reelection campaign. But Ron was extremely aware of the consequences of a strike. "Ron Carey would not keep people recklessly on the street," said Tony Magrene, one of Ron's more respected Local 804 officers. "He knows it's the last card you play. He knows that strikes are very hard."[77]

UPS continued to lobby for Clinton to intervene. Clinton's spokesman, Mike McCurry, put out a statement saying, "We can't solve a labor-management conflict for the parties. Ultimately, the two parties have to negotiate their own agreement."[78] Clinton wanted a fair settlement. "He never pushed Ron to settle early. He wanted a fair deal and for both sides to settle on their own," said Secretary Herman.[79] "I want to let the collective bargaining process function," added Clinton. Collective bargaining and the use of the strike were tactics that unions used as economic warfare in order to level the playing field with powerful companies.

On Tuesday, Secretary Herman met briefly with AFL-CIO president John Sweeney to "pick his brain" on the ongoing strike. Appearing impressed, Sweeney called the secretary a "quick study." She later briefed President Clinton on the condition of the talks saying that she was encouraged by what she saw. "Alexis Herman was very helpful," remembered John Calhoun Wells. "She kept the White House in the loop. She brought both sides in and kept them motivated to keep talking; she got them into the room."[80] But it was Wells who worked with them when in the room and sat with both sides.

Later in the day, Sweeney joined Ron at Teamster headquarters for a rally. Sweeney announced that the nation's labor unions would lend the Teamsters $10 million a week for "many, many weeks" in order to help finance the $55 per week in strike pay for 185,000 striking Teamsters.

In 1995, Ron was instrumental in helping to get Sweeney elected to the top spot taking on longtime conservative AFL-CIO president Thomas Donahue. Sweeney declared that the "Teamsters' fight is our fight." He said, "This is about a greedy, hugely profitable employer who wants to make even more money by shortchanging workers on their wages and benefits." Standing next to the AFL-CIO leader, Ron said that they are establishing a "defense fund that will cover a long strike if necessary."[81]

Once again, Kelly warned of 15,000 layoffs. "I don't think it is accurate that they are losing business permanently," Ron replied. "The Post Office and other companies can't manage the volume. They shouldn't be dictating. They should be negotiating. What they are doing is intimidation. It is threats. That won't get the job done That is a mistake."[82]

On Wednesday, Secretary Herman called the leaders of both sides and convinced them to return to the bargaining table. Proving how committed she was to a settlement, she cancelled her trip home to Alabama to attend "Alexis Herman Day" in her hometown of Mobile.[83]

She also recommended a change in venue. Wells offered that, since the mediator's offices couldn't handle everyone, they needed to move to a larger venue that provided separate bargaining tables and rooms. He added, "Plus the media was always watching who was going in or coming out of my office. It was very distracting, so we decided to go off site." The talks were now to continue bargaining at the Washington Hyatt on Capitol Hill, not too far from Teamster headquarters.[84]

Ron issued a statement affirming that "while there is no reason for optimism at this point, we will be there, ready to negotiate a reasonable agreement." UPS continued to push that the workers vote on their "last, best, and final" offer. They had seen polls showing that even though the American people sided over two to one with the Teamsters, another poll showed that nearly two-thirds agreed with the company that the striking workers should vote on that latest offer.[85]

The markets had not reacted positively to the ongoing strike. On Friday, the Dow Jones dropped 3.1 percent. It was down 4.37 percent for the week. This labor unrest, this "labor nationalism," was unsettling the status quo. Powerful people were starting to notice and point fingers.

Both sides negotiated from 9 a.m. Thursday until 3 a.m. Friday morning. They got a few hours' sleep and were back at it at 8 a.m., continuing until 5:30 a.m. Saturday morning. Then all day Saturday into Sunday morning. Ron hadn't slept but a handful of hours since the talks began.[86] Secretary Herman was seen going from room to room relentlessly helping each side focus on the issues. "It was brutal," recalled Wells. "Some people didn't sleep at all."[87]

The *New York Times* reported, "The rooms in the second floor of the Hyatt Regency Washington Hotel where each side gathered started to look lived in, with used coffee cups, newspapers, and half eaten club sandwiches strewn across the table." [88]

Ron decided to turn the heat up on UPS. He affirmed that his Teamsters would be having over two-dozen rallies across the country the next Thursday called an "Action Day for Good Jobs," with similar events in Europe. He was asking for Americans who supported the strike to wear Teamster blue ribbons. "We are fighting not just for Teamsters but for every working family in America."[89]

Federal mediator Wells conveyed to the media how he had compared both parties to the United States and Soviet Union and how they both could have blown up the world. He actually borrowed Robert Oppenheimer's famous term for the nuclear superpowers: "two scorpions in a bottle." Fortunately, it seemed things had begun to thaw a bit. Secretary Herman updated the president on where they stood. She told him she felt some progress. On Sunday, August 17, Ken Hall announced a breakthrough when UPS suggested it might withdraw its pension demand. On *Meet the Press*, Ron told the panel, "There has been some movement."[90]

Clinton decided to take a tactical change in direction. He recommended both parties do a rhetorical push since he heard that they were now 95 percent in agreement on the outstanding issues. He told reporters, "It's my gut feeling they'll settle. It's a good deal. It will set a precedent for unions. They're that close."[91] He was right.

By early Monday afternoon, an overall package had emerged. It was a "wholesale swapping of demands." UPS dropped its pension demand and accepted the Teamsters' demand to create 10,000 new full-time jobs. Late that night, an agreement was reached. But it almost didn't happen. It was delayed for about two hours because the settlement almost fell apart at the last minute.[92]

But it did get settled. At 12:30 a.m. Monday night/Tuesday morning, Secretary Herman held a press conference to announce the tentative agreement. The Teamsters Union got a commitment from UPS of 10,000 new full-time jobs over the life of the contract, not the 200 to 1,000 full-time jobs UPS was offering. Starting pay for part-timers was to be raised by 50 cents an hour, making it the first increase in part-time pay since 1982. Full-time pay would go up by $3.10 and part-timers by $4.10 over the life of the agreement. Full-time pension control would remain as before in both hands. There would be no more subcontracting unless it was approved by the Local. The only real concession by the union was the length of the contract. It went from three years to five years, giving the company five years of labor peace.[93]

The media reported as a concession the fact that the union agreed that full-time workers would handle more packages that were presently being handled by supervisors. They were clueless that Teamsters wanted to stop supervisors from working: "It's our work." Hence it was not a concession but another win.

Ron praised the agreement as a "historic turning point for working people in this country. American workers have shown they can stand up to corporate greed!" UPS lead negotiator Murray solemnly commented, "We believe it's an agreement that we'll be able to remain competitive with." President Clinton thanked both sides, saying that he was "pleased the parties negotiated in good faith."[94]

It was agreed that all workers would be able to return to work on Wednesday, August 20, after two Teamster committees approved the agreement. The first committee consisted of the fifty-member bargaining committee itself. They easily gave their approval. The second group was a committee of the two top officers of each UPS Local, about four hundred people. When Ron entered the room, the group gave him a standing ovation. They too voted unanimously for the agreement. The agreement was then to be mailed and voted on by the rank and file, but the strike was over.[95]

"Tonight the elected leaders of the local unions unanimously approved the agreement with UPS," Ron said Tuesday evening. "They were united and extremely enthusiastic about the break-throughs that we had won. Our members will be going back to work as soon as the company calls them back." As usual, Ron spread the credit around. He thanked the strikers "for making it happen, staying united, going into the communities." He announced, "This victory would never have been achieved without the support of working families all across America." He then thanked the American people and the customers for supporting the strike.[96] He was right: the strikers had won the strike.

Ron ended the press conference with a warning: "Non-union workers will be talking about how this victory has inspired them for fighting for their futures." He mentioned how FedEx workers walked picket lines with UPS Teamsters in several localities. He proclaimed, "FedEx, here we come!" There was that "momentum" again.[97]

It proved the new direction that Ron had brought to the Teamsters was working. Unlike his predecessors, Ron did not see the company as a partner. He showed that when unions are on the offensive and dictate the narrative, they win. When union leadership methodically plans a strategy for taking on the company, unions win. When union leadership educates and mobilizes its rank and file, the rank and file win. When the union leadership includes the rank and file in the actual bargaining, the rank and file win.

The successful strike added leverage to the 2,000 unionized UPS pilots who were still negotiating with the company. They supported the strike wholeheartedly, joining the Teamsters on the picket lines. Moreover, while the strike was still ongoing, fifty workers at RDS, a package delivery company in Indiana, voted to join the Teamsters Union.[98] Good things were starting to happen.

There were important lessons learned from this strike. As labor historian Professor Nelson Leichtenstein assessed after the settlement, "It ends the PATCO Syndrome, a 16-year period in which a strike was synonymous with defeat and demoralization is over."[99]

It demonstrated how workers can turn production on and off if provoked. Employers fear that. It gave workers, and the union movement, in particular, the confidence and power to create positive change in the workplace. It pointed to a resurgence in the labor movement. It highlighted sympathetic workers who were experiencing economic insecurity, worried about losing their full-time jobs to part-time workers.[100]

"With the Teamsters' astonishing victory against UPS," commented Pulitzer Prize–winning author Studs Terkel, "a word long considered quaint—solidarity—has found a new resonance among the great many hitherto unconcerned."[101]

By legitimizing mobilization and militancy, the strike awakened a sleeping union movement that was dead in the water since the 1982 PATCO fiasco. According to Cornell's Professor of Labor Studies Richard Hurd, "The UPS strike resonates with a segment of our society that is concerned that corporations had reduced their commitments to their workers." He continued that corporations "are doing too much downsizing and using too much contingent labor and temp agencies."[102]

These points were not ignored by the powers that be and its corporate press. In the wake of the strike, *Business Week* wrote, "It was a wakeup call for Big Business. The Teamsters' win means that workers can no longer be taken for granted. For the first time in two decades, the public sided with the union, even though its walkout caused major inconveniences."[103] It was the perfect storm for the labor movement: with the perfect villain, UPS, and the perfect leader, Ron Carey! This was not the Ron Carey from Brill's book. The country had changed, the economy had changed, and Ron had changed.

Years later, in an interview with author Deepa Kumar, Ron looked back on the 1997 strike against UPS:

> The company gave us what they claimed was a final offer. I felt that their strategy was to keep us confused and fearful and I was not going to let that happen. They were playing the bluff game.

I knew the strike was inevitable but I didn't want it to be on their terms. They miscalculated. We anticipated their strategy and we had 6 moves already planned. Whatever they brought up, I made sure we had the ammunition, the research, the communication already there.[104]

Yes, the strike was over, but Corporate America would not let it go. They needed to get Ron Carey and make him pay for their defeat. It seems that in America you have the theoretical right to strike as long as you don't win.

Ron recalled, in that same interview with Kumar, "I remember the last day, right after the negotiations were settled, I was in the room with Secretary of Labor Herman and the company. The company's top negotiator, Dave Murray, got up and said, 'You will be sorry till the day you die.' I said, "Are you threatening me?' I turned to the Secretary and said, 'Did you hear that?' She said, 'I didn't hear a thing.' I knew my demise was in the works."[105]

Federal mediator John Calhoun Wells, when asked about this particular incident, said that he "never heard that." He went on that "they were all pretty professional," but conceded that it might have happened "behind the scenes."[106] During an interview, Secretary Herman told me she too did not hear any threats.[107] Or maybe they didn't want to hear any threats. They just wanted to move on. But without a doubt, the backlash was beginning.

CHAPTER 8

The Scandal

For the "crime" of leading a successful strike against a huge and powerful corporation and being the new spokesman for the anti-corporate movement of workers' rights, there was a tremendous and swift backlash against Ron Carey. He became Enemy of the Corporate State. And this Corporate State used its power and got its political and governmental puppets to "Get Carey!"

UPS couldn't win at the bargaining table, so they attacked Ron in the political arena. They were aware of the investigation of the previous year's campaign, with some of Ron's campaign people being questioned by federal officials. UPS publicly pressured the federal elections officer Barbara Zack Quindel to overturn the recent Teamsters election. They and the rest of Corporate America got their political puppets in the Republican Congress to attack Ron and investigate him. Anti-union conservative congressmen like Florida Republican Joe Scarborough and Bob Barr of Georgia led the attack.

The UPS strike ended on August 18, 1997, and within days of this, election officer Barbara Zack Quindel overturned Ron's reelection. On August 22, she released a 134-page report ordering a new vote between Ron and Hoffa. She ordered a new election

after finding that the supporters in the Carey campaign had participated in a swap scheme in which the campaign received $221,000
in illegal contributions that she believed could have unfairly tipped
the election to Ron: "There was a complex network of schemes to
funnel IBT funds to the Carey campaign that may have affected
the outcome of the International election."[1]

However, she did not find that Ron was involved in any of the
improper activity. Ron denied having known anything about the
illicit funding. Quindel stated that "there is no evidence that Carey
or members of the GEB knew of or participated in the various
improper fundraising schemes."[2] Ron and his board all pledged to
cooperate fully with the decision. She called the misconduct "egregious violations by high-level campaign functionaries who believed
winning at all costs was more important than abiding by the 1996
Election Rules and the law." Those "high-level functionaries" were
Jere Nash, Martin Davis, Michael Ansara, and Bill Hamilton.

Hoffa, Jr., seeing an opportunity, called for an independent special prosecutor to investigate the issue while on Fox News show
Sunday and called for Ron to step down. Ron immediately rejected
the plea to resign but agreed to an independent investigation.[3] Ron
never appeared on the anti-union Fox News network.

RON HAD KICKED OFF HIS reelection campaign in September 1995
and hired the November Group, the Washington-based political
consulting firm, to work on the campaign. The November Group
was run by Hal Malchow and Martin Davis, who had also worked
on Ron's 1991 campaign. Davis was responsible for the effective
"battle page" ads in *Teamster* magazine, portraying the Old Guard
as "pigs feeding at the trough." He also did some direct mail for the
campaign. After the election, Ed Burke had the November Group
stay on and provide services to the IBT.

"Burke wanted to reduce the dependency and political debt to
TDU so they hired the November Group," recalled Steve Early. "It
was your typical liberal hive of hustlers. Davis had worked on the
1984 Mondale campaign; he excelled at persuasion mailings; he

created the 'pigs in the trough' ad. That's how they got their foot in the door."[4] From 1992 through 1996, the November Group made $650,000 from contracts with the IBT. In addition to the Teamsters, the November Group's other clients were the Clinton-Gore campaign, Citizen Action, and the National Council of Senior Citizens.

Davis was considered one of Washington's top Democratic Party political operatives, who could get virtually anything done. He was known as a "savvy middleman who could make deals happen," while always getting a piece of the action. Some who knew Davis agree that he was "a political broker who played the system and saw opportunities to get rich at every turn." He was also known as a high-stakes gambler.[5]

In late Februrary, Jere Nash, the Mississippi-based political strategist and consultant, was hired as Ron's campaign manager. He was known as the guy who got a Democrat elected to the governor's mansion in Republican Mississippi. Nash had been involved with Carey since early 1992, heading up the transition. He had been chief of staff to former Mississippi Governor Ray Mabus, so he had administrative experience and knew how to run and organize staff and transitions.[6]

"Nash sold himself that he can get anyone elected," remarked Paff. "He got a Democrat elected in Mississippi. So Ron went that way. Away from the more grassroots campaign." Paff admitted, "Nash was a smart guy, folksy but a bit of a sleazeball. He was an insider, arrogant asshole as well. Nash always made fun of TDU. When he took over, what does he do? He hires focus groups. TDU does focus groups everyday meeting with the rank and file in the local. He came to see just how valuable TDU was."[7]

Though early polls had shown Ron up by twenty points over Hoffa, Nash and Davis walked into a campaign without a campaigner. Their candidate was not on the campaign trail.

This was not going to be like 1991. Ron was no longer the crusading outsider fighting to get in; he was the incumbent. Whereas in 1991 Ron faced a split opposition, this time he was up against an empowered Old Guard united behind one person: Hoffa, Jr. Early on they realized how weak the campaign was as the convention approached; Ron's slate did not even have a majority of delegates. Though Ron and the Reformers controlled the Marble Palace, the Old Guard still controlled many of the smaller marble palaces around the country.

The new team worked the individual locals to get as many delegates as possible. "The big thing was the failure to elect Carey delegates to the convention," said Muehlenkamp, who basically worked full-time on Ron's reelection. "Hoffa had a small majority and Ron, with Judy's help, basically filibustered the convention. They were able to drag out the proceedings, run out the clock. Joe Morris got up there and his assignment was to talk for an hour or two. It worked."[8] They felt good that they had come from behind to bring it to a draw. They left Philadelphia feeling as though they had survived. But they had their work cut out for them.

Nash and Davis agreed to put out a huge mailer to find a way to communicate with the 300,000 or so Teamsters who were going to vote in this election. It would supplement whatever was going to be done on the ground; it was the air cover for the ground troops. Davis and Malchow had used direct mail in the 1991 campaign, and it was effective.

After the convention and as the summer progressed, more polls showed Ron's lead down to ten points. By October, polls showed a tie race. The campaign strategists became nervous, and some got desperate. They feared Hoffa might actually win. Nash met with Davis, and they agreed that the November Group would conduct the large direct mail to coincide with the mailing of the ballots. Davis, who was considered the mastermind of the plan, thought it essential to Ron's reelection. They agreed $700,000 was to be spent; Nash would get $300,000 from the campaign coffers and Davis would obtain the other $400,000 from fundraising.[9]

Davis became a true believer in Ron as a charismatic figure who was cleaning up the Teamsters and boosting the labor movement. But he was also a capitalist who saw an opportunity to make his firm a lot of money. Nash, who also was a believer in Ron and his reform agenda, saw an opportunity to become the new James Carville if he was able to pull off this national election in Ron's favor. (In the 1990s, Carville was a Democratic strategist and guru who helped elect Democrats.)

The plan developed involved four distinct schemes. One scheme, hatched by Davis, involved extracting, or "leveraging," contributions from the Democratic Party in exchange for IBT contributions to the DNC and its state affiliates around the country. Prior to the campaign, the Teamsters had already intended to make large contributions to the DNC, about $1 million. So Davis "leveraged" this money in order to get donations for Ron's campaign.[10]

Davis proposed to his friend Terry McAuliffe, a DNC fundraiser and head of the Clinton-Gore reelection campaign, that the Teamsters would donate $1 million to the DNC state affiliates. Davis used to work at the DNC. In return, the DNC would arrange for one of its wealthy supporters to contribute $100,000 to the Carey campaign. The Democrats found a wealthy DNC supporter, a Filipino woman, Judith Vasquez, to give $100,000 to the Carey campaign. However, she turned out to be an employer, which was against the election rules. Her check was never cashed, but the Teamsters had already given over $300,000 to DNC affiliates in thirty-five states. (Perhaps the campaign strategists assumed the other $700,000 they "planned" to spend on the Democrats could be used to leverage other organizations.) According to Federal Election Commission records, the IBT contributed $2.9 million to individual Democratic campaigns for the 1996 elections.[11]

The second vehicle for raising funds for the campaign was asking other large unions to contribute. This was illegal according to the consent decree. Nevertheless, Davis conspired with leaders of the AFL-CIO, SEIU, and AFSCME to get each union to contribute $50,000 to the Carey campaign.

The third funding scheme involved the Share Group. In April, Davis had recruited a friend, Michael Ansara, to assist with some fundraising for the campaign. Ansara was also the head of the Boston-based telemarketing firm, The Share Group. Both had a history of seeking Teamster contracts in 1992 and beyond. Davis asked Ansara to come up with some "creative solutions" to help raise the needed funds for their mailing.

Davis informed Ansara that the IBT rules prohibited employers from contributing or soliciting contributions. He also mentioned that the spouses of employers could contribute as long as those spouses did not themselves employ anyone. Ansara thought up a plan to get progressive "trust-fund babies" to donate to the Carey campaign. He even was able to get his own non-employer wife, Barbara Arnold, to contribute $95,000 to the campaign. It was later discovered that this was illegal, because Ansara himself was an employer, and he solicited the donation from his wife. On the other hand, it seemed patently ridiculous since Ansara was not a Teamster employer and his wife was not his employee.[12]

Sometime in September, Nash spoke with Cohen, Weiss, Simon (CWS), the law firm that oversaw Ron's campaign, to get them to set up an entity that would collect all of the large donations that would be arriving as they got closer to the ballots going out. CWS established the group Teamsters for a Corrupt-Free Union (TCFU), which accepted all the funds from rich individuals who were non-Teamster, and then transferred the funds to the November Group in order to pay for expenses related to the mailing.[13] They picked Gene Moriarity to be its treasurer.

Besides being an International rep, Moriarity was Ron's Eastern Regional Coordinator for the campaign. He recalls:

> Late in the summer, Nash tells us that poll numbers were looking bad and we needed to do a mass mailing out of the November Group. He also told me Ron wanted me to contact Nate Charny, a lawyer from Susan Davis's firm, and that Ron wanted me to be the treasurer for this group called TCFU. Nash said, "All the checks will be going to you. All you got to do when you get the checks is deposit them and then you will be directed where to send it to." The money was being solicited from what Charny called "trust-fund babies" who had an interest in the labor movement.[14]

On October 6, Ansara traveled to California for a meeting of the Social Venture Network, a group of 400 wealthy individuals who generally give to progressive causes. There he met an old friend, Charles Blitz, a big fundraiser for liberal causes. Ansara convinced Blitz to solicit contributions from wealthy supporters of Citizens Action, which was a national, progressive consumer and public activist organization, as well as other progressive groups such as Project Vote and the National Council of Senior Citizens. The plan was for him to send the checks from these wealthy individuals to TCFU, and Ansara would hold the checks until the corresponding IBT contributions had been made to Citizens Action.[15] In return, the Teamsters would contribute large amounts from the IBT treasury to these groups.

Multiple streams of donations were coming in and going out. But Nash was not a Teamster official and therefore couldn't simply allocate IBT funds. He needed inside help. So, he recruited IBT Governmental Affairs Director Bill Hamilton to arrange for the Teamsters to make financial contributions to various political organizations. Hamilton's job was to recommend to Ron which political organizations were worthy of an IBT contribution and how much. It was timed so that the big money was being spent in October and early November, during an election year for Congress and the President of the United States.

Hamilton offered some background on the process of how money was raised in Washington in those days:

> That judge [Edelstein] hoisted this on us. He didn't offer any way to raise a lot of money in order to reach over 1 million members going to worksites and union halls and mailings. Drivers aren't gonna write a check for $1,000. Executive board members could, and they mostly gave to Hoffa. But the rules allowed you to raise money from outside the union. So we went to progressive groups.[16]

They couldn't give to Clinton directly because the IBT under Ron's direction didn't endorse Clinton because of NAFTA. Hamilton continues:

> I was being pushed to get Ron reelected and raise money. We needed a lot of money. Nash approaches me and said it would help raise money if I were to give some IBT money to some designated organizations. I said, "It depends if they are compatible and share our causes and values." So he came back with a bunch of recommendations. Some we already gave to; others we had not. I said Yes to some and No to others.[17]

When Hamilton was asked to contribute another $150,000 to Citizens Action, he personally rejected it. "We had just given $475,000 to them. I couldn't. I turned it down. It could not be justified." However, Martin Davis then went to AFL-CIO president Richard Trumka for the money. Trumka couldn't. He said the AFL-CIO had no money, but if the IBT gave the AFL-CIO $150,000, then Trumka would be able to give it to Citizens Action. Hamilton agreed and sent a memo to Ron for approval, saying it would "help finance GOTV activity in selected Labor '96 states." Ron approved it.[18]

Nash also met with Ron's personal secretary, Monie Simpkins. He needed someone on the inside to approve the requests that Hamilton would be recommending when they came to Ron's desk for approval. He explained how the requests for funds would be coming from Hamilton and how she should handle it as soon as possible. With Ron so much on the road campaigning, the disbursement of money did not require a formal signature. An "OK" or a memo followed by Ron's initials and Simpkins's was all that was needed. Simpkins was told that the treasury would be reimbursed and that Ron knew and that the campaign lawyers had approved it.[19]

Besides trying to find creative ways to raise a lot of money fast, they had to work around Ron finding out. "They knew he was a clean, by- the-book Marine. Ron would not stand for any shenanigans," said Bob Muehlencamp.[20] The wrecking crew knew he would never allow the scheme. He'd rather lose than play around with illegal or unethical schemes. If Ron had found out, he would have fired all those involved and exposed it.

But they were keenly aware that it was a very political year. Besides Ron's reelection, there were national elections: the IBT was trying to get Democrat Bill Clinton reelected and for the Democrats to take back Congress from the anti-union Gingrich Republicans. Considerable Teamster funds were going to GOTV to support candidates and groups. Everyone was hyperaware how important it was to defeat the GOP Congress. "Ron decided not to endorse Clinton because of NAFTA but he didn't want to tell people not to vote for him either," recalled Eckstein.[21] They needed extra funds for GOTV to help register union voters and make phone calls. But this was normal for such a supercharged political year. Maybe he wouldn't notice.[22]

The key was to keep Ron in the dark, unaware of any funny business going on and especially from his grassroots supporters inside the administration. Many spoke about how Colleen Dougher, Ron's scheduler and old friend of Martin Davis, saw to it that Ron was on the road busy campaigning and out of reach from his most loyal supporters.[23] This was before cell phones. During this period, Ron was frequently on the campaign trail, and disbursement of contributions did not require his actual signature on any checks. Simpkins had a system in which when Ron was in the office, it only required an "OK" on a memo followed by his initials. If Ron was out of DC, his initials or hers would suffice. The actual checks were later signed by a signature machine.[24]

Bill Hamilton confirms that Ron did not know of the schemes. In early November 1996, Hamilton ran into Ron at a Local 135 shop stewards' banquet. They spoke for about a minute right in front of the stage:

I saw Ron at a banquet in Indianapolis that November. He asked me, "Why are we using dues money, general funds, instead of

PAC money?" I said, "We're using dues money because it's legal and PAC money is hard to raise. We use PAC money for the places where we can only use PAC money, for candidates to the House and the Senate." He seemed out of the loop. I mean he was aware that money was being donated to groups and politicians. This was a huge election not just for him and he knew it. But Ron bought it.[25]

All parties were told not to mention any of this to Ron. Things looked bad for Ron's reelection. Ron might lose. This needed to be done. The very fact that all involved in this clandestine venture believed wholeheartedly in Ron made them push even harder to make this scheme a reality and not let on to Ron about its existence.

From the middle of October until early November, the IBT contributed about $735,000 to these friendly progressive groups: $475,000 to Citizens Action, $175,000 to Project Vote, and $85,000 to the National Council of Senior Citizens. When more money was needed (to pay back Ansara's wife), Davis went back to Citizens Action for another $100,000 contribution in exchange for the IBT to give another $150,000 to the organization. Citizens Action sent a request to Bill Hamilton for another $150,000.[26]

In total, about $885,000 was taken out of the IBT treasury in return for about $221,000 to the Carey campaign. When you add the funds raised from the trust-fund babies and unions, the illegal swaps raised around $538,000.[27] Truth be told, the contributions to the political organizations were not illegal. The agreement, the scheme, the quid pro quo, to swap the IBT donations for guaranteed contributions from these groups was.

When the election was over, Ron's close associate Bob Mueklencamp had a heart-to-heart with Ron about what needed to be done in the second term. "Ron said he was 'going back to 804 now,'" recalled Muehlenkamp. "He said he was gonna be in Washington as little as possible and run the union out of Local 804. He also said he wasn't running anymore." Muehlenkamp continued:

When he first told me my mouth dropped. I said, "This is at least a ten-year project to reform this union and if you're not here, physically, nothing will get done." It was the constant incoming on a daily basis. It's hard to appreciate what they did to him. The attacks on him. The planted stories of corruption and ties to the mob. The daily demands. He said it was not what he signed up for when he ran. Who could have known how relentless these bastards would be from day one.[28]

"The campaign was very physical on Ron," said Bob Hauptman. "His knees were in terrible shape. He was in constant pain. It kinda made him cranky."[29] Bob Muehlencamp concurred: "Ron could hardly walk. He was in terrible pain all the time. At times he couldn't pay attention to any details. I'd ask him if I could do something and he'd say, 'Don't bother me with it, just go do it, take care of it.'"[30]

Dave Eckstein agreed: "His knees were a huge problem. He wanted surgery on both of them, but he knew it would mean riding in some kind of golf cart or scooter and he didn't want to look weak. So he dealt with the pain for the good of the campaign."[31] Soon after the election, Ron got both of his bad knees replaced.

Nevertheless, Ron won the election. But things started to unravel. Both campaigns handed in the final campaign financial reports to the EO. First, Hoffa supporters discovered a large, suspicious donation of $95,000 from a "student" in Massachusetts to TCFU. The Hoffa campaign filed a protest alleging that the Share Group, Michael Ansara's firm, had done little or no work to justify the IBT payment of $97,000. They believed it was actually a quid pro quo for Barbara Arnold's original $95,000 check. Hoffa had several spies in Teamster headquarters. They smelled blood in the water.

Because the donations happened so late in the campaign and could have affected the outcome, Hoffa's managers demanded an investigation into the alleged violations of the 1996 election rules by the Carey campaign.[32] It seems Hoffa operative Richard Leebove

recruited several moles inside Teamsters headquarters who fur-
nished sensitive internal documents to the Hoffa campaign.

On January 30, 1997, Patrick Szymanski, a Hoffa lawyer, joined
John F. Murphy, a Hoffa supporter and president of Local 122
in Boston, to review Carey campaign filings in the EO's office in
Washington. They found TCFU spent $200,000 on mailings all
raised by seven non-Teamsters. This is where they found the infamous $95,000 donation from Barbara Arnold, Michael Ansara's
wife. Leebove used false names to call those seven donors, which
led to a complaint from one donor to the EO, alerting her to the
donor scheme. Later the EO ruled that the seven donations were
improper because they were solicited by an employer.[33]

The mole Leebove had used was a mid-level administrator,
Gregory Mullenholz, whose job was to issue checks for the Teamster
PAC to go to certain political groups. Mullenholz sent notes and
documents to Leebove. By February, John Murphy sent all the
information they had to Mary Jo White, EO Barbara Zack Quindel,
certain news outlets and columnists, and Republican friends in
Congress. In July, Mullenholz was caught faxing a Teamster memo
about a grand jury subpoena probing possible improper Teamster
donations to the Democratic Party. He was later fired.[34]

In January, EO Quindel agreed after finding several other
questionable donations. On January 11, 1997, the EO postponed
the certification of the 1996 election until a thorough investigation into the Carey campaign operation was complete. While still
investigating the validity of 13,000 questionable ballots, Quindel
did not intend to certify the results until the completion of the
post-election protests and appeals process.[35] Ron's office issued an
IBT Constitutional Interpretation that the incumbent IBT officers
would remain in office until the EO certified the results and the
winners were sworn in.

Then in late January, Nash was asked to come back from
Mississippi and run another transition/new term in office. Nash
agreed. He arrived at the Marble Palace and held a few meetings
and created a transition for Ron's new team. On March 10, he was

summoned to New York City to sit down with Susan Davis and her law firm, CWS. Responding to Quindel's ongoing investigation of the 1996 campaign finances, Davis asked Nash what he knew. That was when Nash told her about the entire swap scheme Martin Davis had masterminded.

Immediately, Susan Davis informed a shocked and angered Ron of the entire scheme. Ron said that they had an obligation to go to the government and disclose what they had discovered. They did. People who are hiding things don't normally do this. He also called for an internal investigation into his campaign's own finances and operatives. Ron was incensed that anyone under his watch might have jeopardized his administration and his good name.[36]

Furthermore, he and his lawyers at CWS waived their attorney-client privilege regarding communications between Nash and the lawyers to demonstrate full cooperation and transparency. At a follow-up meeting, Nash was told this. He was also told that he should get his own lawyer since the campaign lawyers could not represent him going forward. Nash was beginning to panic. He at first refused to testify in the case, invoking attorney-client privilege. He tried to get his lawyer to stop Ron's attorney from revealing the misconduct.

Meanwhile, Monie Simpkins read in Burrells, a media monitoring service, that there was going to be an investigation into donations to TCFU. She was well aware of her involvement with the donations and TCFU during the campaign. Simpkins was nervous. She spoke with Susan Davis on March 12. Simpkins told Davis that Nash had informed her that the transactions were all approved by the legal department (a lie) and Ron did not know about it.[37] She described her actions and told Davis she did all this without Ron's knowledge. According to Susan Davis's later testimony, Simpkins said to her that Nash told her to initial the requests when Ron was out of town. Davis also told Simpkins that she, as the campaign lawyer, did not OK these arrangements, which made Simpkins cry. It had been a Carey policy that no risks were to be taken in regard to the financing of the election and to "play it clean."[38]

A few days later, on March 14, Simpkins met with IBT in-house general counsel Earl Brown, Jr., and outside counsel Michael Smith, who were investigating the scandal. Initially, she told them that she had not obtained Ron's approval for the contribution requests at issue. When Smith showed her paperwork for the requests suggesting she would be in a lot of trouble if she didn't tell the truth, she changed her story. Now she was saying that Ron had approved one of the requests.[39]

She too was advised to get her own legal representation. She began to panic. After consulting with her new lawyers, Simpkins retracted her statement. All of a sudden, she remembered that Ron had approved one of the donations but not all four. The narrative was beginning to change.

But Theresa Sherman, the secretary at Teamster headquarters, when questioned by EO Quindel, told a different story. Sherman said that in 1996, Simpkins admitted privately to her that it was Simpkins herself who had approved at least one of the swaps without discussing it with Ron. Sherman relates that Simpkins was worried that she could go to jail for it. Simpkins was a single mother with three children. She also told Sherman that Nash had pressured her into putting Carey's initials on the documents without obtaining Carey's approval.[40]

On March 14, IBT Director of Government Affairs Bill Hamilton spoke with an attorney at Zuckerman Spaeder, outside counsel retained by the IBT. Hamilton mentioned that he did speak with Ron about the Citizens Action contribution on November 3, 1996, at a Local 135 shop stewards' meeting.

By March 19, Hoffa was accusing Ron of illegal reelection campaign activities. Ron, of course, dismissed any allegations of wrongdoing. He was not only fully cooperating with the EO, but he also wanted to dispel any appearances of illegal actions. So he decided to return the $95,000 check to Barbara Arnold (A check was given to Arnold's husband's firm.) as well as the other "trust-fund babies" donations. In total they returned $221,000.[41]

Charny was assigned to vet potential donors to make sure that they were not employers. He approved seven of them. Others were rejected. But he didn't vet those donors properly. He spoke with five of the seven donors directly and the husbands of the other two. One of those husbands was Michael Ansara. As we have seen, he was an employer at the Share Group and husband of Barbara Arnold, who had donated $95,000 to Ron's campaign. Charny was unaware of the connection to the Carey campaign or the money laundering going on. Regardless, he submitted a false affidavit to the EO, which was discovered or assumed by the Hoffa campaign. In its complaint to EO Quindel, the Hoffa campaign noted that under the 1996 election rules, contributions from the spouse of an employer "will be deemed contributions received from such employer or employer representative."[42] (During this time Susan Davis was out on maternity leave.)

Nevertheless, on March 22, which just so happened to be Ron's birthday, Ron Carey and twenty-six other officers of the IBT were sworn in, with hundreds of members and their families watching on.[43] During his inaugural speech, Ron hit on a theme that proved prescient. With negotiations just beginning with UPS, Ron spoke forcefully about the "culture of corporate greed that had created so many 'throwaway workers' who are only part-time or temporary."[44]

Ron appeared calm and unworried about the ongoing investigation of the campaign funds. Most members weren't even aware that an investigation existed. Most thought the election was over. Behind the scenes, however, people were worried.

Not only was the EO now investigating six donations, but on March 26, it was acknowledged that a federal grand jury in Manhattan was considering whether the $95,000 contribution to the campaign was an illegal kickback.[45] Mary Jo White, the U.S. Attorney in Manhattan, immediately jumped on the case and began questioning people involved in the alleged swap.

For some in the administration, that was the "Oh shit moment." But others took it in stride. "As soon as the election protests came in, people started to worry," recalled Bob Hauptman. "No one at first really knew. Maybe five or six of us knew what was going on.

But Ron never worried. He was already gearing up for the UPS negotiations." Nevertheless, "everyone was on notice right away when it started coming out in the papers. Anything you say can get you into a perjury trap. And if you took the Fifth, you were out, period."[46]

To add wood to the fire, on April 1, Monie Simpkins, through her new lawyers, agreed to a "proffer," which meant that the prosecutors agreed that they would not use anything she told them against her in a criminal case. She chose to protect herself and her kids; she did not want to go to jail.

Now, the EO and federal officials started to focus on the four other contributions that the IBT had made to Citizens Action, Project Vote, the National Council of Senior Citizens, and the AFL-CIO. The indictments and resignations were about to begin. According to Hamilton, "The irony is that none of these groups were profit-making employers. They gave money because they cared about the environment or labor reform. When the organization that they were contributing to said, 'Hey, if you help get Ron Carey reelected, the IBT will give our organization some funds.' These were honorable people, so they wrote a check."[47]

On June 6, the federal government charged Martin Davis, the notorious mastermind behind the swap scheme, with mail fraud and embezzlement for scheming to have the Teamsters' union and other groups illegally funnel at least $95,000 to the Carey campaign. Davis had arranged for the IBT to pay nearly $97,000 to Michael Ansara, who, in turn, asked his wife to contribute $95,000 to the Carey campaign. Ansara had already agreed to plead guilty to conspiracy and admitted that he used IBT funds and other questionable funds to reimburse his wife, Barbara Arnold. He also agreed to cooperate with the government's investigation.[48]

Though Arnold was not an employer, it was illegal because it was solicited by her husband, who was an employer. Federal law prohibits employers from soliciting donations for union candidates. Though this is certainly debatable since Barbara was not an employee of her husband.[49]

On July 16, Ron testified before the federal grand jury. The next day he testified before EO Quindel. During both inquiries, Ron denied he knew anything about the illegal swaps. No serious person was accusing Ron of being involved in this. "It was a rogue operation. This would be out of character for Carey. He's had a lifetime of building his clean reputation," commented trucking industry expert Dr. Michael Belzer.[50]

Also in July, Bill Hamilton testified before the grand jury. "They bring you in before the grand jury without a lawyer," remembered Hamilton. "They asked me a bunch of questions and you have no choice: you either answer the questions or take the Fifth. Of course, if you take the Fifth, you are presumed to be guilty so I gave them very protected answers. The thing that I really feared was just having to run the election again. And it would have been my fault that Ron had to run again and raise another $2 million. Well, when you give the FBI an evasive answer, they consider it a lie. I was about to cry."[51]

He was feeling the pressure. On July 29, Hamilton submitted his resignation. Because he wasn't going to lie to give up Ron, Hamilton was never offered a deal. Feeling a bit self-righteous, he basically told the FBI to go fuck themselves. He released a letter taking a few shots at federal prosecutor Mary Jo White defending what he did.[52]

In the letter, Hamilton called the investigation a "circus" and said he "was not able to get work done in the current atmosphere." He attacked Mary Jo White, claiming that "after several encounters with the US Attorney of NY and her retinue that there is no merit to further cooperation by me with this investigation." Furthermore, documents he submitted wound up in the hands of Hoffa operatives, "who spun them to the press, while those of us who tried to assist in sorting out the questions raised by their investigation are unable to respond."[53]

Hamilton tried to explain the actual scheme and "the system" as he knew it. It was "politics as usual, everybody did it, Democrats and Republicans":

I didn't fully understand the scheme at first until it fell apart. It seemed legit: we give money to a progressive group and supporters of that group would give to Ron's campaign. It made sense to me. These groups shared our politics and values. I was asked to give money to Citizens Action. I mean they had honored Ron at a banquet earlier, so I gave. I had reason to believe that in turn Citizens Action was doing something to help Carey. I didn't learn until later that they had all arranged a money swap.

I've worked in Senate campaigns where a donor gives the maximum allowed so you get them to give to another Senate campaign instead. You talk to someone at the DSCC (Democratic Senatorial Campaign Committee) and they find you a donor who matched you up to another candidate and simply do a donor swap. It's a common practice. So that other Senator will get his donors to give to your campaign. That was the system as I knew it. Someone can give $20K because you ask him to; he gives it because he figures, OK next time I need to raise money I can go to you to reciprocate and give to him . . . that's the system.[54]

When pressed about the consent decree and all the eyes looking at the Teamsters in those years, Hamilton admitted:

Yes, I thought it broke the rules but it wasn't illegal; at best a violation of Labor Department rules. I mean we were collaborating closely with the U.S. attorney's people and we didn't do much without their prior approval. Judy [Scott, Ron's General Counsel] was very close with Quindel. I truly thought that the worst-case scenario was they would make us rerun the election.[55]

Meanwhile, the Teamsters were now on strike against UPS. The strike ends on August 19 and Ron's Teamsters score a huge victory. Ron Carey, the slayer of Corporate America, Ron Carey, the face of a now energized and more militant labor movement. There was talk of a massive campaign to organize FedEx. Labor was back and on the move.

Three days later, on Friday, August 22, election officer Barbara Zack Quindel released a report overturning the 1996 Teamster election won by Ron. It called for a new election to take place within the next 112 days. She found that a "complex network of schemes to funnel IBT funds into the Carey campaign may have affected the outcome" in a close election won by Ron by around 16,000 votes. In addition, she labeled the schemes as "egregious violations by high-level campaign functionaries who believed winning at all costs was more important than abiding by the 1996 election rules and the law."[56]

The EO's report did not disqualify Ron from running again because she had not found evidence that he knew of or participated in the scheme, though "important questions remained unanswered."[57] Ron remarked, "I'm very angry and infuriated by this." He continued that he was confident that he would win a rerun election against Hoffa, Jr., especially so close to his huge win against UPS.

Ron's supporters criticized Quindel for ordering a rerun while ignoring Hoffa campaign violations; EAM Conboy then instructed Quindel to investigate any Hoffa campaign-finance violations. Supporters of Hoffa criticized her for not disqualifying Ron. Hoffa himself called for Ron to resign. Ron responded on the Sunday news show *Meet the Press*, on August 31, calling Hoffa "a real pro in terms of smear and distortion who never negotiated a contract, never walked a picket line, never been elected to any position in this union!"[58]

EO Quindel admitted that she reached her decision to overturn the 1996 election results during the Teamsters' strike against UPS. She decided to wait until it ended in order not to affect the bargaining. "I didn't want this to be a factor in the labor-management dispute," claimed Quindel. "I was criticized for running the election in the capacity of a union lawyer. I was not going to do anything that would hurt the union as a whole if I were to release my decision during the strike. We sort of knew already by the time of the strike, but we waited. I had a job to do and the chips had to fall where they did."[59]

This action angered UPS. They attacked Quindel; they attacked Ron Carey. Within days, UPS sent a letter to Judge Edelstein accusing Quindel of siding with the union, complaining how "the delay contributed to the length of the strike." The EO responded to UPS's attack: "UPS seems to misunderstand. The election officer's duty as a court officer is to run the election process for the benefit of the members. The members of the union can't have faith in the consent decree if they see it as interfering with their economic livelihood."[60]

Regardless, UPS and Corporate America saw an opening to strike back. What they couldn't win at the bargaining table opposite Ron, they tried to do in the political and legal arena. On August 26, Republican Congressman Pete Hoekstra, chairman of the House Subcommittee on Oversight and Investigations, announced he was convening hearings on the 1996 Teamster election. The anti-union Gingrich Republicans had recently taken over Congress and were taking aim at their enemies. Unions were one of those enemies. Unions stand up to corporations, the GOP's puppet masters, and generally fund Democrats. Furthermore, Ron Carey had shifted the Teamsters from supporting the GOP to the Democratic Party.[61]

Democrats began to question Hoekstra's motives. When told that Hoekstra had called six Hoffa-supporting witnesses and only one Carey supporter, the ranking Democrat on the Subcommittee, Representative Patsy Mink of Hawaii, called the hearings nothing but a "partisan event." Moreover, the IRB opened an investigation into the campaign allegations of financial wrongdoing.[62] Seeing an opportunity to hurt unions and the Democratic Party, Senator Fred Thompson also opened hearings on the connection between the Teamsters and the Democratic Party.

On September 3, 1997, EO Quindel informed Judge Edelstein that she would be stepping down after he approved the 1998 rerun election rules. During the investigation, it came to her attention that a political group, Citizens Action of Wisconsin, for which her husband served on the board, had played a role in the scheme to provide improper contributions to the Carey campaign. Moreover, her husband, Roger Quindel, was also affiliated with the New Party, which received $5,000 from the Teamsters' PAC under the direction of Bill Hamilton.[63] Judge Edelstein then appointed Benetta Mansfield as interim EO and got Conboy to take over the investigation into whether to disqualify Ron from the rerun. Regardless, on September 11, a Thursday, Ron launched his rerun election campaign outside the huge NYC hub on 43rd Street with hundreds of devoted members cheering him on.[64]

But Mary Jo White and her office were putting intense pressure on the witnesses. They were threatened with long sentences in jail and expensive fines. She strong-armed three key witnesses to plead guilty and receive no jail time or fines, all in order to "get" Ron. White was a very assertive prosecutor who was super ambitious. Many people I spoke to agreed with the statement that "she would prosecute her mother in order to get what she wanted." She saw how her predecessor, Rudy Giuliani, used his office to make the front page of the daily papers in order to run for higher office. (Mary Jo White was awarded the position of head of the SEC from 2013 until 2017.)

A week later, on September 18, Nash, Davis, and Ansara pleaded guilty to funneling illegal contributions to the Carey campaign. Nash pleaded guilty to one count of conspiracy to defraud the government, one count of making false statements and encouraging others to do the same, one count of using phone or mail to defraud the union, and one count of embezzlement of union funds. Martin Davis pleaded guilty to one count of conspiracy, one count of embezzlement, and one count of mail fraud. Ansara pleaded guilty to one count of conspiracy. In pleading guilty, the trio agreed to cooperate with both the EO and the federal government.[65]

Their cooperation and testimony plus new evidence (notes of Ron's scheduler Colleen Dougher) forced the EO to reopen her investigation into whether Ron was involved in the scheme. Until now, Nash and Davis had refused to be interviewed by Quindel. Ron's personal lawyer, Reid Weingarten, said that "Ron Carey is not implicated in any way at all by today's charges." He maintained that Ron and the union were "victims" of these admitted criminals.[66]

In his first public defense since the three guilty pleas, Ron maintained that he was the victim in this case. Speaking before reporters at the AFL-CIO convention, he made the case that the EO should not disqualify him from the upcoming rerun election. "If there is a victim here, I certainly am the victim," stated Ron. "What went on here is a complete betrayal of everything we stood for." Ron described himself as the type of candidate who used methods that were more hands-off when it came to running his campaign. He had a reputation for delegating authority and trusting in his underlings. "I don't think any one man can know everything that's going on in a large organization," he explained. "I didn't rely on crooks. I relied on what I thought were capable, trusted people."[67]

On September 29, Barbara Zack Quindel was officially replaced by the Election Appeals Master Judge, Kenneth Conboy, a Reagan appointee. Two days later, Ron, cooperating with the investigation, appeared before a federal grand jury in Manhattan. He was questioned for three hours and was told he was not the target. Ron told them what he had told everyone who has asked: he knew nothing of the swap scheme and would have stopped it if he had known.[68]

Meanwhile, Congressman Hoekstra's subcommittee began their investigation into the Teamsters. He hired the partisan, anti-union right-wing lawyers Joseph diGenova and his wife Victoria Toensing to serve as his special counsel. Retained for $150,000 for six months of work, they were allowed to keep their lobbying clients, powerful corporations, while running the investigation.[69] Hoekstra was also putting pressure on the IRB and the Department of Justice to void the 1996 election entirely and disqualify Ron.

No friend of unions, Hoekstra had a long history of representing the interests of corporations against working families. Hoekstra and Gingrich were not trying to protect the Teamster treasury or demonstrate care about Teamster members. They hated the fact that the Democratic Party was now partly funded by the Teamsters, who no longer gave money to the GOP. They wanted to use this scandal to hurt and intimidate the labor movement on behalf of their corporate masters. They wanted to cut worker safety regulations and actively went after the AFL-CIO and all their donations to other groups to get Democrats elected.

On October 14, Hoekstra began his hearings into the Carey campaign. Ron sensed it was to be a show trial, so he sent a letter to the Hoekstra subcommittee denying any wrongdoing or retaliation for any Teamster official for not giving any donations to his campaign: "Anyone who feared retaliation was not telling the truth." No Teamster official was fired or suspended for not contributing. A Teamsters' spokesperson, Nancy Coleman, called the Hoekstra hearings "a circus for anti-labor Republicans. There was an unfounded understanding by these people that if they didn't give money, they'd be retaliated against . . . and none of these people have been retaliated against."[70]

The Gingrich GOP had many motives for going after the Teamsters. The IBT under Ron gave $2.5 million in PAC money to Democratic candidates in the 1995–96 election cycle. Only $106,000 was given to Republican candidates. Hoekstra and company offered the public excuse that they wanted to save the government from paying for the rerun election. But in reality, they wanted to force the IBT to spend another $20 million on the election, in the hope that this would mortally wound the Teamsters' financial health, thus cutting off a major source of future Democratic funding.

Activist leaders like Ken Paff also questioned the motives and intentions of the subcommittee. "The Hoekstra committee was a joke. They got people like Bob Simpson to say 'Carey forced me to give money to the campaign.' No one, no one on that committee even asked Simpson the reason why he was no longer a Teamster. He was expelled on corruption charges. Expelled! And now he's working for the hospital group he used to bargain with! These so-called hearings have no legitimate purpose, and are designed to showcase one candidate, Hoffa, in the Teamsters election, in hopes of gaining millions of Teamster dollars for the Republicans."[71]

Bob Muelhenkamp was asked to testify, and he refused to do so. Pro-Hoffa Teamster staff members testified that they got "pressured" for donations to Ron's campaign. It is common to ask staff members to donate. It's not illegal or unethical. But there was no retaliation. No Teamsters ever lost their jobs for not contributing.[72]

The Director of Field Operations, Dave Eckstein, detected a Hoffa-inspired conspiracy to the charge of people being forced or coerced to contribute:

> These folks all worked for us and were encouraged by the Hoffa campaign to make false allegations to get jobs if Hoffa won. We held non-mandatory meetings after work hours and said that if anybody was interested in donations and/or working on the campaign after hours, it was OK under the Election Rules. Nobody was forced or led to believe they had too. . . . I testified to the Elections Officer and the investigation found no merit to their accusations.[73]

Ron said of the Hoekstra subcommittee, it "couldn't put a hat on a drunken sailor in a bathtub."

On October 20, Ron appeared before the National Press Club in Washington. This was his big opportunity to set the record straight. He was not only a great union leader. He was also a keen political observer, analyst, and critic. For about an hour, he stated his record of accomplishments and took questions mostly dealing with the 1996 campaign. He displayed anger at the embarrassing situation the three campaign officials brought to his union. Ron called the scandal "a betrayal of everything I stand for"; he said he was "not involved" and that he was cooperating fully to the extent that he voluntarily gave up his right to attorney-client privilege by turning over all information to the government and the EO.[74]

While defensively stating that "they betrayed me, I am the victim," Ron also said he looked forward to a new election to "set the record straight." He also ridiculed Hoffa for claiming to raise almost $2 million from "cake sales."

During his opening remarks, Ron said, "Despite all of the attacks from corporations, anti-labor politicians, the mob, and even corrupt officials in our own union, we have made enormous progress." He spoke about the seventy-five trusteeships he imposed to clean up corruption, how the Teamsters were training members to organize FedEx, as well as reaching out to FedEx workers. He mentioned the strong opposition from management from FedEx and UPS in Washington: "UPS gave $2 million in campaign contributions in the 1996 election cycle to anti-labor politicians," and "Republicans are trying to stop OSHA's federal inspections from making UPS protect its workers on the job."[75]

Ron took on the powers that be in Washington. He attacked the relationship between the Republican Party and corporate donations: "UPS gave corporate contributions to Speaker Newt Gingrich, Congressman Pete Hoekstra, and four others on Hoekstra's Subcommittee," which was investigating him and the Teamsters but not corporations for real corporate crimes. He said that Hoekstra was in bed with the industrial lobbying group, the American Trucking Association, and with the National Association of Manufacturers and the Chamber of Commerce. Those corporate funds/bribes were used to move the GOP Congress to investigate unions, cut funding for the NLRB, and ban corporate campaign tactics that are so effective at winning strong contracts with companies.[76]

"The real scandal in Washington," Ron declared, "is the power that big corporations have over our government, our major political parties, and over our economic lives." After quoting Lincoln about a government "of, by, and for the people," he asserted forcefully that "we have a government of the Corporation, by Big Business, and for the Special Interests!" He went on to recommend that politicians "ought to wear the logos of their corporate sponsors on their suits just like athletes wear them on their uniforms." He called for people to support public financing of elections.[77]

He ended his press conference with some soaring progressive rhetoric. Saying that the goal of unions was to "take on the fight against Corporate America and the Radical Right," Ron was proud that the "union reform movement was becoming more militant and was scaring Corporate America." Politicians like Hoekstra "want unions to go back to doing what they've always done, just marching up and down the street with pickets. . . . But what labor unions just said with the UPS strike is we had enough of taking it on the chin. . . . We are implementing new strategies and new ways that go beyond the picket line. Unions have a new energy and they don't want that to happen!"[78]

On October 22, Bill Hamilton was charged by the IRB of scheming with Nash, Davis, and Ansara to funnel embezzled money to the Carey campaign. A week later, Ron testified before IRB Chief Investigator Charles Carberry. Once again he denied knowledge of any swap schemes. On November 10, Ron testified before Judge Kenneth Conboy. He repeated to Conboy the same denials of any knowledge of the swap scheme. Conboy also questioned Nash and Simpkins under oath. The next day Conboy announced that candidates for IBT office must declare their intentions to rerun by November 20, 1997.[79]

Nash also testified before Conboy. During the interrogation, Nash told Conboy that he told Ron about the contributions and the swap scheme. He also admitted, "I knew what we were doing was wrong but I felt compelled to do it," acting out of some devotion to Ron and the reform movement. He envisioned a Hoffa win as "just unthinkable. I acted in an attempt to save the campaign of a candidate I admired. I made the calculation that we had to do this to get money. I broke the law."[80]

On Monday, November 17, Conboy released a 74-page decision disqualifying Ron from running in the upcoming election. His report was based mostly on the former EO's report as well as new evidence and testimony from Nash and Simpkins. Conboy found it "difficult to believe Ron Carey would have no recollection of authorizing any of these contributions . . . and unaware of the specific condition of the IBT and the financial condition of DRIVE ... and never inquired as to whether any portion of the $885,000 expended from General Funds had been reimbursed."[81]

Moreover, Conboy believed the word of Nash, a proven liar, over Ron Carey. He deduced that Ron must have known about the swap, and since he failed to put an end to it "in order to protect the integrity of the IBT and the process," Conboy stated that Ron therefore "tolerated and engaged in extensive rules violations." He further inferred that even if Ron had a plausible explanation for each illegal swap, it was highly unlikely that he was innocent in every instance. Conboy "found Carey's denials unbelievable, not credible."[82]

Conboy concluded acknowledging that "disqualification is by nature an anti-democratic remedy which removes in part the choice of union leadership from the rank and file and places it squarely in the hands of the government." But since he accuses Ron of "rules violations . . . misusing his power . . . self-dealing," Conboy calls these actions a "breach of his fiduciary duty," which "constitutes one of the core types of misconduct the consent decree was designed to eliminate." Hence, Conboy determined that "the appropriate exercise of discretion in this case is to disqualify Mr. Carey from participating as a candidate in the rerun."[83] The reality was that Ron Carey was being punished for successfully striking UPS and being a working-class rebel.

As soon as the decision came down, Ron immediately denounced it as "unbelievably wrong." He declared his innocence, stating, "I have done nothing wrong and I will fight this decision until it is overturned." Ron's personal attorney Reid Weingarten called the decision a "strained and wrongheaded decision that turns justice and common sense on their heads."[84] Ron objected to the fact that his lawyers were not allowed to cross-examine any of the witnesses before the Conboy Report was assembled.[85]

"Labor's foes everywhere surely see this as a happy hour," wrote Alexander Cockburn, a journalist with *The Nation*, in response to Conboy's decision. "The prime imperative of election rules is that the will of the electorate prevails, and Conboy lost track of this central point. Who can doubt that, in the wake of the successful strike against UPS, Carey would have swept to victory over Hoffa? Just who is being protected by the rules? The members? Or are they protecting the trucking companies from Teamster power?"[86]

Gene Moriarity remembers the day of the decision:

> On the day the decision came down, Susan Davis called me. She told me that she had just dispatched one of her lawyers to get a copy of the decision. She told him to just flip to the last page. Then she told me she'd call me back in fifteen minutes. But Susan never called me back. After an hour I called her office; there was no answer. Finally, I found her cell number. She answered. She was crying, and I knew it wasn't good news. He was disqualified. I think she blames herself for not being around.[87]

On Thursday, November 21, Judge Edelstein granted the Interim EO Mansfield's request for a 45-day delay in the rerun election in order to give investigators more time to investigate allegations of Hoffa campaign financial irregularities.

After consulting with his lawyers, advisers, and family, Ron took an unpaid, temporary leave of absence on Tuesday, November 25. In a letter to Tom Sever, the Teamsters' secretary-treasurer, who would take over as Interim General President until a new president was elected in the rerun election early in 1998, Ron wrote: "It is a sad day when the word of a convicted criminal prevails over the word of a man who has stood for integrity all his life . . . I fully intend to clear my name."[88]

"When Ron decided to take a LOA," recalled Aaron Belk, "he came down to my office and said, 'I'm going to take a Leave of Absence. I need to hold myself to the same standard I expect of everyone else.' He wanted to hold himself to that same standard that if you are under investigation, you gotta step down. I called a board meeting on the phone to tell everyone."[89]

Dave Eckstein spoke with Ron earlier at the Teamsters Women's

Conference in Cleveland. "I said to Ron, 'Don't step aside.' He said, 'Listen I've taken people out all over the country for the same things or less. I can't stay here until this thing is fully investigated and done.' He really believed he was coming back."[90]

Tim Sylvester recalls his last meeting with Ron: "We were in the Local 804 union hall. I told him, 'When you get cleared of this stuff and you're back in office, you need someone in that building who reports to just you and whose sole job is to tell you what is going on in that building around you.' I laid out who in his building or on his staff was sleeping with who. Ron said he didn't know this or that one was sleeping with anyone. He paused and said, 'I deserve this. I should have seen this.'"[91]

Later in the day, Chief Investigator of the IRB Charles Carberry issued an Investigative Report recommending that Ron be charged for being "in breach of his fiduciary obligations" as stated in the Conboy Report; he issued his Report to the GEB, which filed the charges against Ron (and Hamilton) and returned the matter to the IRB for hearings to follow.[92] Weingarten tried to explain how busy Ron was during this period of the campaign: he was on the road campaigning 24/7, and his leadership style lent to delegating responsibilities to his subordinates. Recalling how much Carberry and the IRB members charge the IBT for their lawyerly services, Ron berated "these folks [Carberry] who were lining their own pockets" with Teamster dues money.[93] Nice gig if you can get it.

But Ron understood what this IRB charge represented. The IRB had a 100 percent conviction rate. "Over the previous 5 years, the 217 Teamsters charged by the board were found guilty by the board, admitted to the charges, or just quit the Teamsters," wrote Ken Crowe.[94]

The events of the day sent a shock wave throughout the union movement. It certainly threw the Teamsters election into chaos. The Reform slate was now without a leader. Tussling ensued among Reformers and so-called Reformers: Tom Sever, Ken Hall, and Tom Leedham. (Tom Leedham wound up getting the nomination as the standard bearer of the Reform slate.) Unfortunately,

Ron did not groom a successor. According to Bob Muehlenkamp, after the LOA, there was no one of Ron's caliber to fill his shoes: "There was no one. That's the job of a union leader. Very few union leaders actually plan a transition. He should have. He had a high opinion of Tom Gilmartin. Not so much in Ken Hall and certainly not Tom Sever. Ron didn't even endorse Tom Leedham when he became the candidate of the Reform ticket in 1998."[95]

Moreover, the fall of Ron led directly to the breakup of the Reform coalition he had led of militant TDUers, other genuine union reformers, some traditional Teamster leaders, and a few opportunists. He also was the leading voice against NAFTA, the man who helped reformer John Sweeney take over the AFL-CIO, and moved the Teamsters from supporting Republicans to supporting Democrats.[96] It demonstrated that whoever is in charge of the Teamsters has the power to influence the entire labor movement and even the national political scene.

It seems Ron's lawyers recommended he take the LOA, while his grassroots activist friends and advisers wanted him to stay and fight. According to Doreen Gasman:

> Some of us felt we could inhabit the building, the Marble Palace, and just refuse to leave, chain ourselves to the furniture. I wondered if the Feds were gonna come in and take him out. What's the worst thing that could happen? Ron told me later in life that he "was lawyered. They wanted me to go quietly . . . I could kick myself for listening to them." He said, "We should have stayed and refused to leave. Who leaves without being declared guilty?!" he yelled. There was an assumption that if you were a Teamster you are guilty already.[97]

Gene Moriarity tells a similar story:

> There were people screaming for him to stay. Doreen Gasman was unbelievable through all that. I was in the rerun office and Doreen was calling me saying, "You're there in DC, can't you

call people, get people up there, we need to form a human chain around the IBT and not let anyone come in and take him out." I ran that by Meuhlenkamp, who was gonna be meeting with Ron. But Ron said no. I told Doreen that and she said, "Bullshit we have to defend him," but in the end, Ron didn't want us to do it.

I think it was Doreen who wanted Bob to approach Ron about forming a human chain around the IBT. There were about twenty people in this tiny little office in the campaign headquarters waiting for the decision to come down and waiting to hear from Susan Davis.[98]

Days later, Ron appeared at the TDU convention in Cleveland. "Hundreds of rank-and-filers cheered him on when he walked into that ballroom, urging [him] to FIGHT FIGHT FIGHT," remembered Ken Paff. Ron said that "if he had known that anything was improper, I would have stopped it dead in its tracks!" He continued, "I've spent the last forty years with many of you fighting arm in arm against wrongdoing." He asked for their continued support and received a thunderous ovation.[99]

Federal prosecutors named an independent auditor to "oversee the day-to-day financial operations" of the Teamsters. Two weeks later, U.S. District Judge David Edelstein appointed Michael Cherkasky the new Teamster EO to oversee the rerun election in 1998.[100]

Subsequently, Ron filed with the U.S. District Court for the Southern District of NY an appeal of EO Conboy's decision disqualifying him from running in the rerun. His appeal charged that he was denied due process because he was not afforded a hearing before the EO where his lawyers could have cross-examined witnesses, and that he was issued discipline by the EO, whose role under the consent decree was to supervise elections, not dole out punishment.[101]

On December 30, his appeal was rejected on the grounds that "individuals have due process only against the government, not against private organizations such as the IBT—even though Carey was actually disciplined by a court-appointed officer acting pursuant to a court-appointed consent decree. The court also stated that Ron "could be disciplined without a full and fair hearing because his disqualification was remedial, not disciplinary."[102]

Ron applied to the Southern District of New York on January 14, requesting an order authorizing his lawyers to be able to issue subpoenas to compel the attendance of key witnesses and the production of vital documents in connection with the IRB hearings. Two days later, the court rejected his request.

The IRB hearings began on January 20, 1998, a Tuesday, and ran through Thursday. They were headed by former federal judge Frederick Lacey, former CIA and FBI director William Webster, and labor lawyer Grant Crandall. Former prosecutor Charles Carberry, the IRB's chief investigator, did most of the questioning of the witnesses. This cabal was to be investigator, prosecutor, judge, and jury as to whether Ron would be allowed to remain in the union.

Ron's lawyers opened their remarks by stressing that the whole "investigative process" was flawed because the IRB's case, as well as Conboy's report, was based on unchallenged and uncorroborated statements by witnesses that they couldn't cross-examine.[103]

Furthermore, the main witnesses, Jere Nash and Monie Simpkins, did not appear in the courtroom to be cross-examined that day, a point Reid Weingarten, Ron's lawyer, made throughout the hearings. While Simpkins was refusing to attend Ron's IRB hearings and be subjected to cross-examination, she was meeting with FBI agents and prosecutors. Again, she chose to protect herself and her kids and throw Ron under the bus. I'm sure she was told that she already had given several versions of her story and speaking again might jeopardize her position.

Carey campaign lawyer Susan Davis testified that Simpkins had told her that Nash wanted Simpkins to initial the expedited documents sent over from Hamilton when Ron was out of town. Davis also refuted Nash's affidavit claiming that Davis was aware of the contributions and had approved them, saying that Nash simply lied to Simpkins to get her to cooperate.[104]

Then, Ron's administrative secretary and friend of Simpkins, Theresa Sherman, testified that Nash had indeed pressured her into putting Ron's initials on the requests without getting Ron's approval or knowledge. The next witness for Ron was Barry Colvert, who was a retired polygraph expert for the FBI. Colvert testified as an expert that Ron had passed a lie detector test, concluding, "I did not find any indication of deception" in any of Ron's responses.[105]

The final witness was Ron. *The Nation* columnist David Corn, who attended the hearings, described Ron looking tired with "dark bags beneath his eyes." He wrote that Ron testified that he knew nothing of the illegal schemes his campaign aides pleaded guilty to, as Carberry was "hurling one brutal question after another at the beleaguered Teamster president…. With each question, Carey's shoulders drooped further" as Hoffa supporters in the back of the courtroom chuckled.[106] Weingarten managed a point-by-point rebuttal to each accusation, but the panel appeared "skeptical."[107]

Nevertheless, Ron testified to prove his innocence and remain in office as a way to protect his reputation and legacy. He contradicted the affidavit submitted by Monie Simpkins that he approved the money going to Citizens Action. "Had she mentioned to me about any swaps I would have known something was up," recalled Ron under oath.[108]

Ron admitted to approving money to progressive organizations that would help with GOTV (Getting Out the Vote) in November. There was nothing wrong with that. Political directors are supposed to recommend optimal donations to allied political groups. But Ron insisted that Nash never suggested any political contributions because Nash was not a Teamster and therefore was not allowed to interfere in union affairs.[109] When asked about the large contributions to these progressive groups, Ron answered, "They were out there on the issues that were important to us, Medicare, Getting out the Vote, getting people educated about the issues that would confront them."[110]

Lacey got frustrated and asked Ron, "With the heat that was

going on around this money, it is beyond my comprehension you heard none of this," to which Ron responded that he too agreed that it was "beyond my comprehension as well."[111]

In the course of the investigations and hearings, Weingarten hired a private detective to do a forensic exam of Martin Davis's firm, the November Group, as well as of Teamster finances. He revealed that while Nash was managing Ron's campaign, receiving $2,500 per month, he was also being paid $18,000 per month by the November Group.[112] He was in charge of the Carey campaign account for Davis's firm. It was a shady conflict of interest. Nash had a financial incentive to convince the Carey campaign, which he was running, to spend more money on mailings so that he could collect more; he was ultimately given a $50,000 bonus from the November Group. That could be called self-dealing. It was also revealed that Martin Davis also owned stock in and was on the board of Michael Ansara's firm, the Share Group.[113] No one besides Nash, Davis, and Ansara (NDA) were in the know about these business and financial ties.

At the conclusion of the hearing on January 22, the IRB relented to Ron's arguments on the injustice of not being able to question those who were accusing you of wrongdoing. (Actually it was the Southern District of New York that gave the OK.) They announced that they would allow Nash to testify at a supplemental hearing in March. On March 11, Nash took the stand. Nash testified that when Hamilton told him that Ron turned down the $475,000 for Citizens Action, he called Simpkins at Teamster headquarters on October 16 or 17, 1996, who supposedly patched his call to Ron on the campaign trail. Nash then explained to Ron that "it would help Davis in fundraising." According to Nash, Ron responded with "No one ever explained it to me like that" and the contributions were approved.[114] At the previous hearing, Ron had denied that conversation ever took place.

During cross-examination, which lasted over five hours, Ron's lawyers went about exposing Nash's deceptions. Weingarten was able to get Nash to admit that the so-called phone conversation lasted no more than fifteen seconds. Moreover, no mention or allusion to any swap was spoken about or how it might help Ron's campaign. After explaining how all or most of that money raised from the scheme went to Davis's November Group, Nash was asked, "So the big winner was Davis?" Nash replied, "One can come to no other conclusion."[115] As documented by Ken Crowe, "Weingarten complained that he wanted to cross-examine Simpkins, but was denied the power to subpoena her, and her lawyer refused to produce her voluntarily."[116] Ron's other attorney, Mark Hulkower, was able to get Nash to admit that he never talked to Ron about donating to Project Vote or the National Council of Senior Citizens.[117]

David Corn called the hearings a "process short on due process on the basis of underwhelming evidence." His point was that even if one believes or can prove that the call took place, nothing was explained about any swap deal; there is nothing illegal about contributing to friendly political groups in the hope that you might get a legitimate benefit in the form of donations to your campaign. In addition, Ron was banned from running because of a scheme he says he didn't even know about. There was no direct evidence that Ron had any knowledge of a quid pro quo. The short talk with Hamilton in Indianapolis was about PAC money, nothing about swaps.[118] It came down to vague, uncorroborated statements by a person, Nash, who admitted to lying and who was facing years in prison, and suggestive testimony from Simpkins who had given several versions of events to stay out of prison.

In the end, according to Corn, "Neither Conboy nor Carberry nor SDNY had produced direct incontrovertible evidence from a reliable source that Carey was in on the money exchange." Too much was inferred by Conboy. Furthermore, "a union should not turn on the inference of one man, especially when the process is not open to challenge," despite not holding hearings, sharing evidence, or allowing Ron's lawyers to cross-examine witnesses. Corn ends his column warning that "those who challenge the status quo have to be damn careful. Carey took on powerful forces, in and out of the union, and his foes were forever on the lookout for ammunition."[119] And whoever controls the Teamsters influences the entire labor movement and the national political landscape.

Gene Moriarity was also asked to testify before the IRB. He understood the nature of the hearings. He saw them as more of a political witch-hunt then a true investigation:

> The last thing they asked me was "Before you came over here today, did anybody at the International advise you what you should say here?" I said, "Matter of fact, someone did." "Who was that?" they asked. I told them, "Ron Carey." As I was walking out the door he spotted me and he said, "I understand you have your deposition today. No matter what happens just tell the truth about everything because if anyone in this organization did something they should be held responsible for, then let it be." But that's not what they were looking for.[120]

In April, the new EO, Cherkasky, revealed that the Hoffa campaign had also committed several 1996 election-related violations. Hoffa was fined $31,000 for misreporting the source of donations. He also failed to testify truthfully about receiving a donation from a former president of the IBT. Nevertheless, EO Cherkasky did not disqualify Hoffa from the rerun.[121] In June, Judge Edelstein criticized Hoffa's behavior in the election as "disturbing, worrisome and suspect," calling it a "deliberate attempt to mislead IBT members," yet he allowed Hoffa to run in the rerun.[122] On April 27, a grand jury in the Southern District of New York returned an indictment charging Bill Hamilton with multiple felonies.[123]

The IRB panel released its decision on Ron and Bill Hamilton on Monday, July 27. It was no surprise. The die was cast when Conboy concluded his one-sided "investigation" without allowing hearings, sharing of documents, or cross-examining of witnesses. Carberry had his marching orders from this anti-Carey IRB.[124] In the end, the IRB believed Nash over Ron.

In their majority ruling, Webster and Crandall wrote: "Given all of the facts and circumstances that surround the IBT contributions

... and having in mind our incredulity as to Carey's denial regarding those contributions, we must conclude that a conversation did take place as Nash testified. While the information provided to Carey was not sufficient to establish Carey's knowledge of the nature of the scheme, it was sufficient to impose on Carey a fiduciary duty to inquire further about any relation or tie between Carey's own campaign fundraising and the IBT's payment to an advocacy group like Citizens Action."[125]

However, they stopped short of stating that Ron was guilty of participating in the scheme: "A fair inference to be drawn from all the facts is that Carey closed his eyes because he knew or suspected that those contributions were to generate a personal benefit for him." Lacey issued a separate, more stern concurring decision. "I find Carey was not a credible witness," Lacey wrote. "I am convinced that he did authorize the contributions."[126] All three agreed to expel Ron and ban him and Hamilton from having any connection to the Teamsters union or Teamster members

"In a fit of regulatory overzealousness," said Weingartern, criticizing the decision, "the IRB found Ron Carey did not have actual knowledge of an illegal fundraising scheme and then imposed severe sanctions upon him solely on the basis of his failure to prevent misconduct that he knew nothing about." He continued, "Under this reasoning, every bank president who has been unable to stop a teller from embezzling money can be tossed out of his job and industry."[127]

"The social forces underlying all of this is that when labor raises its head and begins to fight they get beaten down," wrote Stanley Aronowitz. "Labor had begun to raise its head and fight back. Ron epitomized that new activism, the new militancy of unions." Tim Sylvester, former organizer under Ron and now a friend, commented, "Ron was taken down by a system that didn't allow anyone as good as he to remain in power."[128]

The enemies of reform and Ron Carey needed to gloat. Hoffa made a statement saying the decision to ban Ron "is a small step toward returning honest, competent, and democratically elected leadership to the Teamsters."[129] Congressman Pete Hoekstra called expelling Ron a "positive step" and was happy that Ron "will not be a part of this union in the foreseeable future."[130]

People have asked why a labor lawyer, Grant Crandall, would have joined their decision to expel Ron. It was no secret that Ron ticked off some powerful people over the years, including Lacey himself. I'm sure he didn't make friends with Webster, whom he was trying to prevent from becoming a member of the IRB in 1992. As for Crandall, no one understands why he sided with Lacey and Webster. Both Bill Clinton and Newt Gingrich experienced election financial scandals while they were in power. Neither were removed or banned from office. Neither were forced to rerun elections.

Weeks later, Judge Edelstein affirmed the expulsion, finding it "utterly incredible that Carey had no knowledge of contributions and loans totaling $1.485 million" and "at the very least turned a blind eye to the improper fundraising." Reporter and author Ken Crowe called the decision "an almost medieval stricture banning all Teamsters from even associating with him. Any Teamster, other than a relative who even speaks to Carey risks a similar excommunication from the union and the IBT."[131]

HOW DID WE GET HERE? Only a year before, Ron Carey was riding high, labor was riding high. There was talk of a new militancy in the union movement. Corporate campaign strategies made companies fear unions again. There was talk of organizing FedEx. Unions were on the move, on the offense. Then it all came crashing down.

For a while, there was much finger-pointing and blaming people and factions in the Teamster headquarters: grassroots rank-and-filers blaming the more educated, non-Teamster "outsiders" and vice versa; there was the corporate media; overzealous prosecutors; his lawyers; the "bubble" around Ron; the political right wing; "his bad knees"; good intentions and greed; and, of course, Nash, Martin Davis, and Ansara.

In truth, it was more a collection of failures. Most people involved in the 1996 campaign blamed the main campaign people: Nash, Davis, Ansara, and Hamilton—the people who were indicted or pleaded guilty to charges. Grassroots activists like Doreen Gasman, who was also an International Rep, recalled, "Back in '91, we [the rank and file] were in the thick of things at the local level. By '96 we were stuck in DC or working around the country, doing our jobs and things got out of control. They brought in outsiders, people who didn't know the system or union people."[132] They seemed oblivious to or didn't care that the Teamsters were being monitored closely under the consent decree. They just wanted to win. And lots of decent people with some good intentions did some awful stuff.

Though they helped Ron win the 1996 election, this crew ultimately cost him everything. They failed Ron. It might be true that all four believed in Ron and union reform. But they allowed greed and a winning-at-all-costs mentality to dominate their part of the campaign. They lied to Ron, and they hid things from him. They failed Ron. Three of them made lots of money from their association with Ron, got caught, pleaded guilty, and cooperated with officials in order to save themselves from prison time and huge fines.

While Jere Nash truly believed in Ron and seems to have had a good heart, he ultimately kept things from him, such as the actual swap deal and his employment at the November Group. He also manipulated Bill Hamilton and Monie Simpkins into the plot. And in the end, he lied to investigators and prosecutors to stay out of prison. The mastermind, Martin Davis, appears to have lied to everyone to help Ron win as well as make a lot of money. He also pleaded guilty to lesser charges and cooperated with officials looking to take down Ron.[133] Michael Ansara, who today has heartfelt regrets for his role in Ron's downfall, also misled people.[134] And let's not leave out Nathaniel Charny, of CWS, for not properly vetting those trust-fund babies.[135]

Hauptman agrees that Martin Davis was the worst actor in all this. But he refutes the line that Davis lied to everybody. "He didn't have to lie to everybody. Martin made a million dollars that year, 1996; we saw the W2. He paid Nash over $100,000 over that same year to have him under his control. He bought Nash. Martin didn't have to lie to him."[136]

Gene Moriarity recalls when he suspected something wasn't right with the fundraising. He started questioning things sometime in November 1996:

> Because at one point I said to Nash, "You know I see pockets of money coming from Boston from these trust-fund babies, who believe in Ron so strongly they are sending a check for $75,000, $95,000 to get Ron reelected. Next time Ron is in Boston why not have a little cocktail reception for these people." Nash said, "That isn't going to happen." That didn't make any sense to me. I said, "Well, maybe that is a decision Ron should be making." Nash said, "This is not something that should ever be discussed with Ron!" Right there I thought, "Now this is not good."[137]

Some blame political director Bill Hamilton. He failed Ron too. He brought the DC mindset with him to the Teamsters where these sorts of arrangements are made all the time. "I've worked in Senate campaigns where a donor gives the maximum allowed, you get them to give to another Senate campaign instead in the expectation that that other Senator's donors will give to your guy's campaign. . . . But I did what I thought was in the interests of Ron's campaign." Hamilton went on to rationalize what he did as more of a systemic failure:

> Of course, it was easy for investigators to blame Ron. He was the president, the ultimate fiduciary. But Ron delegated. It's what he did. That is what I loved about him. He trusted you. He gave you the freedom to run a program. He'd listen to me and others and say, "OK, you're doing it right."[138]

Hamilton then went about disparaging Ron's executive assistant at the time, Aaron Belk. There seemed to be some class conflict in the headquarters. Hamilton believes Belk failed Ron as well:

> A good executive assistant would have protected Ron. Belk was just incompetent as an administrator. He was a warehouse guy; he wasn't a bad guy, he just didn't know shit. He was not very educated, a religious fundamentalist. He believed in a very simplistic way that things were getting bad and never got a sense of how the world worked.
>
> If Aaron had understood his job to protect Ron and be a strong gatekeeper and to run the union when Ron was busy campaigning, none of this trouble would have happened.[139]

IBT organizing director and close adviser to Ron, Muehlenkamp, agreed with Hamilton's assessment of Belk and his role. "That is exactly it," affirmed Muehlenkamp. "A big part of that job was not just helping to run the union but also to guard the door and everything to protect Ron."[140] "Over his head is a good description of Aaron," stated Bob Hauptman. "But in Aaron's defense, he was trying to protect Ron. He just had a more small-town view of the big city. He certainly wanted to protect Ron; his motivations were 100 percent pure, it's just that his ability to implement them and get the bigger picture was not."[141]

Tim Sylvester also came to Belk's defense. "His detractors love to tell how he was 'in over his head,'" commented Sylvester. "In truth, Aaron was genuinely too nice of a guy who was not used to dealing with the scum of the earth. He was one of the most honest, loyal people I've ever known. He told the IRB, 'When Ron was not in the office, I was in charge. The money deal was done under my watch! If you are charging anyone, you should be charging me!' Only an Aaron Belk would have done that." [142]

Hamilton also took aim at Ron's secretary-treasurer, Tom Sever, for not inquiring about the contributions:

> I did what I thought was in the interests of Ron getting reelected

and the interests of the union; I was not a fiduciary, Sever was. So we had this system in place where I recommend a contribution to certain groups that share our values. Nobody at the top ever stopped me from giving money to these groups. Sometimes, they [Belk and Sever] held it up for a week or so, but no one ever said you can't do that. They asked me for an explanation, I gave them one. They signed off on it. Tom Sever, the same thing. He almost never asked any questions about contributions as long as I was able to give money to his favorite golf charity two or three times a year. He was incompetent, at best disengaged.[143]

IBT political director Hamilton then went about demonstrating how "the real world worked" and how he broke the election rules as laid out in the consent decree that all staff people were made aware of. He believed there was a gray area, which he went about exploiting. Hamilton had done similar acts numerous times over the years for many campaigns and never run into a problem. "I thought it broke the rules, but it wasn't illegal. I ran it past Judy Scott [Ron's general counsel] who didn't say it was illegal. I thought at best it was a violation of Labor Department rules. Worst-case scenario they would just make us rerun the election," said Hamilton.[144]

The class conflict was reiterated in Belk's take on what happened as well. Belk took a more conspiratorial perspective of Ron's downfall. According to executive assistant Belk:

Ron's biggest flaw was he trusted people and delegated authority to people he trusted. Those people on the campaign didn't understand we were under government scrutiny of our election process. This wasn't some senatorial race. Burke, Judy [Scott] called the shots, the November Group, Hamilton. They stepped over boundaries and didn't care.

At the end there was a bubble around Ron. Even I couldn't get to him. His problem was that he had a group around him that isolated him, kept Ron from the rank-and-file people like me and Dennis Skelton.[145]

Belk named names:

> People like Burke, Scott, Muehlenkamp. They kinda controlled
> things around Ron, setting the agenda. Colleen [Dougher] kept
> his scheduling, controlling where he went and who he had
> access to in DC. [Dougher was a DNC fundraiser in the late
> 1980s.] They controlled Ron like a rock star, kept him isolated
> on stage to the point that Ron wasn't in touch as he was earlier.
> He was less active in decisions now. Scheduling him to be out of
> the building so they could kinda control things more.[146]

But Belk had some of his harshest criticisms, as did Hamilton,
for secretary-treasurer Tom Sever. In order to have the requests
approved, they had to be signed off by both Ron and Sever. Every
penny spent by the IBT required a sign-off by the president and
the secretary-treasurer. But during the campaign when Ron was
on the road, he delegated that stuff to Belk or Simpkins. Belk
remembered:

> Sever allowed those checks to go out even though they violated
> the IBT constitution. He knew. I turned down every request on
> Ron's behalf; that's why he put me there. Anything over $10,000
> went against the rules. It required a GEB vote and approval.
> Sever should have stopped those checks. He and I had heated
> discussions.[147]
>
> If Ron had been more plugged in at the time, this mess never
> would have happened. People in that building, were overriding
> my decisions, going around me. I couldn't operate like that. I
> quit at one point. Ron called me at home. I said, "You've got four
> or five people constantly going around me when they disagree
> with my decision." I came back of course.[148]

Others also close to Ron observed similar things. Many agreed
they saw Ron in some sort of a bubble. "With Ron what you see is
what you get," argued Bob Hauptman. "He generally saw through

the bullshit, but I don't think he was always able to do that. In the '96 campaign, he was definitely not hearing from the right people. People who had easy access to him distorted his view. Colleen Dougher was good at that. She was very good at keeping people away from Ron. She helped create that bubble."[149]

According to Dave Eckstein, "Ron did get pulled away from the goings-on in DC. He trusted some people that he shouldn't have. Nash mainly. They thought they knew what's best for Ron. As though he was a child. Hiding stuff. Colleen Dougher she was good friends with Martin Davis, she's another one. They had no clue."[150]

However, others like Bob Muehlenkamp discount the idea that Ron was in any bubble. "I think he was just busy," said Muehlenkamp. "There was no hidden plot. He wasn't isolated from anyone. He was just overwhelmed and busy dealing with everyday stuff, the constant barrage, the daily incoming." Yet he conceded that Ron "was isolated in comparison to the start when he was closer to the rank and file, sure, but it wasn't a conspiracy." [151]

Some people blamed the lawyers. Moriarity believes that "Ron got fucked by his lawyers."[152] "Ron had incompetent people around him including his legal advisers," added Sylvester.[153] Hauptman also put much blame on the lawyers: the law firm "CWS have a lot of responsibility for what happened, and they tried to push it all on Charny."[154]

Bob Hauptman implicates Charny's superiors: "Those checks passed through his hands. He is guilty as sin; the fact that he only got two years suspended pisses me off! The idea that hundreds of thousands of dollars passed through his hands and that none of his bosses had any clue what was going on is horseshit!"[155]

People like Steve Early didn't see any conspiracy. "You had people pleading guilty in order to save themselves and they implicated Ron," he said. "After they took advantage of him, made money off him, saving their own skins. Bill Hamilton sort of fell on his own sword, he even went to jail."[156]

With noted exceptions, the corporate media failed massively.

They got caught up in a lazy groupthink mentality. They were used by the enemies of Ron and reform. The media accepted lies and distortions about Ron under the assumption that he was just another "union boss" to be taken down. Generally, these were white-collar reporters who seemed to look down on the blue-collar union truckers and their leaders, whom they assumed were thugs and mob associates.

They were all too eager to report on Ron's downfall. Gene Moriarity recalls a moment on the day of the decision as to whether Ron would be disqualified from running in the rerun:

> Just before the decision came down, I got a call from UPI who called the campaign office and asked me where the news confer-ence was going to be. I told her we haven't made a confirmation yet but either the Washington Courtyard or the Marriott. She said, "OK, can I call this number and find out what the deci-sion is before I go to the press conference?" I said, "I don't know if you can do that." She replied, "If Mr. Carey is cleared then I have no interest in your press conference. It's news if Carey is not cleared." I called them the biggest fucking whores in the news business and hung up! Hauptman comes over and says, "That's it, you're not taking any more media calls."[157]

Others blamed the political right, which was jealous and fearful of Ron's success. The right-wing editorial page of the *Wall Street Journal* was appalled that Ron had been a wise investor in real estate over the years. Republicans in Congress saw how Ron pulled the Teamsters from supporting the GOP to a union that generally supported Democrats. And with that support came funding. That was why suddenly the GOP Congress had multiple investigations of the Teamsters. When the Teamsters were controlled by corrupt leaders associated with mobsters, the Republican Party protected the Teamsters from investigations because the corrupt leaders of the Teamsters funded their campaigns. The election of Ron Carey altered that.

Certainly, Kenneth Conboy and the IRB failed. They took out a proven reformer because they wrongly believed the word of a Jere Nash over a man who lived and breathed integrity his entire life. "To be fair," noted Ken Crowe, "neither Conboy nor the three members of the IRB were aware as the jury of the extent of Nash's lies."[158]

But stepping back, it appears the government overseers were simply biased. For Judge Lacey, it seems after years of fighting corruption in New Jersey, he started to see it everywhere, in every mistake or oversight made by human beings. Appointed to the bench by President Nixon in 1971, Lacey had a biased arrogance about unions and specifically the Teamsters. Lacey also had a pro-business record: On Jan 6, 1980, Lacey ruled against striking members of Local 177. UPS had fired three workers on Leave of Absence. They were serving as business agents, and they organized brief work stoppages. When he retired from government service, Lacey joined a huge, powerful corporate law firm. According to lawyer Alan Dershowitz, Lacey was "predisposed toward the prosecution ... and has no sense of fair-mindedness."[159] Bob Hauptman described Lacey as "the most dogmatic" of the three whose "judgment was much more pro-police, pro-prosecutor than union."[160]

A similar story could be told about Judge Webster, who was appointed by President Nixon in 1973. After his stints as CIA director and FBI director, Webster used his credentials to land on numerous corporate boards, including the Teamster employer Anheuser-Busch, as well as Pinkerton Security and Investment Services, which had a long and disgraceful history of breaking union strikes. Both he and Lacey saw things through corporate eyes. But every mistake, even the mistake of not knowing an illegal scheme was ongoing, was not corruption. They had just removed one of the greatest labor leaders of our time.

Ron's lead attorney Weingarten agreed that Lacey and Webster were pro-prosecution: "They saw all Teamsters as mugs. Lacey was monstrous; he was so used to dirty Teamsters that he couldn't differentiate. Webster was a disappointment, but I thought he'd be straight up and up."[161]

As for Crandall, the former general counsel of the United Mine Workers, many in the labor community were left dumbfounded. Some made apologies for Crandall, remarking that he already knew that, at best, if he voted against banning Ron, it would still be a two to one vote. Why rock the boat? I'm sure he was thinking about the upcoming Teamster election with Hoffa now favored to win, and possibly feared a dissent here might lead to his replacement by a Hoffa administration. Others felt that Crandall got too comfortable in his position. "He was pulling down a good $100,000 back then from his position for sitting there a couple of days a month," recounted Hauptman. "He should have known better, but in the end, it was go along to get along."[162]

Others blame overzealous prosecutors. It was no secret that Mary Jo White wanted to be the next Rudy Giuliani. She wanted to be a dragon slayer and make headlines and maybe obtain a job boost. She spotted her target, a "union boss," Ron Carey, and started off with the little guys, pressuring them with the possibility of prison and large fines and then methodically worked her way up to the Teamster leader. She had glory not justice on her mind. Never once did she think maybe this is just a bunch of knuckleheads doing stupid things in the heat of an important election. Both Bill Clinton and Newt Gingrich were involved in campaign financing scandals, yet neither one was prosecuted nor persecuted. It seems some people, powerful people, were protected, while others, union folk, were not. This was Big Government siding with Big Business over unions and the little guy.

White and her attorneys strong-armed these union folk, leaving some with no choice but to "give up" someone involved in the scandal or insinuate Ron was either involved or knew of the swaps. These people had spouses, children, and careers to think about. So when confronted with the weight and power of the federal government, they gave in and told investigators what they wanted to hear. They saw their only option was to give them Ron.

In this case Big Government came down on the side of Big Business in taking down a leader of Big Labor. Many said that they believed the FBI and the attorneys had a preexisting notion of all Teamsters as corrupt thugs. Grassroots supporters like IBT Director of Field Operations Dave Eckstein believe there was some kind of conspiracy between corporate America and the government to get Ron Carey. "They decided they were gonna take him out as well as the Republicans in Congress browbeating him," Eckstein said. He explained how Mary Jo White just couldn't understand the genuine love and respect the rank and file had for Ron:

I was at Mary Jo White's office many times testifying. Now I donated lots of money to Ron's campaign. And she just couldn't get that. She wanted to prove that we were funneling money to him. She looked at all my finances to see if I was taking big gobs of money and funneling it somewhere else.

At one point she sees that I'm wearing my "Putting Members First" windbreaker every time I'm at her office. She said, "You're pretty proud of that jacket." I said, "I wouldn't expect you to understand. You don't know what our union was like before Ron Carey came along. And what you're doing is trying to take out a person who was making our members feel like they were in charge again. And you're putting back in there the same trash [Hoffa] Ron Carey's been trying to take out!" She didn't get it. She wanted to prove that we were all crooks.[163]

In the end, many decent people, progressive people, who only wanted to see Ron succeed, had to make a difficult choice. The prosecutors were looking to get a big name to bring down. They didn't necessarily care whose lives or careers they were destroying in order to move their own careers along nicely. People like Nash and Simpkins said whatever they had to say in order to avoid jail time. Both had families to think of. They gave investigators exactly what they thought the investigators wanted. They might even be sorry for what they did, but they put their personal struggles first and with that helped take down Ron Carey, the leader who constantly Put Members First. [164]

Finally, Ron can be blamed for some of this as well. After blaming everyone from Nash to Ron's lawyers, Moriarity explains that this whole affair happened because "of one minor fuck-up by Ron. For a very brief period Ron pushed away people like Judy Scott and Tom Gilmartin, people he relied on for advice for a long time. He started listening to people like Jere Nash and Burke, people who play a little fast and loose with the rules."[165] These characters didn't really know Ron. If they did, they would not have embarked on such a perilous path. Or maybe some of them wanted to cling to power a little bit more than Ron did. He had integrity and principles. He certainly did not believe in winning by any means necessary, even if it meant allowing the corrupt Old Guard back in.

Tim Sylvester, who became a close friend of Ron later in life, agreed that Ron trusted the wrong people at the end. "In Local 804, he had people he could trust. He worked with them for over twenty years. They did their jobs. . . . Then he goes to Washington and started trusting people there that he never knew well and never should have trusted."[166]

Generally, in the world of politics, there are no do-overs. Campaigns pay fines. The candidates are not removed by judges and other unelected bureaucrats. It is the people or the members who make the decisions of who wins or loses, who stays and who goes. In Ron's case, the government overstepped its authority and removed a democratically elected union leader. Stanley Aronowitz summed it up precisely: "The social forces underlying all of this is that when labor raises its head and begins to fight, they get beaten down!"[167]

The scandal not only harmed Ron personally and professionally, but it allowed the enemies of reform to kill reform for the next twenty-two years. It made some rank-and-filers look skeptical at any reform, because now "everyone" looked corrupt. Ron himself was now in legal jeopardy. Mary Jo White kept the grand jury grinding and digging for evidence in order to link Ron to the crimes.

In April 1998, EO Cherkasky announced that the Hoffa campaign had committed several violations as well. The first violation involved two vendors improperly contributing over $167,000 to the Hoffa campaign by underbilling for work they had done for the campaign. The second violation revealed that a $44,000 cash contribution was never reported.[168] The third violation stated that Thomas O'Donnell, a vice presidential candidate on Hoffa's slate, hid the fact that a convicted felon, Kevin Currie, was on the Hoffa campaign payroll.[169] Nevertheless, Hoffa was not disqualified from the rerun.

Meanwhile, there was uncertainty about who would carry the banner of Reform. In April 1998, TDU's steering committee endorsed Ken Hall, who was the head of the Teamsters' Small Package Division and was Ron's top negotiator during the UPS strike. But a few weeks later, Hall dropped out of the race because he had a serious eye condition. Tom Leedham, the IBT's Warehouse Division Director, and a favorite with TDU, entered the race as the new leader of the Reform slate.[170]

After a compromise between Congress and the IBT over who would fund the rerun, Cherkasky was allowed to conduct the new election between Tom Leedham, the head of the IBT's 250,000-member Warehouse Division, who was also endorsed by TDU, John Metz, the head of St. Louis Joint Council 13, and Hoffa, Jr. Ron's secretary-treasurer, Tom Sever, jumped ship and ran with John Metz as did Aaron Belk. On December 5, 1998, Hoffa beat Leedham and Metz. After 365,000 ballots were counted, Hoffa received 55 percent of the vote to Leedham's 39 percent and Metz's 6 percent.[171] The Hoffa, Jr., era had begun.

Meanwhile, Nash was able to remain free because in 1997 he agreed to testify truthfully and commit no further crimes and cooperate fully, which meant he had to provide "substantial" assistance in the Carey case. He was promised a 5K1 letter. By definition, "A 5K1 letter is a document that the US Attorney Office files with a federal district court judge in order to seek leniency on one's behalf. They are given to defendants who cooperate with the

Government and provide substantial assistance in an investigation." It is also called a "snitch letter" or "snitch credit."[172]

But investigators found more embezzlement and lies by Nash—double billing. On April 20, 1999, Nash was back in federal court in Manhattan. He pled guilty to two more felonies: lying again to the Feds and embezzlement after they discovered a transaction in which Nash billed the Teamsters' treasury for $21,000 to be paid to the November Group for a Carey campaign expense. Nevertheless, the prosecutors again allowed him to remain free if he pleaded guilty, and a 5K1 letter was again promised. Otherwise, Nash could have been sentenced to twenty years in prison and assessed a $1.2 million fine.[173]

Ron wanted to use this new evidence as a way for the IRB to "consider his motion for relief from judgment." But on July 19, the IRB issued a Supplemental Decision denying Ron and Bill Hamilton motions for "post-judgment relief." One month later, August 27, Judge Edelstein ruled that the "new evidence"—Nash admitting to more lying—was not enough to overturn their expulsion from the IBT. In November 1999, a federal jury convicted Bill Hamilton of fraud, conspiracy, embezzlement, and perjury. He was sentenced on March 14, 2000, to three years in federal prison.

CHAPTER 9

The Trial

Ron went about his life in Queens. He consulted at times with his lawyers and was kept updated on his cases and what Mary Jo White was doing. He traveled a lot between New York and his Florida place.[1]

The fact that Ron was still walking the streets agitated conservatives. Right-wing commentator Anne Coulter was irked that Mary Jo White had not yet indicted Ron and top Democratic officials. She wrongly accused Ron of being "at the center of the money laundering scheme." Coulter also accused Mary Jo White of "sitting on evidence for four years that implicated Carey."[2] Conservative *New York Times* columnist William Safire and the *Wall Street Journal* editorial board had an obsession with Ron, other unions, and their connections to the Democratic Party. The *Washington Times*, run by the religious "Moonie" cult, also attacked Mary Jo White. The right-wing attack machine accused her of "shielding Ron Carey" because he was a prominent supporter of the Democratic Party. These reactionaries also wanted the head of Ron's friend, Richard Trumka, secretary-treasurer of the AFL-CIO, who took the Fifth at the Hoekstra subcommittee. Ron honestly answered everyone's questions.[3]

Others like Bill Hamilton disagreed with the idea of White "dragging her feet" to help Ron. They describe her as a vicious zealous prosecutor. Ron's lead lawyer during the trial, Reid Weingarten, commented, "I knew her as a professional. I was profoundly disappointed in her that she actually authorized this prosecution. I really believed the SDNY would decline." He went on:

> As for her motivations, let's look at the facts: there was sort of a technical election law violation that he should have been more alert to—the fact that these operatives were fucking around. So Ron had to be crushed for that technical violation.
>
> She was appointed by Clinton, so to be seen as even-handed, sometimes you have to prosecute one of your own to show you are not politically biased.[4]
>
> I'm not a conspiracy nut. But we finally had an honest Teamsters leader and now they're gonna indict him over some election horseshit where he wasn't the moving part and allow the return of the bad guys? It seemed preposterous to me, but the SDNY authorized it. It surprised me. As for her motivations, I assume at the trial she probably had some regrets.[5]

On whether there was any conspiracy in this scandal, Hauptman responded, "Was it a conspiracy to make all the bad things happen? No. The swap scheme was for Martin Davis to make money. On the other hand, the prosecution and persecution of Ron and the shape that it took is, in part, because of what he accomplished."[6]

In December 2000, the Supreme Court handed George W. Bush the presidency. Usually when a new president wins, they remove all the federal prosecutors throughout the country. Three of the four New York State federal prosecutors were told to hand in their resignations. For some reason, Bush retained Mary Jo White. (Did she promise to indict Ron if she was allowed to stay on?) On January 20, 2001, Bush was inaugurated.[7] Five days later, January 25, a Thursday, a federal grand jury under the direction of SDNY federal prosecutor Mary Jo White indicted Ron Carey on charges that he lied in the investigation of the 1996 Teamsters election.[8]

The indictment, announced in Manhattan by White herself, accused Ron of five counts of violating the federal false statement statute, which states, "Whoever, in any matter, within the jurisdiction of the executive, legislative, or judicial branch of the government of the US, knowingly and willfully makes any materially false, fictitious or fraudulent statement or representation, is guilty of a crime,"[9] and two counts of violating the federal perjury statute, which states, "Whoever, under oath in any proceeding, before any court or grand jury of the U.S., knowingly makes any false material declaration, is guilty of a crime."[10] The government could not get him on embezzlement of union funds, so their last resort was to go after him on perjury charges.

White said that Ron lied repeatedly (sixty-three times) to federal government officials EO Conboy, IO Carberry, the IRB, and a federal grand jury. In truth, Ron was being charged seven times for the same "offense" of consistently and truthfully maintaining his innocence of any wrongdoing.[11] Weingarten broke down what the charges amounted to: "False statements to federal officials are usually when you get interviewed by an FBI agent, called 1001—the number of the statute. Perjury is typically when you are under oath in a legal proceeding. Both are lies. It just depends on who you are lying to and when you're lying."[12] Each of the seven charges against Ron carried a possible punishment of five years in prison; that's a 35-year sentence.

According to Ed Burke, throughout the process prosecutors tried to force Ron to plead guilty for a reduced sentence. "They offered Ron a deal, three deals actually," asserted Burke;

> The first deal was offered as it all happened. All he had to do was basically say Sweeney and Trumka were involved, and he could walk. Then, prior to the trial, they offered him a second deal. And then after they closed their case after the prosecution rested, they offered him a third deal. Each time he told

them, "Fuck you!" That's why you had to admire this man. They
wanted him to roll on the labor movement and he said NO, even
though he was facing like thirty years in prison. He just wanted
to clear his name."[13]

Ron's lead lawyer, Weingarten, concurred with Burke's version:
"Ron was making no admissions of wrongdoing. He was strong
and unflappable. First, he didn't think he did anything wrong.
Second, he was outraged that they were going after him. He was
going to take it on. That little guy who was strong as an ox."[14]
Outside the courtroom, Weingarten spoke to reporters. He stated,
"Ron Carey is guilty of no crimes. We will contest these charges
until he is fully vindicated. His proper place in history is as a hero
of the labor movement."[15]

On February 1, Ron was back at U.S. District Court at 500 Pearl
Street in Lower Manhattan to be arraigned. He pleaded not guilty,
and Magistrate Henry Pitman released him without bail after he
turned over his passport and was fingerprinted and photographed
by U.S. marshals.[16] Weingarten described the process of Ron handing over his passport as "routine."

The trial began on August 27, 2001, a Monday, on the twentieth floor of the federal courthouse. Presiding was Judge Robert L.
Carter, the respected former civil rights lawyer. The jury was com-
posed of eight women, four men. Among the jurors were Blacks,
Latinos, and whites. Their occupations ranged from college stu-
dents to hospital supervisor.[17]

Wearing a navy-blue suit with his "hair far whiter than when
he led the Teamsters," Ron was mostly silent that first day during
jury selection. Weingarten commented that "we're satisfied with
the jury and we're looking forward to the trial."[18] On the following
day, both sides gave their opening statements.

In the courtroom, Ron was greeted by some friendly faces. Tim
Sylvester and Jim Reynolds, both devoted members and friends
with Ron, attended the trial dates religiously. They came after work
or took days off. They showed true loyalty and courage. Sylvester

described the scene in the courtroom: "Ron's three daughters were the only ones there. His wife didn't show. Then Ron saw us, and he lit up and smiled. He comes over to us and says, 'What are you doing here?' I told him 'I'm here for you, Boss!' I always called him Boss." [19]

Supporters like Sylvester had to be careful. The IRB ruling in July 1998 prohibited current members of the Teamsters from any contact with Ron. "The Executive Board [of Local 804] knew I was going," Sylvester said. "[Local 804 Trustee Pat] DeFelice warned me. He said, 'You gotta be careful.' I said, 'It's federal court that is open to the public. They could go fuck themselves!'" The Executive Board at the time, under Howard Redmond, "didn't go because they didn't need him anymore."[20] Bob Hauptman commented, "Tim and Jim sat there with the threat of disbarment hanging over their heads. Besides being loyal friends and supporters, they were heroes as well."[21]

The prosecutors, Assistant U.S. Attorneys Deborah Landis and Andrew Dember, opened the trial, accusing Ron of lying "to be sure that he would not be implicated in a scheme to defraud the union." They alleged that Ron must have been lying when he denied being told about the contributions and that "he knew were schemes to violate the law and violate the election rules because he wanted to keep his position as General President of the Teamsters Union."[22]

Ron's team consisted of Reid Weingarten, Mark Hulkower, Bruce Bishop, as well as Bob Hauptman, who was Ron's former Special Assistant for Management and Budget. Bob was invaluable as "the defense team's researcher, analyst of the documents used in evidence, and a source of insight into the operations of the complex union."[23] His defense team represented Ron pro bono.

Hulkower gave their opening statement, calling Ron a decent and honorable man who was "neither a liar nor a perjurer," who "would not be and was never party to a scheme to divert money from the union."[24] He took the jury through the entirety of Ron's career as a Teamster leader.

The government put on the stand numerous witnesses to assist their case. Ron's defense team meticulously took apart the government's case, witness by witness. The defense destroyed the credibility of the prosecution's two main witnesses: Jere Nash and Monie Simpkins. Other witnesses were used by the defense to their advantage as well.

Nash was the prosecution's first witness. Though he had pleaded guilty to four felonies in September 1997, he was not currently in prison. "They caught Nash and twisted his nuts," recalled Weingarten.[25] He pledged to cooperate fully with the prosecutors. If Nash provided "substantial assistance" in the prosecution, the prosecutors would write a 5K1 letter[26] to the judge who was presiding over Nash's case and recommend leniency.

This amazing team defending Ron thoroughly prepared for the trial, and Bob Hauptman had a big hand in preparing Ron's legal team. Hauptman worked for Reid as a volunteer during the summer of 2001. They went through sixty boxes of documents and evidence that the government had turned over as part of discovery, which the government was obliged to give to Ron's legal team.[27]

Unfortunately, these rules had not applied to the hearings before the IRB. But, as Ken Crowe stated at the time, "What a difference a trial makes."[28] Ron's superb legal team never truly got to cross-examine the IRB charges at the hearing. (Ron's lawyers were not allowed to cross examine any witnesses that Conboy had spoken to. During the IRB hearing, Nash was cross-examined but Simpkins was not.) Their job was to destroy the credibility of the government's witnesses. We can only wish they had had the opportunity to take apart the IRB's case with all the information they found during discovery for this trial.

"That's where I found the smoking guns against Nash," described Hauptman. "At the trial, my job was to poke holes in Nash's credibility. To show what a liar he was. Granted, Nash had some pressures on him: his kid was sick. But he was so dishonest." Hauptman recalled the IRB hearings:

They had their hooks into Nash, so he was confessing to get himself off. So, he shared his phone records with them since it could not be disproved. The only thing he could identify, the call, he just made up. But during the IRB hearings, it was just left there as a statement that we couldn't disprove at the time. But we did at the trial. He was making it up in order to give the prosecutors what they wanted even though it didn't actually take place.[29]

Once again, Nash testified that he "vividly remembered" going into the hallway outside his office at the campaign headquarters to make the notorious 15-second phone call. He claimed his call was "patched" into an ongoing phone call between Ron, who was in Los Angeles campaigning, and his campaign office in DC,[30] a "super-complicated and barely possible technical process."[31] Nash claims it was on this call that he told Ron that the contribution to Citizens Action would "help Martin Davis in the fundraising." He testified that Ron said, "Hell, no one ever told me about it," and approved the $475,000 contribution.[32] Even if one believes a call did get made, it seems to have been made to Monie Simpkins, who, if you believe her first version to Susan Davis, approved the contribution herself.

But Nash made up the long elaborate story that didn't follow with the actual phone records. "It was a short call but he kept adding detail to it," recalled Hauptman. "Here's a case where somebody lies too much and gives too much detail. So, when I got the records, I started going through Nash's expense accounts for that day, October 17, 1996, at that exact time and I saw he had a receipt from a restaurant a few blocks away from the office. It nailed him. He made up the call."[33] Indeed, while cross-examining Nash, Weingarten explained to the jury that he couldn't have been "outside in the hallway" of his office at the time of the call, 1:24 p.m. Nash's own expense records revealed that he paid $33.22 for lunch at the Holiday Inn. He concluded that the phone call was never patched through to Ron.[34] He later called Nash "a completely dishonest, untrustworthy, little thief."[35]

Hulkower went on to expose more dishonest behavior by Nash. In the years leading up to the trial, Nash had to do two separate plea agreements. The first one, in 1997, was for his complicity in the actual quid pro quo swap. He pleaded guilty and agreed to cooperate and tell the government everything he knew. A year later, they found a second scheme that he hadn't told them about. "Even when Jere Nash goes to court," Hulkower pronounced, "and promises to take a plea, promises to tell the truth, he can still look his new partners, the FBI, and the prosecutors in the eye and lie to them."[36] Besides Nash, this scheme involved Martin Davis and Trish Hoppey.

"Nash, Davis, and Trish Hoppey, an unindicted co-conspirator, took work that the November Group did for the campaign and stuck it on an invoice titled IBT Convention," recalled Hauptman. "The invoice was originally billed to the campaign but Nash didn't want to use up the campaign funds, so he got Trish to rewrite the invoice and give it to the union, the Teamster treasury." Hoppey was the 1996 IBT convention coordinator at the time and would later go to work for the November Group. "Trish signed off on the false invoice, saying it was OK, and told the union to pay for it. They stole from the union," concluded Hauptman.[37]

When the investigators found out about this scheme in 1998, they threw the book at Nash. Now he was part of a federal crime. Nash claimed that he didn't remember that particular activity. He was desperate and now facing a twenty-year sentence and a $1,250,000 fine. In order to sweeten the deal and avoid prison, Nash then all of a sudden produced the long lost "chart" on a computer disk that he supposedly showed Ron explaining the entire swap scheme. Nash originally claimed that he didn't have the chart because he "erased it" from his computer. Hulkower called Nash "a fellow backed into a corner" who was grasping for anything and used the idea of the newly "found" chart as a get-out-of-jail-free card.[38]

However, there was a problem with the chart testimony during the trial. The government was unable to find any of the faxes of the chart that Nash alleged he sent to Ron. Moreover, Ron's legal team demonstrated that the government couldn't prove when the disk was created. It could have been made any time after Nash was indicted. Regardless, the government didn't rely on it that much in the end.[39]

Furthermore, Ron's defense team uncovered more instances where Nash lied or cheated that the government did not know about. It was revealed that Nash had cheated the IRS by not paying taxes on the $50,000 bonus he received from the November Group in December 1996. Later on, Hulkower asked Nash on the stand, "Would you steal money from the campaign?" Nash answered, "No." It was then that Hulkower provided the jury with invoices showing that Nash had double-billed the November Group and the Carey campaign for numerous airline tickets and cab rides. Nash claimed they were "accidental," but Ken Crowe, who attended every trial date, observed the jurors shaking their heads in disbelief.[40]

It was a devastating account, one that decimated Nash as a credible witness. Nash hid things from the FBI and the prosecutors just as he had hid stuff from Ron. Nash was a pro at having a selective memory. "Nash seemed to remember everything his lawyer asked but nothing that Ron's lawyers asked," observed Sylvester.[41] Hulkower concluded, "That is the history of the deceit of Jere Nash."[42] At the trial, it was revealed that the November Group provided Nash with other lavish perks such as first-class air travel for Nash and his family between Mississippi and DC.

By the end of Nash's testimony, it was evident that Nash was not a very good witness for the prosecution. During redirect, prosecutor Landis asked Nash: "Was Ron Carey involved in any way in the swap transaction?" Nash testified, "No, ma'am." He had been so discredited that Landis later told the jury: "They turned up some good stuff to show Jere Nash was a liar."[43] Crowe observed that Nash's "value as a witness was totally destroyed by Carey's defense team's revelations drawn from his own mouth that lying and cheating were woven into the fabric of his life."[44] In sum, Ron's lawyers called Nash a "completely dishonest, untrustworthy, greedy, manipulative little thief."[45]

The trial was temporarily interrupted by the September 11 terrorist attack on the World Trade Center, which occurred only a few blocks from the courtroom. It resumed two weeks later. For a slight moment, with the delay, the added security, and a new sympathy for the government, the defense team wondered how this was going to turn out for their case. "I don't think the feeling changed in that room. If anything, we feared the FBI would be given the benefit of the doubt on these issues like the chart," said Hauptman.[46]

Ron had great faith in the jury and in his defense team. As Weingarten put it:

> Ron was always confident. He was the President of the Teamsters Union, a pretty big monster to run. So he was used to being in charge, but he deferred to us. He never questioned us. We had to decide whether to put him on the stand, who to call.
>
> Ron was the perfect client: smart, trusting, and optimistic. Early on I knew we didn't need to put him on the stand so his role in the courtroom was limited to an adviser on a few issues relating to witnesses and his wisdom was valued.
>
> He participated but was deferential. Deep down he had come to peace that he did nothing wrong. That he was getting fucked by the government. But he was optimistic that in the end justice would prevail. He had an innate consonance that this was gonna turn out OK. Throughout I felt that I had the Rock of Gibraltar sitting next to me.[47]

Ron must have had a lot of faith in his knees as well. Ken Crowe recalls a little of what happened on that horrific day:

> On the morning of September 11, the judge came in late that day. Carey always got to the court early. He would drive from his house and park his car in Jackson Heights where he would take the subway, the 7 train, into the city.
>
> When the buildings crashed down, he walked with his two

bad knees from downtown Manhattan to the Queensboro Bridge [six miles] over to his car [another two miles]. All on adrenaline.[48]

The trial resumed on September 24. The next witness was Monie Simpkins. In order to bolster their case, the government had her wear a frumpy housedress so that she appeared to be "a simple, innocent, unsophisticated attractive woman," thus more sympathetic to the jury.[49] Weingarten pointed out that she had worked at a large law firm before coming to work at the IBT, so she was very cognizant of the term "liability." Needless to say, Simpkins was no simple housewife. She had years of experience and knowledge.

Weingarten did a brilliant job in showing Simpkins's vulnerabilities without attacking her. He chose to be delicate, like a surgeon navigating the delicacies of an operation. At first, he reminded the jury how convenient it was that "for every contribution, Ron Carey was out of Washington."

After the prosecution attempted to make an October 21, 1996, meeting at LaGuardia Airport between Nash, Ron, Susan Davis, and Simpkins vital to their case as told by Simpkins, Weingarten sternly pushed back that it was irrelevant since the first two contributions were approved on October 17. In other words, Simpkins was already in on the plan, which further undermined the government's case. "There is no reason to bring in Monie Simpkins into this at all," Hulkower stated, "if you believe that Ron Carey was part of the scheme."[50]

In borrowing from the OJ Simpson trial, Weingarten, in his closing later, asserted that "if the timeline don't fit, you must acquit." In summation, Weingarten professed, "Monie Simpkins is not a co-conspirator. She was a person manipulated by Jere Nash. If he had Ron [in the scheme], he wouldn't need Monie Simpkins."[51]

Then Weingarten demonstrated how Simpkins had altered her story numerous times. In version one, Simpkins tells Susan Davis that Ron approved none of the contributions. That story was confirmed by two of her co-workers, Theresa Marie Sherman and Gary Heying, who testified that Simpkins had told them that she herself had approved the contributions without informing Ron because Nash was putting pressure on her. She even told Sherman that the government "had twisted" the details to suit their needs.

In her version two, after speaking with the IBT lawyers two days later, Simpkins repeated her first version that Ron had not approved any of the contributions. When the lawyers informed her that they had seen what she herself had initialed and warned her that she could be in legal jeopardy, she panicked and told them that maybe Ron had approved one of the contributions. Days later, she consulted her old law firm for legal advice, where she became aware of cases in which prosecutors offered deals of immunity to underlings who gave evidence against their bosses. With high-powered legal assistance, she cut a deal with Mary Jo White's office and signed the "proffer" with the government, agreeing that it wouldn't use anything she told them against her in a criminal case. This leads to version three, where she tells the government that Ron approved all four of the contributions.[52]

Some of Ron's supporters believed Ron's side was too soft on Simpkins. Sylvester implied that she was a hypocrite because she tried to offer herself as some kind of born-again Christian while having relationships with more than one member on Ron's staff: "At one point, while she was testifying, I went up to Ron's attorney, Mark Hulkower, and said, 'This woman is trying to portray herself as this little mouse. Go after her!' He said in response, 'Ron wouldn't let me. Talk to your boss.'"[53]

But instead of attacking Simpkins, Weingarten eased off the accelerator. He tried to demonstrate that she was just another victim of Jere Nash: "I don't believe for a second that Monie believed she was engaging in wrongdoing. She was told by Nash that Susan Davis blessed the scheme. Those pieces make her a victim." Then Weingarten spoke directly to the jury and asked, "Why did she do this? Monie realized she had the potential for serious legal trouble. She was concerned about going to jail. She had two little kids. From that point on, Ron approved it. She made a decision to protect her family and lay it off on her boss."[54]

"Every prosecution witness who had working knowledge of the Teamsters was turned into a character witness praising Carey for his dedication and honesty," wrote Crowe.[55] Bill Hamilton, who was the IBT's political director under Ron, testified for the prosecution. Throughout the entire process, the government had put tremendous pressure on Hamilton to screw Ron, but he never gave in to their strong-arm tactics.

Hamilton testified that he never told Ron about any swap or his dealings with Nash. He repeated his narrative that the only conversation he had with Ron was about why they were using money from the Teamster treasury and not PAC money. Almost his entire testimony was beneficial to Ron's defense. He immediately became a hostile witness for the prosecution.

"I was in federal prison in Cumberland, Maryland, when Mary Jo White's prosecutors came for me," remembered Hamilton. "They sent three FBI agents in a private car and drove me to NYC. I met up with Ron's lawyers a few times and the prosecutors as well. They thought I was gonna hurt Ron, but I wanted to do whatever I could to help Ron. Then the testimony wasn't what the prosecutors wanted. My lawyer felt that I had betrayed the U.S. attorneys. So instead of chauffeuring me back or putting me on a bus back to Maryland like others had done, they sent me on Con Air in chains on a plane to Oklahoma City at the airport prison. Three weeks there, then back to Baltimore."[56]

Weingarten commended Hamilton for his toughness and honor. "Hamilton was an important witness. I had a great deal of respect for him," contended Weingarten. "He was completely honorable. To his core, he believed Ron was utterly a decent human being and had greatness in him."[57]

Another witness for the prosecution, Aaron Belk, testified that Ron was "the most honest Teamster officer who ever held the General President's office. I never saw him do anything that was not in the best interests of the union."[58] Then the government put Bob

Muehlenkamp on the stand, hoping he would reaffirm a statement that Ron had made about AFL-CIO secretary-treasurer Richard Trumka, that Trumka "wasn't delivering." Muehlenkamp clarified that the remark had nothing to do with the swap. He said since Ron had helped Trumka win office in 1995, he was "disappointed in the AFL-CIO's lobbying performance on issues important to the Teamsters in Congress."[59]

To prove that Ron must have known about the large contributions, the prosecution put on the stand Joseph Selsavage, the IBT's accounting director, and Hal Malchow, the partner of the November Group. Under cross-examination by Weingarten, Selsavage admitted how huge the IBT was, with sixteen divisions and twenty-three departments, 550 locals, 1.5 million members, and an annual income of around $90 million. Selsavage was there to say that there was a budget deficit and the IBT shouldn't have been spending so much. But Weingarten got Selsavage to admit that the real sum in the IBT treasury at the time was closer to $80 million, not the $16 million figure the government was saying.

Moreover, in his opening statement earlier, Hulkower repeated a line that Hauptman had used at Bill Hamilton's trial: "A labor union is not a credit union. It's not in the business to make money. It's in the business to carry out the fundamental needs of and to protect the working people that belong to that union."[60] In other words, the union isn't there just to balance the budget. It is there to make important expenditures in their members' interests: lobby to pass or stop legislation, fund campaigns of politicians or parties that support labor.

When Malchow took the stand, Weingarten used him to make the defense's case of the enormity of the IBT and Ron's style of delegating authority. In discussing Malchow's business, he got him to state that "in the process of handling $11 million there's a lot going on. I don't think I looked at ten invoices. To operate a big business like this you have to trust and delegate responsibility." Weingarten then told the jury that "the government bought that. They didn't prosecute Hal Malchow. Ron Carey ran a union with

1.5 million people and a \$90 million budget, and he's got to know everything."[61]

Weingarten added, "All of the government's witnesses felt terrible that Ron was in this position. They knew fundamentally that Ron was a decent guy. The Teamsters were shifting to the Democratic Party and that was a sea change, but for Ron, that wasn't his top priority. He cared about the working conditions of his members. He let others take the lead on that and he got fucked!" [62]

After summations, the case went to the jury for a verdict. "We were cautiously optimistic," recalled Hauptman. "We presented a good, solid case. Then it was just the waiting. During deliberations, Reid had this Blackberry. Ron would love to play with it. He had a lot of fun with it."[63]

After deliberating for only twelve hours over a three-day span, on Friday, October 12, 2001, at 2:43 in the afternoon, the jury came back to the courtroom with a verdict. After being seated, the young jury foreman stood and read out the jury's decision. As one writer described it: "On Count #1, the jury finds the defendant, Ron Carey, not guilty. On Count #2, the jury finds the defendant, Ron Carey, not guilty. As he read on and the suspense built… On Count #7, the jury finds the defendant, Ron Carey, not guilty, one could say with certainty: justice is sweet."[64]

Listening to some of the jurors speak afterward, one got a sense that they too got to know the real Ron Carey. They saw through the lies of Nash and the different versions of Simpkins. They too learned of the smart, passionate, dedicated, genuine, tough, honest person and leader Ron was. The twelve jurors rejected the government's case that Ron lied to government officials in order to cover up an illegal swap scheme. One juror said, "I felt sorry for him. I actually believed he was a good guy trying to carry out good things for the Teamsters."[65] Some jurors evidently learned a lot about unions and the labor movement.

They found Ron not guilty of the seven counts of perjury and making false statements. Whereas the IRB panel believed Jere Nash and Monie Simpkins, a jury of Ron's peers believed in "the unshakable Ron Carey, the most distinguished labor leader of modern times."[66] Ron's defense team exposed a "rotten conspiracy" by the government and its agents to go after an honest and committed union leader. The powerful prefer that union leaders be weak, corrupt, and for sale. Ron was none of those things. The jurors detected that.

After the not guilty verdict was read, Ron walked to the rear of the courtroom to hug his three daughters, Sandra, Pamela, and Barbara. There were tears in their eyes. He then thanked his outstanding legal team. Hulkower afterward described the moment, comparing it to "a Greek tragedy with a happy ending. He has his life back and his good name back."[67]

"We are delighted but not surprised," Weingarten professed. "We had every confidence that Ron Carey would ultimately be vindicated. We are relieved at the result because when the government comes at you with guns blazing, a lot can happen. This is the first opportunity for him to present his story, and the jury accepted it. They wanted to put Ron Carey in jail. In the SDNY, the percentage of times defendants are convicted was 95 percent. With 9/11, the world seemed to be coming apart, and yet the jury came back and acquitted him. Vindication. Justice was done!"[68] A spokesman for the prosecution stated, "We are disappointed but we respect the jury's verdict."[69]

Outside the courtroom, Ron spoke to the press, sounding conspiratorial, relieved, and then optimistic. "It's somebody else pushing the buttons here," Ron suggested. "They just don't want to see a revitalized labor movement. They sat around a table and said, 'We've gotta get this guy!'" He told the reporters that he'd like to get back in the Teamsters: "It's been in my blood for forty years. This verdict opens a lot of doors. We'll move on at this point and move on in a positive way and look at opportunities down the road. I want to sit back and shake off this tragic aspect of my life."[70]

CHAPTER 10

Legacy

Indeed, it was a joyous day. It was a day for justice. But it was also a sad and disheartening day. Only around sixteen people were in that courtroom on that October day: Ron's daughters, a few dedicated reporters, members of Ron's legal team, some assistant prosecutors, an observer for Hoffa, and the ever-present Tim Sylvester from Local 804, who watched from a safe distance.[1]

It was disheartening and ironic to see this great man, who once spoke at length about the "Forgotten Teamster" at the 1991 Teamsters Convention, now seemingly forgotten by so many. Not even TDU had a presence at the trial. There were no activists, no protests, and no signs in solidarity with Ron. They too seemed to have moved on from the man. All one heard was "reform was bigger than one man." That seemed a long way from "No Justice No Peace!" But in fairness, TDU was busy trying to get Tom Leedham, who did support Ron through it all, elected at the end of the year.

By this time, the Old Guard had been firmly back in control of the Marble Palace since 1999. Hoffa and his minions made it a point to label Ron as corrupt and guilty. It forced many to toe the Hoffa line or possibly risk trusteeship of their locals, even leaders and locals that should have known better. Beside Sylvester or Jim Reynolds no one from his Local appeared, including Local 804's Executive Board, people he personally picked, colleagues he had known for decades. Instead, they ran for cover.

Fear had a lot to do with it. Fear of the IRB. Fear of pissing off Hoffa and getting a trusteeship. Some were just straight up traitors. Others were opportunists who after coming to power on Ron's name and coattails, were now toeing the Hoffa line. The "leaders" of Local 804 were now taking their marching orders from Hoffa. Some stayed loyal in their hearts, but publicly they too bent the knee for Hoffa. As Sylvester remarked, "They didn't need Ron anymore." They ran from him.

Some rank-and-filers didn't show because they didn't want to brave the gauntlet of possible banishment by the IRB; others were absent because not many rank-and-filers knew or remembered that Ron was on trial. The Hoffa locals were mum. In Ron's Local 804, the Executive Board never called for any shows of solidarity or protests outside the courtroom. Members were kept in the dark. It wasn't spoken about at union meetings or mentioned in their newsletters.

Remarkably, at the very next Local 804 general membership meeting after the acquittal, no one from the Executive Board even mentioned it. No one. It took Tim Sylvester, who waited for new business at the end of the meeting, to announce it. President Redmond reacted with an "Oh yeah, by the way . . ." attitude.[2] It was a real low point for the home of Ron Carey. "His own Local leadership shunned him. It was disgraceful," Bruce Carey angrily recalled. "He carried those guys. It was a slap in the face."[3]

In the end, the powers that be got what they wanted. They didn't want a militant union leader riling up the peasants. They didn't want another Eugene Debs or John L. Lewis. They wanted to be able to control them or exploit them. Democrats supported unions but certainly not a militant one. The GOP simply despised unions altogether.

Now Ron Carey was "vindicated" but soundly out of the picture. Collusion among the Old Guard, the Corporate Media, Big

Business, and reactionary forces in government took him out in a bloodless coup. The corporate press obliged by keeping it quiet. When Ron was expelled by the IRB and then indicted by the government, it was on page one of the newspapers and condemned on CNN. Ron gets acquitted of all charges, and you had to be careful not to pass up the small article on page A21 of the *New York Times*. But Ron's story transcends the attacks and the lies made up about him. It's a major reason why I wrote this book.

It was a huge victory for Ron, but he was not completely satisfied. His next task was to get Weingarten to appeal the original IRB decision. The trial demonstrated how disreputable those IRB witnesses were. It should be enough to overturn the IRB decision that was based on such unreliable sources.

However, the courts rejected any appeal, stating that the IRB was not a government actor and therefore none of the rights he had could be sued for in court. Only the IRB itself could possibly overturn the charges. But after Hoffa appointed reactionary lawyer Joseph di Genova to replace Grant Crandall as the IBT's member on the IRB, that possibility was now gone. This very likely was why Hoffa, Jr., chose a ferociously anti-union lawyer to be the sole union voice on the IRB. Ron was dejected. He spent his entire adult life fighting injustice for his members. And now there was no one and no entity that was going to restore his reputation, his "rightful place in history."

At this point, all he wanted was his union card back and the restoration of his reputation. He no longer had any interest in getting involved in the union. Hoffa wouldn't lift a finger. He needed to keep Ron Carey as the bad guy. It made him look better. The government wouldn't do anything, but then it never admits guilt or wrongdoing on its part for anything. His old Local didn't do a thing. Some activists moved forward, trying to ger rid of Hoffa and push for reform. But over the years, even Ron gave up trying.

After the trial and appeal, Ron took it easy. It was quite a shock to be out of the union. He had lived and breathed union for over forty years. But he kept busy with odd jobs around the house and at his kids' homes as well. Instead of suits, he wore paint-stained clothes while he painted, spackled, tiled, or poured cement.[4]

"Even though he wasn't allowed to have contact with the members, his heart was still in it," recalled Ron's brother, Bruce. "He read a lot about what was still going on. Later, he became disenchanted. Some of the fight was out of him. I think he blamed himself."[5]

He spent a good deal of time in Florida at their family condo in the Keys. According to Ron's daughter, Sandra, "He would travel to the Keys, our place on the ocean, to get away. It was very peaceful."[6] "When he was retired, he would fly down alone and stop by our house in Fort Lauderdale," remembered Doreen Gasman. "Ron was very fond of my husband. He was like family. He wouldn't dwell on the bad times. He was coasting at this point. He was never miserable and never complained about it. Ron Carey was not a look back kind of guy; he was a look forward guy; his internal makeup was 'OK, that was yesterday.'"[7]

Ron had developed close relationships with certain people he worked with in Washington. One was Gasman. Another was Gene Moriarity, who recalls:

> We'd see each other at Doreen's place in Florida. When he came down, Doreen had this great house with an in-ground pool. Ron loved to swim laps. One day, I got there and Doreen said, "He's out by the pool with a glass of wine," looking relaxed and happy.
>
> Doreen had just told him that I had been making phone calls to certain people who worked for Ron and then crossed over to Hoffa. One of them was Ken Hall. I told him off and called him a "scumbag and a liar and a cheap con artist."
>
> Anyway, I sat down next to Ron. He says, "How are you, Gene, I understand you've been making some interesting phone calls." I said "Yes, I had to because it really bothered me." Ron paused for a second and said, "Those are not phone calls that I can make . . . but I'm sure glad someone did. Thank you."[8]

Moriarity agreed that Ron didn't miss the power of the office or anything like that. He did miss his members. But he tried to put it all behind him. However, "it did bother him how it ended," recalled Moriarity. "He blamed people like Nash, but when it was over and I'd see him in Florida, he was OK. It didn't take a toll on him. He wouldn't bring that stuff up."[9]

In 2006, Ron tangentially got involved in Local 804 politics. The Redmond-led Executive Board in Local 804 was planning on going to the Teamsters convention that year and supporting Hoffa. Local 804 had supported Tom Leedham, the Reform Candidate, in 1998 and 2001 by 80 percent to 20 percent. Tim Sylvester and Jim Reynolds put together a slate of delegate nominees to go to the convention and support the Leedham Slate.(I was part of that delegate slate.) Ron got word of this delegates race in his old Local. He knew he had the ban hanging over his head. He couldn't speak out. Ken Paff had spoken to Ron and proposed that Gene Moriarity, who was retired, speak for Ron and put it on a flyer endorsing the Putting Members First Slate, blasting the Redmond Slate. It was simply a few statements by Ron Carey "as told to Gene Moriarity."[10]

Regardless, the Hoffa-backing Redmond slate wound up going to the convention. Our slate, which I was on, lost by a margin of two to one. But it made us realize that our local was not very educated on how the process worked. Members who voted were led to believe they were voting for the positions on the board, not for representatives to the convention. In the 2006 elections, once again Leedham received 80 percent of our vote. This incited me to write a newsletter: before we got involved in any more elections, there needed to be an effort to educate and inform the membership.

A year later, Ron appeared and spoke at the launching of Deepa Kumar's book, *Outside the Box: Corporate Media, Globalization, and the UPS Strike*. "Ron Carey was all fire and no remorse last week when he spoke about the legacy of the successful national strike a decade ago against UPS," wrote Meredith Kolodner of *The Chief*, the civil service and local government newspaper. "The room that Mr. Carey spoke to May 7 was full of labor advocates but devoid of Teamsters."[11] There were just twoTeamsters in that audience: Tim Sylvester and Jim Reynolds.

Ron spoke about the ten-year anniversary of the UPS strike. While happily recalling key moments of the strike, Ron appeared disappointed that no one had stepped forward since then to continue the fight against Corporate America. He spoke of the current "dim picture of the labor movement," that it seemed to be "just moving backwards."[12]

Though he physically looked ten years older, Ron still had fire and passion in his voice. He reminisced about how the labor movement involved the members' families, telling members to bring their families down to the picket lines. "It's always been my philosophy that what happens to Tim Sylvester happens to Gretchen [Tim's wife, in attendance with her husband], happens to the children, when they take away benefits, they take away the future and turn them into part-time jobs." He ended his speech stating that "it was an honor and a privilege for me to serve the Teamster membership."[13]

In 2007, Ron gave an interview to Mark Brenner of *Labor Notes* to talk about the Teamsters contract with UPS, which was to expire July 31, 2008. He spoke about the UPS strike in 1997 as well as the current Hoffa administration's concessionary contracts. During the interview, Ron said that he was "enjoying his retirement, spending lots of time with family, trying to make up for neglecting them during my years in office." He'd also been "talking to retired Teamsters around the country, talking about the state of the union" and was working on a book about his experiences.[14]

He then went on to address the possible elimination of the "25-and-out" pension in Local 804: "They want to eliminate the 25-and-out pension plan for new hires. The union officers who negotiated this rip-off know that the 25-and-out pension was something we fought for and won over 25 years ago and it took a thirteen-week strike to do it." After hearing that a slate of delegates had run in Local 804 on the Members First Slate, Ron smilingly said that he was "glad our legacy was still alive in the Local."[15]

But he regretted how the Local 804 union officers were "selling out the future," knowing that they "won't be around to answer
for their deal making." He was prescient in that statement: in
December 2009, a reform slate running on Ron's name and legacy,
soundly defeated the Redmond slate in the Local 804 election
for the Executive Board. Those officers who were "selling out the
future" were beaten two to one. (I was a part of that winning slate.)
"I always saw it as my job to stand up to anyone who got in the way
of a better future for my members," Ron told Brenner. He criticized the Redmond regime in Local 804: "They have lost that spirit
of independence. Local 804 officers have sucked up to Hoffa, like
sheep, in a betrayal of Local 804 members."[16]

But Ron never was able to see that joyous day in Local 804 history. "My mother got the cancer first," recalls Sandra Carey. "But
by June of 2008, dad had found out he was sick. She got better. Dad
got worse. He never let on to how bad he was. But in September, he
said to me 'You might need to get things together just in case.'"[17]
It was inoperable lung cancer.

"When he was sick he was, of course, very quiet about it,"
remembered his brother Bruce. "He couldn't tell you anything. He
was very private. He'd jump on a bus and just go to his doctor without telling anyone—until he had to be admitted."[18] Ron's daughter
Sandra confirmed, "Then he came home one day and he tells us
that he has to go and stay in a hospital. He didn't want to burden
anyone."

Ron Carey died on December 11, 2008, a Thursday, in New
York Hospital Medical Center in Queens. Four days later, his wake
was held at the Frederick Funeral Home on Northern Boulevard
in Bayside, Queens. It was a workday and peak season at UPS.
Nevertheless, many UPS Teamsters came to pay their respects.
Some even came in their brown uniforms during their lunch
breaks. Others right after work. It was a sad occasion. There were
lots of tears. Most members hadn't even known he was sick.

Though the room was filled with flowers, there were none from
the Local 804 Executive Board. Not only did no one from the

Redmond board show up at Ron's wake, but they didn't even have the decency to send flowers or a card. The Carey family never forgave that insult.[19]

The funeral was held on Wednesday, December 17, at Our Lady of the Blessed Sacrament Catholic Church in Bayside. Over five hundred people attended the service, including members, neighbors, family, and friends. Once again, no one from the Local 804 board attended. "All those years, he carried those guys," said Bruce Carey. "And then they shunned him. It was a slap in the face."[20]

About a week before Ron passed away, Tim Sylvester called Ron's daughter Pamela to see how his old boss was doing:

> Ron answered the phone. He said he was "doing fine." I said, "We need to go to lunch when you feel up to it." I apologized to him for all the times me and Reynolds were with him and we had to speak in code. There were always too many people around. Many times, he had no idea what we were trying to tell him. I felt foolish when he wouldn't understand what I was trying to tell him. We couldn't discuss anything related to the union.
>
> Anyway, after I apologized, he said, "Friends don't let things like that bother them. And you have been a friend to me." Last thing he ever said to me.[21]

Tim Sylvester and Jim Reynolds organized the memorial service to Celebrate the Life and Work of Ron Carey. Members, friends, family, and associates of Ron showed up on March 4, 2009. All spoke about who Ron Carey was and what he meant to them. Speakers included: Sylvester, Reynolds, Pat Pagnanella, William Riley Fernandez, Ken Paff, Ken Crowe, Tom Leedham, Willie Hardy, Aaron Belk, Eddie Burke, Sandra Carey, Dan Carey, and Ron's grandson Daniel Marchese.

Ron's family members spoke of the dad who was always there for them, the warm soul, the playful grandfather. They understood that they had to share him with his members. They looked at the members and colleagues in the audience as their brothers and sisters. Sandra, Ron's oldest daughter, spoke how her family "shared him for all those years." She felt appreciative that at least he got to spend the last years of his life committed to his grandchildren "playing volleyball, basketball, with them and encouraging them to sing and dance." Ron's ten-year-old grandson, Danny Marchese, spoke of how proud his family was for standing up to UPS during the strike.[22]

Ron's close associate in Washington, Aaron Belk, described Ron as "what every leader should aspire to be: honest, frugal, and caring." He went on: "Ron never understood why members reacted the way they did to him. I told him 'You're a human being, put on this earth, for a special purpose and you're doing it every day.'"[23]

He inspired many to get active, attend meetings, step up and run for office. Rank and filers like William Riley Fernandez are an example of that. He stated that Ron "was the heart, the engine that inspired the rank-and-file who admired him so much.... He taught us that it is not what we do for us, but what we can achieve for future generations."[24]

Activists and leaders in TDU were in attendance. TDU Organizer Ken Paff spoke of how "Ron Carey's contributions to the Teamsters and the U.S. labor movement tower over those of his contemporaries." Paff called Ron "a modern labor hero" as well as a "good friend." Willie Hardy, who was hired by Ron in the Organizing Department and was one of the first African Americans in that position, said that "Ron treated me as a man and with respect. If any of us had a problem, we could always go see him and he would take care of it."[25]

The labor reporter and author Ken Crowe had been writing about unions and Ron for years. Crowe saw him as the real thing:

> Ron Carey was the nation's most charismatic and successful labor leader as the twentieth century was coming to an end. He will be remembered as a major figure in American labor history on the basis of just two of his accomplishments: in 1991, running as a reformer with the backing of TDU, he was elected General

President of the IBT. In 1997, he led the successful strike against UPS, the biggest victory organized labor had experienced in at least three decades.

Ron Carey knew that it was time to change the way unions operated, to create strategies that could beat corporate greed by empowering rank-and-file workers and involving their families in the labor movement.[26]

Crowe recalled a moment that demonstrated Ron's genuineness, his regular guy, down-to-earthness, when he was first elected to office:

On the day Ron Carey was elected President of the Teamsters, I rode with him in a cab, interviewing him all the way from downtown Washington DC to the airport. After we were dropped off, we realized we were in the wrong terminal. Carey picked up his two heavy bags, refusing my offer to carry one of them, and we ran, literally, to the right terminal.

That scene sums up Carey: self-effacing and not too ambitious. Most individuals having been elected to head the most powerful union in the nation would have had flunkies carry them [remember Jackie Presser] along with his baggage to the right terminal. And one had to be enormously ambitious to run for GP of the IBT. Not Ron Carey.[27]

Others spoke of his first campaign in 1967, the 1991 campaign, how he was all about "putting members first," his record in DC and Local 804, and, of course, the 1997 UPS strike. When Tim Sylvester finally gave his speech—he was also the emcee of the memorial—he first pointed out the empty seat in the front of the audience: "I'd like to think of Ron as sitting right there, listening to hear us speak about everything he did for us." Sylvester acknowledged the Carey family's sacrifice, sharing their dad with Local 804 members: "To Ron's family, we were all enriched by your sacrifices." He continued:

Ron was a threat to Corporate America and to Old Guard Teamster officials who feared him because he threatened their personal bottom line and made them look impotent in comparison. . . .

He was taken away too early, not just with his death, but he was taken away from us ten years ago by a system that didn't allow anyone as good as he was to remain in power in our union. To those of us who knew him he was Ron or Ronnie. To some in the union he was "the GP" or "Mr. Carey." How jarring that was the first time I heard it because here in Local 804, he was one of us. We are all better for having known him. I miss him already and I am not ashamed to say I loved him. He was my friend.[28]

The enormous outpouring of love and respect for Ron deeply struck Ron's brother Bruce, who attended the memorial. "It truly amazed me," recalled Bruce Carey. "I met three gentlemen from Tennessee and Mississippi. They traveled all the way here to say such wonderful things about Ronnie. Things I never knew about him."[29]

So many have only good things to say about Ron and his legacy, but what consistently comes through is his genuineness. He was not only the leader who Put Members First; he was one of them himself. He stayed grounded with the rank and file; he never lost touch. Even when he was out of office, he liked to be with Teamster members

Earlier, TDU had put out a special remembrance of Ron's legacy in one of their issues of the *Convoy Dispatch*. Many members contributed to the issue, including Joe Fahey. He wrote: "During his entire union life, from rank-and-file worker to General President of the Teamsters, Ron did the right thing. I don't think Ron was fearless; it was just that fear didn't stop him. His bravery and consistency is an important example for all workers and leaders."[30]

Some remembrances focused on how grounded Ron was and how he never had to become Ron Carey. He was always Ron Carey. "He genuinely liked hanging out with working Teamsters in Queens, not politicians or union officials in DC," wrote Rand

Wilson and Steve Early. "He was a workhorse, not a show horse. A hands-on handler of IBT members' daily problems."[31]

In an interview with Deepa Kumar for her book on the media and the UPS strike, Ron said, "A man isn't what he says he is. He is what his deeds say he is."[32] Under that criteria, Ron Carey was surely a success. He ran for higher office, he made promises, and he delivered for his members. Ron was not the type to say it's about the person—he'd say it's about the members.

On a warm August afternoon in 2010, the City of New York renamed the corner of 28th Avenue and 206th Street in Bayside, Queens "Ron Carey Avenue." It was the end result of hard work by Tim Sylvester and Ron's daughter Barbara. It was attended by family members, friends, Executive Board members of Local 804 as well neighbors and members.[33]

Through the ups and the downs, Ron Carey maintained his integrity. Over the years he grew, he learned, he succeeded in changing the Teamsters, changing the labor movement. Ron's life will always serve as an inspiration for all those who champion the working class, the only force that ultimately can change the world forever.

The reforms he implemented are still in place. His accomplishments are still a template for all who follow him to replicate. No one has even come close. Ron Carey was a true, genuine American hero. His record speaks for itself:

- He cut excessive officer salaries as well as his own.
- He sold off the Teamster jet, the limos, and the condo in Puerto Rico.
- He got rid of the excessive perks and free lunches.
- He made the International reps actually work: trusteeing corrupt, incompetent Locals.
- He negotiated strong contracts using innovative strategies.
- He took his members on strike when necessary.
- He brought truth and transparency to the position of Teamster president.

- He made the Teamster bureaucracy work for the rank and file.
- He ended the wasteful area conferences.
- He organized many new members.
- He got rid of mob influence
- He helped reform the AFL-CIO by getting John Sweeney elected.
- He made members feel proud again to be a Teamster.
- He left the Teamsters better than he found it.

Ron Carey was a trusting person. He trusted the people he put in charge of departments and divisions. He trusted the less experienced people he empowered in positions such as the International representatives. He did things no Teamster leader ever considered: having enough trust in putting rank-and-file members on the negotiating committees bargaining with the companies. Some might say he trusted too much, or he just trusted the wrong people at times, hence the 1996 scandal that took him down.

Ron Carey was a fighter who saw how UPS treated his members, his friends in the workplace. He worked tirelessly to fix the injustices he saw and was told about. His daughter Sandra said he fought "to do good and make a difference." He truly had a "righteous anger," as Rick Gilberg called it.

Ron Carey gave the truth and expected the truth from his staff and Executive Board. He hated lazy people. Though his leadership style demonstrated a commanding presence, he was still able to stay connected to his members. That continuing connection kept him real and grounded to their needs and grievances. It made him relentless and unstoppable.

Ron Carey was always the real deal from day one: a working-class guy who preferred a good tuna on toast to fine dining; a working-class guy who preferred a beer with members in Queens than champagne at a Washington dinner party.

Ron Carey was always and consistently an independent-minded leader. Even back in the 1980s when we had conservative union leaders publicly supporting the Solidarity movement in Poland that fought for exploited workers and against the autocracy of the

Communist government, and when left-wing union activists were supporting left-wing governments in Central America, Ron never let such events, important as they might be, distract him from the Teamster work at hand. What mattered most to him was the power of his members.

Ron was a long-term thinker, as well as a leader who chose to take the long road to power. While others could be bought or sold via the fast lane, Ron earned his position. He never accepted "go along to get along" leadership. He stood his ground as he journeyed from driver to shop steward to local leader to General President of the International.

Furthermore, it's what he did with that power. Ron didn't become rich. As Local president he made a little over what the average driver brought home. As General President, he cut his own salary. Ron used power to empower the rank and file. He worked tirelessly to deliver strong contracts, corrupt-free leadership, reform. He was a leader unafraid to strike the largest corporations in America.

He never joined Teamsters for a Democratic Union. Though he was once a conservative Republican, he came to Washington with a fresher outlook on things. He continued to stay nonpartisan, yet he developed a stronger belief in how to attain economic fairness for his members, a belief that bordered on a more radical outlook. Some say he was "Bernie (Sanders) before Bernie."

Though Washington was a place for taking sides, left or right, Ron stayed his ground on politics. Though he did move the Teamsters to support the Democratic Party, he never felt too comfortable with those on the left. However, he was quite aware and fearful of just how anti-union and anti-worker the Republican Party had become. So he advocated for policies and reforms that would benefit his members and all workers' economic interests.

Some like to believe that Ron in the 1990s or the 2000s was exactly the same Ron from Steven Brill's 1977 book, *The Teamsters*. But we all know that people change; they evolve. All the people who worked with or for Ron acknowledge the change in Ron over the years. Traversing the country to help vote down weak contracts in the 1980s and campaigning for two intense years for IBT General President broadened Ron's mind to the economic troubles and grievances of his fellow Teamsters. He never turned into a Marxist, but he felt comfortable enough to give full support to the Democratic Party that was on the union's side.

He lived his life conservatively, but when he spoke about our economic system, the powers that be, corporate greed or pro-business politicians, Ron could easily have been mistaken for a Ralph Nader or a Bernie Sanders. Like anyone else, Ron was a human being. He made mistakes, evidenced by the hiring of certain campaign operatives, but in the main his mistakes were few. Just ask the hundreds of thousands of Teamsters who, like so many others, do society's hard and often unrewarding labor.

In 1996, Ron had the opportunity to back Pat Buchanan, who was railing consistently against NAFTA, but did not, because he believed economic justice was bigger than one issue. Remember, Ron was an early supporter of a single-payer health care system. He saw directly from his twenty-five years as the leader of Local 804 the expensive health care costs that could bankrupt a union, a company, individuals, and their families. Ron believed a government-run single-payer system would relieve the burden of the usual fight over health care during contract negotiations. He felt that too much was at risk. He knew his members wanted reliability, something they didn't have to worry about every three or four years, something that would always be there.

For a while, at least according to Corporate America, Ron Carey was the most dangerous person in America. Ron knew he was a powerful leader. He knew he put fear into Corporate America. He knew after the UPS strike that they would hit back with all they had to hurt him or have him removed. "I had kept telling people that this company would be looking for a victim to pay for this. They would not let it go . . . I made a lot of enemies . . . I have paid a great personal price."[34] He certainly did.

Throughout Ron's remarkable life, he was always looking to

make things better for his members. Whether it was running for shop steward, running for president of Local 804, negotiating for stronger contracts, taking on the corrupt IBT establishment, challenging the political status quo in Washington, taking on Corporate America, Ron Carey was constantly fighting for the rank and file. His final fight was for his own reputation, his legacy, the truth. His exceptional legal team delivered him a sweet victory. But that entire story needed to be told.

I hope this book succeeds and resuscitates his good name. He was unfairly and unjustly taken down by some very powerful forces. I hope it sets the record straight. I hope it educates millions of Teamsters and their families about a great human being who touched so many lives.

Ron's life is also a cautionary tale. If you are going to take on corruption and entrenched power, you have to be careful about those who surround you. One slip can lead to disaster and bring down everything.

In the end, however, Ron Carey took on Corporate America and refused to listen to the corporate-controlled politicians. He was independent and walked to his own beat. Ron was a working-class guy who played by the rules and was true to his word. He remembered where he came from; he stayed grounded and real. He was not just admired and respected. Ron Carey was loved. And no matter what, he Put Members First.

I BEGAN THIS BOOK WITH the "Forgotten Teamster" speech that Ron Carey gave at the 1991 Teamster Convention. It is worth repeating part of it here:

> Our victory for the Forgotten Teamsters will be when they can once again see the huge resources of this great union used to reach out, to organize, to educate, to build the union it once was, organizing the oppressed workers everywhere. It will be when we restore the strength in the membership, the numbers, regain the power that we once had, numbers in power which make it

possible for us to provide these lifestyles for our members and not the country club lifestyles that we see our leaders enjoying today.

It will be that day when the forgotten Teamsters know that if we promise to negotiate good contracts, good wages, good working conditions, good health care benefits, good pensions, and a good secure future for Teamster families, then they'll know that we deliver on our promises because we can and because we have.

Our victory for them will be on the day when they know there is no more Marble Palace, no union official, no union abuse, no union corruption beyond their power to correct, change, and clean up, and no dream for a better tomorrow that we cannot obtain.[35]

Ron Carey guided our union to fulfill that great victory. We were no longer "forgotten." Ron had awakened a great beast, the rank and file, the real and often silent majority. He restored our faith in our union, in our leadership. He fulfilled his promises and empowered us to use the power that we had. Too many so-called leaders refuse to use that power. They fear provoking the anger of Corporate America. Ron Carey never backed down.

In that speech, Ron called out the enemies of labor: "We face powerful roadblocks from within our union and from without our union. . . . The enemy from without, multinational employers, runaway shops, the so-called free trade, scabs which now are politely and disgustingly called 'replacement workers,' and last, but not least, a union-busting government." He was referring to the government under George H. W. Bush. Speaking about those "Forgotten Teamsters," Ron concluded that "they have a right to know that they will never again be Forgotten Teamsters, that they are only Teamsters, brothers and sisters, working men and women, part-timers, full-timers, who stand tall and say, 'I'm a Teamster and I'm damn proud of it!'"[36]

For decades photos and portraits hung in the Marble Palace of thieves, thugs, and felons who occupied the top offices of the Teamsters union. In 1998 the Hoffa cult decided not to hang one of Ron Carey, the first ever democratically elected president of the IBT. Keeping Ron in a bad light made Hoffa look better: "Hoffa was never banned or indicted for lying," they'd say. But in the great light of Teamster history, Hoffa, Jr., is but a place holder. Reform had been put on hold for too long: twenty-two years. Some reformers are once again in control of the IBT. Only history will tell if it is a continuation of Hoffa's years or Ron Carey's reforms. I'm sure this book will enrage some of the Old Guard. Too bad.

Today there is a new regime occupying the Marble Palace. Though I have been a longtime skeptic of current president Sean O'Brien, I feel optimistic about reform in the Teamsters. The jury is still out on whether he is following in the footsteps of Ron Carey or the Old Guard or something new. He has a handful of reformers on his team. I wish them luck.

THE DEDICATED MEMBERS OF LOCAL 804 put together a slate of reformers, activists, and admirers of Ron who took on the Redmond regime. It was a tall order. Redmond had been on the board since 1975. Most of the board had been hand-picked by him. They were used to getting reelected every three years. They assumed this election would be like the others. They thought they owned their positions. But they had grown lazy and arrogant over the years. Many of the BAs stopped caring and hardly showed up at the buildings they represented

But the membership was looking for change, for fresh faces and a new direction with new ideas. The old way of "go along to get along" was not cutting it. The Redmond crew got scared and started putting out lies about our slate, 804 Members United. We took a page out of Ron's campaign book. We visited every building, every shift, every week. We came up with a ten-point platform of goals and promises. Our slate included drivers, feeders, clerks, car washers, custodians, as well as part-timers. That fact alone created a large wave of inside support.

When the ballots were counted on December 3, 2009, 804 Members United had beaten the once mighty Redmond slate by more than two to one. The first thing that newly elected President of Local 804, Tim Sylvester, did when we officially took office on January 1, 2010, was hang Ron's picture on the wall of the union hall. It was once again the Home of Ron Carey.

CHAPTER 11

A Personal Note

C ollectively, we all owed Ron for everything he gave us. To
some he was a friend, to others a leader who delivered a
full-time job, and to still others a famous person who once
occupied our union hall and whom everyone talked about.

I came to the party late. I started working for UPS in 1985. But
by 1997, I had been awakened. The strike was the catalyst. Soon
after, they were going after Ron. That's when I joined TDU. Before
you knew it, I was handing out the *Convoy Dispatch* at my building every month. Getting yelled at by the likes of Tony Donato, the
BA for my building at Foster Avenue in Brooklyn. By this time,
the Executive Board of Local 804 had already turned their backs
on Ron. I didn't know the politics behind it yet, but I knew it was
wrong.

Fast forward to 2006. Over the years I met with Tim Sylvester,
who at the time was organizing a slate to run against the EB, then
led by Howard Redmond. They ran a slate in 2000 and were beaten.
I had transferred to the Melville building on Long Island. I joined
them as they handed out fliers. Sylvester and I became close. In
2003, the reform slate attempted to challenge Redmond once
again, but things fell apart when a big name backed out and the

slate didn't move forward. Danny Katch, a part-timer and activist, and myself offered our names to help fill out the slate so that
at least we could challenge them. Tim looked at us and said, "Do
you think you are ready to be a BA? Say we win…what happens if
a Division Manager walks a driver out, what do you do? He went
through several what-ifs… Kenny, what are you going to do?" I
said, "Call you!" He responded, "I will not put people in important
positions who are not ready. This is a supremely important and
responsible position, and I will not put someone there who is not
up to it yet."

This showed me how responsible a leader Tim was and how
committed he was to the members. Even if it meant waiting
another three or even six years to get it right. Sylvester retired in
2022. Yet he continues to be active. He, Tom Leedham, and some
others have started a go-to website for Teamsters of all stripes
called TeamsterLink.org.

Well, it did take six years, proving that hard work does pay off.
In early 2009, about twenty of us committed, reform-minded drivers and inside workers put together the 804 Members United slate.
Our goal was to take back our local from the Old Guard Hoffa-
friendly EB run by Howard Redmond. It took almost a full year
of campaigning nonstop to defeat the longtime incumbents. Our
slate beat them two to one.

When I started working at UPS, I probably had heard the name
Ron Carey over the years, but it didn't have much relevance. I saw
him as I marched behind him and a Local 804 banner in a 1996
Labor Day Parade. I was with John Mastellone, a fellow driver from
Foster Avenue. I remember being one of many who tore down the
Hoffa signs on several poles along Fifth Avenue on that parade day.
I wasn't very union-minded at the time. I had never attended a
union meeting, even though I had been a UPS Teamster for eleven
years. I just came into work, did my thing, and went home. I never
connected my progressive politics with my union until I attended
that parade.

A year later, the UPS strike erupted. That really radicalized me.

I was reading Howard Zinn's *A People's History of the United States* when we went on strike. The solidarity, the union chants, following supervisors delivering what was left in the system, what a jolt it all was to my consciousness.

Then, when they went after Ron Carey, I decided to join TDU. John Mastellone had told me they were a group of progressive Teamsters who were for reform and rank-and-file empowerment. My career as an activist and agitator began. It hasn't stopped.

SOLIDARITY FOREVER!

Putting Members First:
Lessons from Ron Carey's Career
and Fifty Years of Teamster Reform

BY STEVE EARLY AND RAND WILSON

Books about union presidents are usually penned by professional writers—either academic historians, labor journalists, or paid flacks. Past accounts of the life and work of labor organization chiefs like John L. Lewis, Walter Reuther, Jimmy Hoffa, or Cesar Chavez have run the gamut from hagiographic to constructively critical. Few have had a biographer whose view of their leadership role is rooted in firsthand experience as a blue-collar worker in the same industry and union.

Ken Reiman's personal connection to the subject matter of this book comes from his long career as a UPS driver and activist in the Teamster local that Ron Carey led before becoming national union president in the 1990s. His insights into the workplace culture and organizational politics of Local 804 in Queens, New York; the International Brotherhood of Teamsters, before, during, and after Carey's presidency; and the Teamsters today provide a rank-and-file perspective on the challenges of institutional change in organized labor over the past fifty years.

Carey's story, as told by Reiman, contains many important lessons for younger union activists, whether they are Teamsters or involved in other unions. Organized labor today is in a state of very positive ferment. A reform movement in the United Auto Workers, modeled after Teamsters for a Democratic Union, has had similar success winning direct election of top officers and using that system to oust old guard officials.

By late 2023, newly elected UAW leaders were conducting a major strike against U.S. automakers, after building a membership-based contract campaign of a sort never employed by the previous leadership during national bargaining. Earlier in the year, new leadership in the Teamsters, elected in 2021 with TDU backing, engaged many of the union's 330,000 members at UPS in a national contract fight that drew on the experience of the UPS strike in 1997, led by Ron Carey.

In California in 2023, workers in the state university system staged the largest higher education walkout ever, and union members at Kaiser Permanente conducted the biggest health care industry strike in U.S. labor history. Actors and writers participated in an overlapping work stoppage in Hollywood that involved more than 170,000 workers. Meanwhile, thousands of Southern California hotel workers also struck for a new contract.

Workers in more than 350 Starbucks outlets won collective bargaining rights and dug in for a long first contract fight punctuated by nationally coordinated protest activity and mini-strikes in particular workplaces. The landscape of labor organizing in Amazon warehouses and distribution centers was replete with similar shop-floor skirmishing between labor and management, including worker-led strikes over local issues in many locations with no formal bargaining rights or union recognition.

This dynamic mix of union democracy and reform struggles, at the local and national level, and heightened workplace militancy in many different sectors was, of course, the context for Ron Carey's own late twentieth-century career as a union dissident, who became the first democratically elected president of what was, not long ago, the nation's most corrupt and racketeer-dominated union.

Each phase of Carey's rise and fall, as recounted in *Ron Carey and the Teamsters*, is worthy of close study by those seeking to follow in his footsteps as a shop-floor militant, an opposition candidate for local union office, and a coalition-builder with other reformers. Finally, and most impressive, was Carey's role as a national labor leader faced with the daunting challenge of transforming a dysfunctional organization in the face of employer hostility and the internal resistance of union officials protecting their own perks, political power, and personal fiefdoms.

Below are some of the critical components of union revitalization, as recounted in this biography, that have continuing relevance to present-day reform struggles:

- OUSTING LOCAL UNION INCUMBENTS

Like many disgruntled members before and since, Carey first got involved in union politics because officials of Local 804, in the late 1950s, were so unresponsive to worker complaints and concerns. He ran for shop steward, beating a fellow driver who "didn't want to rock the boat." Rocking the boat became Carey's "M.O." for the rest of his career. But he understood the limitations of being a Lone Ranger. Reiman's account of how Carey assembled a team of like-minded co-workers to take on the union establishment is a good primer for anyone trying to do that, at the local union level, today.

It took Carey a decade, and several election defeats running for lesser offices, before he became 804 president on a platform of cleaning up the local, enforcing the contract, and improving pensions. As he did twenty-four years later in the Marble Palace in Washington, Carey cut his own salary to show that he was serious about putting union resources to work for the membership.

- USING DIRECT ACTION ON THE JOB

The year Ron Carey became a Teamster steward, Local 804 had

twenty wildcat strikes; not long afterward UPS drivers in New York City struck for six weeks, over the objections of local and national union officials. Throughout his three decades in the Local, Carey tapped into, rather than tried to suppress, rank-and-file unrest that took the form of job actions, whether legal or not.

When Carey became president in 1968, after campaigning for a year as part of an opposition slate, his first challenge was striking UPS again. This time, Local 804 members walked out for more than two months to win a first-ever "25-and-out" pension provision with UPS, effectively using contract rejection votes at mass meetings to win a better final offer from management.

• CHALLENGING BUREAUCRATIC CONTROL OF BARGAINING

As Reiman reports, Carey quickly developed a reputation for honesty, transparency, and independence from the corrupt regional and national power structure of the IBT. But, in the Teamsters then, and in many other unions today, islands of militancy have trouble surviving in a sea of business unionism. *Ron Carey and the Teamsters* shows how dissident locals like Carey's 804 must overcome attempts by the union hierarchy to undermine picket-line solidarity among workers bargaining with the same employer, but in different locals or national unions. Carey's methods of thwarting management's divide-and-conquer schemes, aided and abetted by top union officials, are worthy of emulation.

• NETWORKING WITH LIKE-MINDED REFORMERS

In the 1980s, the IBT began negotiating more issues with UPS at the company-wide level—via a tightly controlled national bargaining committee—which reduced the scope and impact of local or regional bargaining. To counter this threat, Carey and Local 804 began to ally with UPS dissidents around the country, including those long active in TDU and equally opposed to a then-provision of the IBT constitution that required a two-thirds vote, rather than a simple majority, to reject any tentative agreement with an employer. Jousting with the International over imposition of unpopular UPS contracts—voted down by a majority of those covered by them—helped build the movement for democratizing the Teamsters, by linking bad bargaining outcomes to denial of membership rights.

- ### WINNING AND USING "ONE MEMBER/ONE VOTE"

Most U.S. union members have no direct say about their national union officers and executive board members. The latter are elected by smaller groups of Local union delegates at national conventions that tend to be leadership controlled, particularly when incumbents are up for reelection. These delegate bodies are resistant to changing national union constitutions to allow the more democratic method used in APWU (Postal Workers), ILWU (Longshore Workers), the NewsGuild/CWA (Communications Workers), and a few others.

The only major breakthroughs in direct voting on top officers have occurred after corruption scandals and resulting judicial intervention involving the IBT, UAW, and LIUNA (Laborers Union). Without a rank-and-file reform movement—of the type that backed Carey during his two Teamster president campaigns, or which developed recently in the UAW—it remains hard for opposition candidates to win any union-wide election. The lesson of this book is to be ready for that political opening when and if it occurs, while fighting for "one-member/one vote" in the meantime.

- ### TACKLING INTERNAL RESTRUCTURING

When Carey and other members of his reform slate took over Teamster headquarters in DC in 1992, the Marble Palace was not just a monument to past Teamster extravagance. It was full of poorly performing departments, with overpaid and/or incompetent staffers hostile to the goals of the new administration. Foes of reform also controlled all the Teamster joint councils, area conferences, and the boards of the many health and welfare and pension benefit funds. These powerful officials wanted Carey and his team to fall on their faces.

Working with TDU activists around the country and a minority of reform-minded local officers, Carey put seventy-five troubled locals under trusteeship, cut waste, stepped up Teamster organizing, hired aggressive new staff and empowered members. As Reiman documents, the elimination of the "area conferences" was a major restructuring victory—and a blueprint worth following, as needed, in other unions saddled with unnecessary layers of bureaucracy and staff featherbedding.

• **STAYING CLOSE TO THE MEMBERS**
To his credit, Carey never felt comfortable in his new inside-the-Beltway world (where a sycophantic culture of political hustling and overpaid "consulting" would, in the end, contribute to his undoing). He liked hanging out with working Teamsters in Queens, not politicians or other high-ranking union officials in Washington. He was a workhorse, not a show horse, a hands-on handler of IBT members' daily problems, large and small. His organizational accomplishments, as Reiman shows, were always rooted in a strong personal connection with the membership, which many elected and appointed officials seem to lose as they ascend through the ranks of their respective union bureaucracies.

• **TAKING ON EMPLOYERS, WITH NEW ALLIES**
Carey's finest hour came in 1997 when the presence of someone at the top of the union who sincerely believed in the power of the rank and file made it possible for 185,000 UPS workers to win the biggest nationwide strike in the last thirty years. The UPS contract campaign employed membership education and mobilization, labor-community coalition building, and outreach to UPS customers and the general public, via the media, that the union had never utilized before.

Two years before, the Teamsters, under Carey, had cast 1.4 million votes in the AFL-CIO's first contested election in a hundred years, thereby helping to secure the victory of a new leadership more helpful in labor-management showdowns like the UPS strike. The IBT joined Jobs With Justice, embraced single-payer health care reform, and campaigned against free trade. The union ditched its traditional ties to conservative Republicans, while maintaining some—albeit not enough—distance from Democrats who disappointed or betrayed labor.

• ANTICIPATING A COUNTERREVOLUTION

When union reformers win, they still face pushback from entrenched internal foes. Carey's crackdown on crooks and leadership perks alienated large sections of the Teamster officialdom. Still-powerful bureaucrats who had split their support between two "Old Guard" candidates in 1991, bankrolled a unified $4 million challenge, fronted by James Hoffa, Jr., five years later. The wealthy Detroit attorney masqueraded successfully as a populist critic of a "New Teamster" establishment that was spendthrift, incompetent, and run by "outsiders."

As Reiman recounts, the Carey campaign fundraising misconduct in 1996 was a self-inflicted blow to the moral authority and public reputation of his administration. It was the result of corner-cutting and top-down campaigning that was very different from the bottom-up approach that propelled Carey to victory five years before. The moral of this story: if you're going to take on union corruption and corporate America at the same time, don't let opportunistic "outsiders," hitch their wagon to your team. Their greed, bad judgment, and lack of any connection to union reform will lead to grifting of a new sort.

WHILE THE TRAGEDY OF RON CAREY'S criminal prosecution and eventual banning from the union makes for painful reading, Ken Reiman's book reminds us that the Teamster reform movement survived "Donorgate" in the mid-1990s and upheld his legacy of opposition to Teamster Old Guard politics and policies. The work of Carey and many like-minded supporters four decades ago raised the bar and set the stage for Teamster reformers to reclaim their national headquarters nearly twenty-five years later.

One result of that most recent national-level reform slate victory was the 2022–23 UPS contract campaign that drew on the lessons, experiences, and, in many cases, the leadership of 1997 strike veterans. In much media coverage and analysis of last year's grassroots contract campaign and its results, Carey's name, memory, and past strike role were often invoked.

To TDU members and the many other Teamsters whose votes made him the first directly elected national union president, Carey remains a heroic, not just tragic, figure. In a union where to this day many local officers are wary of TDU, the pugnacious ex-Marine and former UPS driver from Queens was a unique ally in a vibrant reform movement that has now spanned five decades. During that period, we had the privilege of working with Ron in different capacities and seeing him in action behind the scenes and in public, during several critical junctures in the union's modern history.

We salute Brother Ken Reiman and Monthly Review Press for bringing Ron's story to a new generation of labor activists faced with the unfinished task of revitalizing and reforming the U.S. labor movement. Reiman's book will help ensure that Carey's singular role will be remembered—and rightfully honored—long after his critics and detractors have been forgotten.

In the late 1970s, STEVE EARLY was an organizer, lawyer, and newspaper editor for the Professional Drivers Council (PROD), a Teamster reform group that became part of Teamsters for a Democratic Union (TDU). He assisted Ron Carey's 1989–91 campaign for the Teamster presidency and, while on loan from the Communications Workers of America, served as a member of Carey's headquarters transition team in early 1992.

A longtime labor activist, RAND WILSON worked at Teamster headquarters in the union's communications department under Ron Carey. He helped plan and implement the UPS contract campaign in 1997, and handled publicity for the subsequent two-week strike. In 2022–23, he worked as a TDU organizer aiding membership education and mobilization in support of the IBT's latest UPS contract campaign.

Notes

1. Steven Brill, *The Teamsters* (New York: Simon & Schuster, 1978).
2. Ron Carey, Teamsters Convention speech, 1991, http://fb.watch/h8zcbTEpPp/.

1. Son of a UPS Driver

1. Interview with Bruce Carey, July 2018.
2. Interview with Sandra Carey, July 2016.
3. Larry Reynolds, "Ronald Carey: No More Business-As-Usual in the Teamsters," *Management Review* 82/6 (August 1993).
4. Interview with Barbara Carey, August 2014.
5. Interview with Bruce Carey.
6. Interview with Bruce Carey.
7. Interview with Pat Pagnanella, June 2014. Joe stayed a UPS driver until retirement in 1976. He got many awards for Safe Driving. He also got held up a lot, too.
8. Interview with Bruce Carey.
9. Interview with Bruce Carey.
10. Pat Pagnanella on Ron as a swimmer: "Later in life in the 1970s and '80s, when Ron and Pat and their wives went away on vacations, Pat realized what a good swimmer Ron really was."
11. Interview with Barbara Carey.
12. Interview with Bruce Carey.
13. Interview with Bruce Carey.
14. Interview with Barbara Carey.

15. Deepa Kumar, *Outside the Box: Corporate Media, Globalization, and the UPS Strike* (Champaign: University of Illinois Press, 2007), 186.

16. Ken Crowe, *Collision: How the Rank and File Took Back the Teamsters* (New York City: Scribner, 1993).

17. Interview with Ken Crowe, September 2014. Note that each building had several "centers" or areas that it covered. For instance, a Bronx building would have a "North" Center, "South" Center, etc. Each center had a manager and three supervisors. Each building had around three or four centers, A Division Manager was in charge of the entire building.

18. Kumar, *Outside the Box*, 186.

19. Ibid., 185.

2. The UPS Driver

1. Interview with Ken Spillane, February 2015.

2. Interview with Mike Maloney, April 2020.

3. Steven Brill, *The Teamsters* (New York: Simon & Schuster, 1978), 156.

4. Kenneth C. Crowe, *Collision: How the Rank and File Took Back the Teamsters* (New York: Scribner, 1993), 133.

5. Interview with Tim Sylvester, former President of Local 804, November 2019.

6. "Battle of the Budget: Political Gettysburg," *New York Times*, April 21, 1957

7. http://local804.dreamhosters.com. This was the group that hosted Local 804's Local History page.

8. Ibid.

9. Ibid.

10. Ibid.

11. *New York Times*, April 21, 1962.

12. "United Parcel Strike in New York Illustrates New Union Mood," *New York Times*, June 18, 1962.

13. Ibid.

14. Interview with Spillane.

15. Brill, *The Teamsters*, 156.

16. Crowe interview with Ron Carey, September 1991.

17. Brill, *The Teamsters*, 156.

18. Interview with Pat Pagnanella, June 2014.

19. Interview with Spillane.

20. Interview with Pagnanella.

21. Ibid.

22. Deepa Kumar, *Outside the Box: Corporate Media, Globalization, and the UPS Strike* (Champaign: University of Illinois, 2007), 187.

23. Interview with Spillane.
24. Brill, *The Teamsters*, 166.
25. Ibid., 200.
26. Interview, Spillane.
27. Brill, *The Teamsters*, 168.
28. Ibid.
29. Interview with Pagnanella.
30. Ibid.
31. Brill, *The Teamsters*, 168.
32. Ibid.
33. Ibid.
34. Peter Millones, "Local in Parcel Strike Is Told by Union to Vote on Pay Offer," *New York Times*, July 6, 1968.
35. Brill, *The Teamsters*, 169.
36. Interview with Sandra Carey, July 2016.
37. Interview with Pagnanella.
38. "Accord Proposed in Parcel Strike," *New York Times*, July 10, 1968.
39. Brill, *The Teamsters*, 155.
40. Ibid., 180.
41. Ibid., 176.
42. The term was popularized by Nixon in a television address to the nation on November 3, 1969, when he said, "And so tonight—to you— the great silent majority of my fellow Americans..."
43. Brill, *The Teamsters*, 180. There were numerous other short wildcat actions, such as on October 31, 1969, when Ron pulled his members out on strike over an incident involving a member's haircut and the wearing of turtleneck sweaters. Ron called it a "misunderstanding."
44. Damon Stetson, "Workers Return at United Parcel," *New York Times*, August 12, 1970.
45. The arbitrator was attorney Burton B. Turkus, who was known as the assistant district attorney who prosecuted members of the Brooklyn mafia gang Murder Inc.
46. Richard Phalon, "United Parcel Strike Is Spreading into New Jersey," *New York Times*, August 4, 1970.
47. Ibid.
48. "United Parcel Strike Is Ended by Lifting of Ban on Flag Pin," *New York Times*, August 11, 1970.
49. Interview with Pagnanella.
50. Ibid.
51. Brill, *The Teamsters*, 166.
52. Ibid., 186.
53. Interview with Pagnanella.

54. Ibid.
55. Brill, *The Teamsters*, 184.
56. Ibid.
57. James B. Jacobs and Kerry T. Cooperman, *Breaking the Devil's Pact: The Battle to Free the Teamsters from the Mob* (New York: New York University Press, 2011), 16–17.
58. Edith Evans Asbury, "Delivery Strike Leader: Ronald Robert Carey," *New York Times*, November 21, 1974.
59. Interview with Spillane.
60. Brill, *The Teamsters*, 195.
61. Emanuel Perlmutter, "Strikers Say No to United Parcel," *New York Times*, November 18, 1974.
62. Interview with Pagnanella.
63. Ibid.
64. Brill, *The Teamsters*, 188; John McQuiston, "4000 Go on Strike at United Parcel," *New York Times*, August 29, 1974.
65. Interview with Pagnanella.
66. Ibid.; Brill, *The Teamsters*, 182; Robert McFadden, "Death Postpones the Parcel Talks," *New York Times*, August 31, 1974.
67. Interview with Pagnanella.
68. Brill, *The Teamsters*, 182.
69. Ibid.
70. Jacobs and Cooperman, *Breaking the Devil's Pact*, 14.
71. Brill, *The Teamsters*, 183.
72. Interview with Pagnanella.
73. Emanuel Perlmutter, "United Parcel Strike Ends after 87 Days," *New York Times*, November 21, 1974.
74. Brill, 166.
75. Interview with Barbara Carey, August 2014.
76. Ibid.
77. Interview with Sandra Carey, July 2016.
78. Ibid.
79. Brill, *The Teamsters*, 198.
80. Interview with Bruce Carey, July 2018.
81. Interview with Sandra Carey.
82. Ibid.
83. Ibid.
84. Brill, *The Teamsters*, 159.
85. Interview with Sandra Carey.
86. Ibid.
87. Ibid.
88. Ibid.

3. The Leader

1. Steven Brill, *The Teamsters* (New York: Simon & Schuster, 1978), 160.
2. Ibid., 178.
3. Ibid., 164.
4. Ibid., 167.
5. Ibid., 188.
6. Kenneth C. Crowe, *Collision: How The Rank and File Took Back the Teamsters* (New York: Scribner, 1993), 135.
7. Brill, *The Teamsters*, 187.
8. "U.P.S. Workers Ratify Contract," *New York Times*, June 8, 1977.
9. Brill, *The Teamsters*, 196.
10. Ibid., 195–98.
11. Crowe, 135.
12. Joe Allen, *The Package King: A Rank and File History* (Self-published, 2017), 48.
13. Interview with Rick Gilberg, May 2014.
14. Crowe, *Collision*, 135.
15. Ibid., 137.
16. Ibid.
17. Ibid.
18. Interview with Pat Pagnanella, June 2014.
19. Interview with Ken Spillane, February 2015.
20. Interview with Gilberg.
21. Interview with Pagnanella.
22. Ibid.
23. This was my first contract as a member of Local 804 and UPS. I received that $600 bonus.
24. Crowe, *Collision*, 136.
25. Ibid., 137.
26. Ibid., 136.
27. Ibid.
28. AP, "Teamsters Are Said to Scrap a Rule on Two-Thirds Vote," *New York Times*, October 21, 1988.
29. A few years earlier, the body of a dead Teamster official was found in the trunk of Hyman's car.
30. Crowe, *Collision*, 137.
31. According to Susan Davis, one of Ron's lawyers at the time, when Ron found out about the subpoena, he quickly sent a lawyer to ask Bruce Baird, the lead prosecutor, whether he, Long, or the Local were targets of the investigation. Baird told them no. Jeffrey Goldberg, "Hoffa Lives!," *New York Magazine*, July 31, 1995.

32. Selwyn Raab, "Loan Sharking Inquiry Gives Officials New Insights Into Organized Crime," *New York Times*, August 17, 1984.

33. Arnold Lubasch, "A Federal Jury Finds 8 Guilty in Loan Racket," *New York Times*, April 20, 1985.

34. Ibid.

35. Mahoney was also a former NYC Transit Police officer and NYPD officer for eleven years. He challenged Joe T. for president of the Joint Council 16 in 1975 and lost. Joe T. had been the head of the JC16 since 1965.

36. James B Jacobs and Kerry T. Cooperman, *Breaking the Devil's Pact: The Battle to Free the Teamsters from the Mob* (New York: New York University Press, 2011), 4.

37. Hyman testified that he agreed to pay Long a 1 percent cash kickback for funds invested by Local 804 in Penvest. After Long gave Hyman a check for $100,000 for Penvest, Hyman gave Long $2,000 in cash, a 2 percent kickback, to encourage Long's continuing cooperation in the scheme. A few months later, Long invested another $50,000 with Penvest, and Hyman gave Long $1,000 cash. Hyman also paid Long $5,000 in cash for introducing Hyman to Mahoney.

38. William Rashbaum, "Feds were investigating slain union organizer," UPI, January 5, 1988.

39. Crowe, *Collision*, 138.

40. Interview with Ken Paff, June 2016.

41. Years later, opponents used his acceptance of immunity against Ron in his run for IBT president. He also regretted accepting immunity. He blames his lawyer for coercing him into signing.

42. Trial transcript, September 27, 1988, *US v. Long*, United States District Court, S.D. New York.

43. Ibid.

44. There were errors in the instructions to the jury by the judge and improper administration of unsealed surveillance tapes and hearsay.

45. Law.justia.com/cases/federal/appellate-c.

46. Interview with Tim Sylvester, November 2019.

47. Ari Goldman, "UPS Workers Stage Walkout after a Dispute," *New York Times*, September 10, 1982.

48. Ibid.

49. Interview with Pagnanella.

50. Interview with Spillane.

51. Interview with Sylvester.

52. Interview with Pete Mastrandrea, January 2020..

53. Interview with Gilberg.

54. Interview with Sylvester.

55. Interview with Mastrandrea.

56. Crowe, *Collision*, 25.

57. Jacobs and Cooperman, *Breaking the Devil's Pact*, 17.

58. Ed Pound, "Teamster Leader Indicted for Plot to Offer Bribe to Senator Cannon," *New York Times*, May 23, 1981.

59. The Teamsters were the only major union to support Reagan in the 1980 General Election. As a matter of fact, Reagan's attorney general, Edwin Meese, had a warm relationship with Jackie Presser, another corrupt Teamster leader.

60. William Serrin, "Teamsters Open Convention with Reagan Message," *New York Times*, June 2, 1981.

61. TDU, Teamsters for a Democratic Union, was a national dissident reform organization whose mission was to reform the Teamsters. It was started in the mid-1970s by Ken Paff and Steve Kindred.

62. Crowe, *Collision*, 23.

63. Ibid., 27.

64. William Serrin, "Bribe Convictions: Troubled Union's New Burden," *New York Times*, December 16, 1982.

65. George Lardner and Kevin Klose, "Gangland-Style Shooting in Chicago," *Washington Post*, January 21, 1983.

66. Crowe, *Collision*, 30–31.

67. Jacobs and Cooperman, *Breaking the Devil's Pact*, 17–18; and Crowe, *Collision*, 15–16.

68. Crowe, *Collision*, 33.

69. On October 15, 1983, a caravan of BLAST thugs traveled from parts of Ohio and Michigan and descended upon the TDU convention at the Romulus, Michigan, Hilton Hotel. BLAST members harassed and terrorized TDU members. Crowe, *Collision*, 19; and Jacobs and Cooperman, *Breaking the Devil's Pact*, 7.

70. Crowe, *Collision*, 33.

71. President's Commission on Organized Crime (PCOC), Library of Congress.

72. Giuliani was ambitious and used this to move up the political ladder. Frankly, he couldn't have cared less about union democracy or rank-and-file Teamsters. Giuliani knew that taking on organized crime made headlines and put his name in bold letters. Instead of taking this to the end, he left it cold and ran for mayor of NYC. Jacobs and Cooperman, *Breaking the Devil's Pact*, 3–6.

73. Crowe, *Collision*, 38.

74. Ibid.

75. Ibid., 39.

76. Ibid., 37.

77. Ibid., 44.
78. Ibid., 45.
79. Jacobs and Cooperman, *Breaking the Devil's Pact*, 6–7.
80. Ibid., 19.
81. Ibid., 25: "The Teamster International Union has been a captive labor organization, which La Cosa Nostra figures have infiltrated, controlled and dominated through fear and intimidation and have exploited through fraud, embezzlement, bribery and extortion.... This infiltration, control, domination and victimization has taken the form of multiple violations of the RICO statute and these violations will continue (resulting in irreparable injury to those victimized by such violations) unless and until this Court divests the defendants associated with La Cosa Nostra, those working with them and those under their control (including present and past members of the General Executive Board) of their union interests."
82. Crowe, *Collision*, 90; Jacobs and Cooperman, *Breaking the Devil's Pact*, 20.
83. Crowe, *Collision*, 86–89.
84. The consent decree agreement called for three court-appointed officers: Independent Administrator, Investigations Officer, and Elections Officer plus an election of convention delegates, the secret ballot, direct election of the GEB, no associations with organized crime people, and once a new administration took office a three-member Independent Review Board to investigate corruption.
85. Crowe, *Collision*, 106–16.
86. Ibid., 107–16.
87. Interview with Michael Holland: "I organized my role like a political campaign. We broke the whole country into regions. Then we got people in each region to be regional coordinators and they built part-time staffs. We had adjuncts all over the place to observe nomination meetings and intervene if necessary. The officers didn't want to make any mistakes so they cooperated with us." November 2020.
88. Richard N. Gilberg. Ron's young lawyer, worked out of labor-friendly Cohen, Weiss and Simon.
89. Interview with Gilberg.
90. Ibid.
91. Interview with Susan Jennick, April 2016.
92. Interview with Gilberg.
93. Crowe interview with Ron Carey, September 1991.
94. Crowe, *Collision*, 139.
95. Interview with Ken Paff, June 2015.
96. Interview with Steve Early, April 2021.

97. Interview with Early: "I had invited a guy who would be a potential candidate for campaign manager, Frank Emspak, who was a local union official of IUE at General Electric in Boston. He had lots of organizing and bargaining experience. He was more available at the time but he and Ron didn't click."

98. Interview with Sylvester, November 2019.

99. Until the 1990s, Local 804 had its General Membership meetings at Washington Irving, at 40 Irving Place, Manhattan.

100. Interview with Pagnanella, June 2014.

101. Crowe, *Collision*, 141–42.

102. Crowe interview with Ron Carey.

103. Stanley Aronowitz, unsourced quote.

4. The Insurgent

1.   Kenneth C. Crowe, *Collision: How the Rank and File Took Back the Teamsters*, 8.

2.   Interview with Ken Paff, May 2015.

3.   Interview with Susan Jennick, April 2016.

4.   Crowe, *Collision*, 9.

5.   Ibid., 10; interview with Ed Burke, February 2016.

6.   Interview with Burke.

7.   Ibid.

8.   Frank Swaboda, "Union Maverick Mounts Campaign to Win Control of Teamsters," *Washington Post*, March 11, 1990.

9.   Interview with Rich Devries, August 2023.

10. Crowe, *Collision*, 171.

11. Interview with Burke.

12. Ibid.

13. Ken Crowe, interview with Rick Blaylock. I found this in Crowe's huge trove of files and articles on Ron and the Teamsters.

14. Interview with Burke.

15. Interview with Ken Paff.

16. Crowe, *Collision*, 172–73.

17. Ibid, 123.

18. Ibid.

19. Interview with Michael Holland, November 2020.

20. Crowe, *Collision*, 153–59.

21. F. C. "Duke" Zeller, *Devil's Pact: Inside the World of the Teamsters Union* (Secaucus, NJ: Carol Publishing Group, 1996), 314.

22. Karen Ball, "Front-Running Teamsters' Candidate Picks Running Mate," AP, June 11, 1991.

23. Interview with Rick Gilberg, May 2014.

24. James B. Jacobs and Kerry T. Cooperman, *Breaking the Devil's Pact: The Battle to Free the Teamsters from the Mob* (New York: New York University Press, 2011), 95.

25. Ibid., 258.

26. Crowe, *Collision,* 181.

27. Interview with Ed Burke.

28. Crowe, *Collision,* 176.

29. Zeller, *Devil's Pact,* 332.

30. Crowe, *Collision,* 226–27; interview with Pat Pagnanella, June 2014; interview with Sandra Carey, July 2016

31. Interview with Aaron Belk, August 2015.

32. Ibid.

33. Ibid.

34. Interview with Dennis Skelton, April 2020.

35. Crowe, *Collision,* 175.

36. Interview with Burke.

37. Ibid.

38. Jacobs and Cooperman, *Breaking the Devil's Pact,* 92; Crowe, *Collision,* 168.

39. Crowe, *Collision,* 168; AP, "Hoffa's Son Ineligible for Race," *New York Times,* April 25, 1991.

40. Crowe, *Collision,* 191–92.

41. Interview with Burke.

42. Interview with Burke; interview with Sandra Carey.

43. Interview with Tim Sylvester, November 2019.

44. Interview with Belk.

45. Ken Crowe, interview with Ron Carey in Crowe's files.

46. Interview with Sandra Carey.

47. Interview with Gilberg.

48. Interview with Paff.

49. Interview with Burke.

50. Ibid.

51. Crowe, *Collision,* 210; interview with Burke.

52. Interview with Skelton.

53. Interview with Paff.

54. Michael Holland, *The Cookbook: How the Election Officer Supervised the 1991 Teamster Election,* July 1992, (Washington D.C.: Library of Congress, Manuscript Division, 2009), chapter 2.

55. Disgraced Local 804 former secretary-treasurer John Long showed up at the convention too. He worked the hallways talking to others not to support Ron.

56. Crowe, *Collision,* 204.

57. Interview with Holland.
58. Ibid.
59. Judge Edelstein issued a decision earlier in May declaring that no matter how the delegates voted at the convention, the rank-and-file elections would be held.
60. Holland, *The Cookbook*, chap 2.
61. Crowe, *Collision*, 212; Jacobs and Cooperman, *Breaking the Devil's Pact*, 93; Zeller, *Devil's Pact*, 316.
62. Interview with Sylvester.
63. Interview with Burke; Crowe, *Collision*, 214.
64. Crowe, *Collision*, 214–16.
65. Ibid., 217.
66. Ibid.
67. Frank Swaboda, "Teamsters Vote Cap on Officers' Pay," *Washington Post*, June 27, 1991.
68. Crowe, *Collision*, 223.
69. Interview with Burke.
70. Ibid.
71. Crowe, *Collision*, 227; Jacobs and Cooperman, *Breaking The Devil's Pact*, 94; interview with RV Durham, February 2022.
72. Crowe, interview with Ron Carey.
73. Interview with Ken Spillane, February 2015.
74. Interview with Holland.
75. Holland, *The Cookbook*, chap. 4; Jacobs and Cooperman, *Breaking The Devil's Pact*, 98; Crowe, Collision, 252.
76. Interview with Holland.
77. For a more specific rundown of the counting process, see Jacobs and Cooperman, *Breaking the Devil's Pact*, 259–60.
78. Crowe, *Collision*, 255.
79. Holland, *The Cookbook*, chap. 4.
80. Interview with Burke.
81. Crowe, Collision, 258–59.
82. Stephen Franklin, "Reformer Declares Teamsters Victory," *Chicago Tribune*, December 13, 1991.
83. Ibid.
84. Ibid.; Bob Barker, "Reformer Close to Winning Teamsters Presidency Race," *Los Angeles Times*, December 12, 1991.
85. Peter T. Kilborn, "Teamsters' New Chief Vows to Put Members First," *New York Times*, December 13, 1991.
86. Franklin, "Reformer Declares Teamsters Victory."
87. Bruce Butterfield, "Teamster Chief Rides Reform Wave," *Boston Globe*, December 13, 1991.

88. Zeller, *Devil's Pact*, 334.

89. Interview with Dennis Skelton.

90. Ibid.

91. Belk's testimony at the U.S. Congress House Committee on Education and the Workforce, Subcommittee on Oversight and Investigations, 105th Congress, July 24, 1998.

92. Jacobs and Cooperman, *Breaking the Devil's Pact*, 104.

5. The Reformer

1. Kenneth C. Crowe, *Collision: How the Rank and File Took Back the Teamsters*, 261.

2. Ron's inaugural speech, February 1, 1992.

3. F. C. "Duke" Zeller, *Devil's Pact: Inside the World of the Teamsters Union*, 338.

4. David Levin, *Convoy Dispatch*, January 1992.

5. Zeller, *Devil's Pact*, 338.

6. Interview with Ed Burke, February 2016.

7. Interview with Ken Paff, June 2015.

8. Interview with David Mitchell, August 2021.

9. Interview with Bob Muehlenkamp, March 2022.

10. Peter Kilborn, "Carey Takes the Wheel," *New York Times*, June 21, 1992; interviews with Burke; Diana Kilmury, July 2016; and Muehlenkamp.

11. Interview with Kilmury.

12. Ibid.

13. Interview with Dennis Skelton, April 2020.

14. Interview with Kilmury.

15. Ibid.

16. Interview with Muehlenkamp.

17. Ibid.; interview with Aaron Belk, August 2015.

18. Interview with Burke.

19. Interview with Muehlenkamp.

20. Interview with Kilmury.

21. Interview with Mitchell.

22. Interview with Tim Sylvester, November 2019.. "Later in life Ron told me that chair is the electric chair. The worst thing he ever did was come down here. No matter what you do there is always someone going behind your back."

23. Kilborn, "Carey Takes the Wheel."

24. Ibid.

25. Ibid.

26. Interview with Belk.

27. Interview with Steve Early, April 2021.

28. Interview with Gene Moriarity, February 2014.

29. Herman Benson quote: "Union Democracy Triumphs Over Organized Crime," *Dissent Magazine*, Spring 1992.

30. Interview with Doreen Gasman, August 2015.

31. Interview with Skelton. Ultimately, Skelton had to fire her for faxing stuff to RV in Local 391.

32. Kilborn, "Carey Takes the Wheel."

33. Ibid.

34. Ibid.

35. Interview with Fred Zuckerman, April 2020.

36. Kilborn, "Carey Takes the Wheel."

37. Interview with Muehlenkamp.

38. Steven Greenhouse, "Hoist on Their Own Ad Campaigns," *New York Times*, March 17, 1996.

39. Interview with Muehlenkamp.

40. Bob Baker, "Teamster Brings New Message to L.A.," *Los Angeles Times*, March 14, 1992; Kim Clark, "Teamsters Take New Tack, Union Urges Boycott of Ryder Over Use of Non-Union Labor," *Baltimore Sun*, March 25, 1992.

41. Ibid.

42. Interview with Muehlenkamp.

43. Interview with Zuckerman.

44. Ibid.

45. Interview with David Mitchell.

46. James B. Jacobs and Kerry T. Cooperman, *Breaking the Devil's Pact: The Battle to Free the Teamsters from the Mob* (New York: New York University Press, 2011), 104.

47. Ibid.

48. Interview with Burke.

49. Jacobs and Cooperman, 114; Reuters, August 10, 1992.

50. Interview with Burke.

51. Crowe, *Collision*, 266.

52. Reuters, August 10, 1992.

53. Jacobs and Cooperman, 116.

54. Ibid.

55. Interview with Belk.

56. Jacobs and Cooperman, 117.

57. Interview with Moriarity.

58. Interview with Belk.

59. Ibid.

60. Ibid.

61. Interview with Sylvester.

62. Interview with Muehlenkamp.
63. Interview with Belk.
64. Interview with David Eckstein, July 2019.
65. Interview with Muehlenkamp.
66. Ibid.
67. Interview with Sylvester.
68. Ibid.
69. Interview with Skelton.
70. Interview with Muehlenkamp.
71. Interview with Moriarity.
72. Interview with Ken Spillane.
73. Interview with Eckstein.
74. Interview with Skelton.
75. Interview with Eckstein.
76. Interview with Rand Wilson, August 2019.
77. Interview with Moriarity.
78. An LM-30 is part of the Labor Management Reporting and Disclosure Act of 1958. It requires union officers and employees to file Form LM-30 to make public any possible conflict between their personal financial interests and their union obligations.
79. Interview with Skelton.
80. Interview with Early.
81. CSPAN, September 23, 1992.
82. In return for millions of dollars in campaign donations and Teamster loyalty, the Reagan administration quashed any investigations into Teamster corruption until after Reagan's reelection.
83. On March 3, 1993, the Teamsters union delivered 200,000 Teamster-grams to the White House and House Reform Panel for "One National Medical Plan for All." One can conclude that Ron became a supporter of Single-Payer Health Care.
84. Jacobs and Cooperman, 16.
85. *Roanoke Times*, June 5, 1993.
86. Joe Allen, *The Package King: A Rank and File History* (Self-published, 2017), 69.
87. Ibid., 68–70.
88. UPI, "Teamsters Authorize Strike against UPS," September 4, 1993.
89. Allen, *The Package King*, 67.
90. Frank Swaboda, "UPS, Teamsters Reach Accord, Avert Strike," *Washington Post*, September 28, 1993.
91. Interview with Gilberg.
92. *Los Angeles Times*, December 31, 1993.
93. *New York Times*, January 5, 1994.

94. Ibid.
95. Staff, "Teamster Members Reject Dues Increase," *Buffalo News*, March 25, 1994.
96. Interview with Kilmury.
97. Interview with Skelton.
98. Interview with Muehlenkamp.
99. Unknown source.
100. Keith Bradsher, "The Free Trade Accord: Reaction; After Vote, Labor Is Bitter but Big Business Is Elated," *New York Times*, November 18, 1993.
101. Louis Uchitelle, "NAFTA and Jobs: In a Numbers War, No One Can Count," *New York Times*, November 14, 1993.
102. News Wire Service, "Clinton Presses Free-Trade Talks but Labor Rejects Olive Branch from President on NAFTA," *Buffalo News*, November 19, 1993. Many unions refused to endorse or support pro-NAFTA politicians. Anger over NAFTA pushed union members, especially Teamsters, to sit out the 1994 midterm elections. Only 40 percent of Teamsters voted. The Democrats went on to lose Congress in a massive Republican wave.
103. CSPAN, November 10, 1993.
104. Interview with Paff
105. Ibid.
106. Interview with Skelton.
107. Paul Blustein, "Mexico Agrees to Delay Trucking in Border States," *Washington Post*, December 19, 1993.
108. Interview with Bill Hamilton, August 2019.
109. Ibid.

6. The Incumbent

1. UPI, "Teamsters end one-day walkout," February 7, 1994.
2. Interview with Aaron Belk, August 2015.
3. Peter Applebome, "Teamsters and UPS Settle after Short, Scattered Strike," *New York Times*, February 8, 1994.
4. "Teamsters end one-day walkout," February 7, 1994.
5. Interview with Belk.
6. Interview with Dennis Skelton, April 2020.
7. J. Sanchez, "Short-Lived Strike Against UPS Has Little Impact on Deliveries," *Los Angeles Times*, February 8, 1994.
8. Interview with Gene Moriarity.
9. Tom Leedham at Ron Carey's Memorial, March 2009.
10. Applebome, *New York Times*, February 8, 1994.
11. Sanchez, "Short-Lived Strike Against UPS."
12. Interview with Moriarity.

13. Interview with Bob Hauptman, April 2020.
14. Interview with Ed Burke, February 2016.
15. Leedham, Ron Carey Memorial.
16. Michael Janofsky, "Teamsters to Shut Down 4 Offices," *New York Times*, June 12, 1994.
17. Ron Carey's FBI File, U.S. Department of Justice, Federal Bureau of Investigation, Records Management Section.
18. Kim Clark, "Leadership Rift in Teamsters' Ranks," *Baltimore Sun*, April 20, 1994.
19. Catherine Manegold, "Teamsters Strike Stops Activity of Big Haulers," *New York Times*, April 6, 1994.
20. This was Ron's first step in addressing "Part-Time America." In 1997, he would focus like a laser beam on fighting it.
21. Interview with Skelton.
22. Ibid.
23. Catherine Manegold, "Teamsters Reach Accord to End Strike," *New York Times,* April 29, 1994.
24. Ibid.; AP, "Teamsters OK New Trucking Pact," *Los Angeles Times*, June 6, 1994.
25. Ken Crowe, interview with Ron Carey, September 1991.
26. Gene Giacumbo, "Ousted From Teamsters, Will Fight Charges," *Journal of Commerce*, November 19, 1995.
27. Interview with Burke; *Journal of Commerce*, July 13, 1995.
28. Selwyn Raab, "Obstacles to Cleanup; Mob Hinders, Teamster Trustee Says," *New York Times*, June 29, 1993.
29. IRB Report, July 1994, 39. Kenneth Crowe Papers, Tamiment Library and Robert F. Wagner Labor Archives at NYU.
30. Jeff Gerth, "Despite Change, Reform Is Slow in the Teamsters," *New York Times*, June 28, 1993; interview with Rick Gilberg.
31. Interview with Burke.
32. Gerth, June 28, 1993.
33. Interview with Susan Jennick, April 2016.
34. Ibid.; Interview with Michael Moroney, April 2020.
35. 1994 IRB Report; Selwyn Raab, "Panel Clears Top Teamster of Mob Link," *New York Times*, July 12, 1994.
36. *U.S. vs International Brotherhood of Teamsters*, No 88 CIV. 4486 (DNE).
37. Selwyn Raab, "Chief of Teamsters Union Ousts a Leader of a Powerful Local," *New York Times*, January 12, 1994.
38. AP, "Corruption Is Cited in Suit on Dismissals," *New York Times*, December 17, 1995.
39. Interview with Jennick; Raab, *New York Times*, July 12, 1994.

40. Interview with Jennick.

41. William Serrin, "Hacks and Hatchet Jobs: Misled by a disinformation campaign, the press is smearing Teamster President Ron Carey," *In These Times*, February 19, 1996.

42. Ibid.

43. Ibid; Joe Calderone, "Union Big Had Ties to $2 Million in UPS Stock," *Newsday*, August 1, 1993.

44. Frank Swaboda, "Teamsters Strike Talks Bog Down," *Washington Post*, April 28, 1994.

45. Interview with Sandra Carey, July 2016.

46. Swaboda, "Teamsters Strike Talks Bog Down,"

47. Ibid.

48. Serrin, "Hacks and Hatchet Jobs."

49. "Old Style Smear of Carey," *Extra!*, July/August 1994.

50. 1994 IBT Report.

51. Ibid.

52. Interview with Ken Crowe.

53. 1994 IBT Report. The report dismissed accusations that Ron tried to help the Lucchese crime family by appointing William Genoese as Trustee of Local 295 in 1992. The report debunked the allegation that Ron knowingly associated with William Cardinale, a Trustee of Local 804, who was a cousin of a Colombo crime family member and that Ron had appointed Cardinale. Cardinale was actually elected in 1973 by a vote of the members. The Report explained that Ron had not known that a Local 804 shop steward at Macy's, John Conte, was a Lucchese crime family associate when he testified as a character witness for him. The report debunked the allegation that Ron had a relationship with Louis Sunshine, a mob associate and former BA of Local 804 in the 1950s and early 1960s. There was no evidence of any association. (Selwyn Raab, "Panel Clears Top Teamster of Mob Link.")As a matter of fact, Sunshine visited Local 804 once while Ron was in charge and it was to speak to John Long. When Ron found out, he told him to leave, as per Ron's FBI File. The investigators probed Ron's finances from the 1970s through 1994 and found he was able to afford those listed investments.

54. 1994 IRB Report. For a time, Ron and his wife were separated or "estranged."

55. Ron Scherer, "Cleared Teamsters' Head Continues Union Reform," *Christian Science Monitor*, July 14, 1994.

56. Ron Scherer, "A Look Under the Hood," *Christian Science Monitor*, May 24, 1996.

57. Peter Kendall and John O'Brien, "Two Labor Kingpins Toppled," *Chicago Tribune*, August 9, 1996.

58. *Javits Center: Q & A;* "4 Years in the Face of Corruption," *New York Times,* March 6/12, 1995.

59. Interview with Pete Mastrandrea, January 2020.

60. Interview with Moriarity.

61. Ibid.

62. Ibid.

63. AP, "Union Suspends Local President with Alleged Mob Ties," August 22, 1994.

64. Interview with Burke.

65. By 1998, Hoekstra and his committee spent over $1 million investigating Ron Carey.

66. Dan Morgan, "Pressure on NLRB Turns Into a Doubled Budget Cut," *Washington Post,* July 20, 1995.

67. Joe Allen, *The Package King: A Rank and File History* (Self-published, 2017), 109.

68. James Tyson, "Teamsters Union Shows Its Clout in Auto Strike," *Christian Science Monitor,* October 11, 1995.

69. Michael McKesson, "Teamsters Strike Hits Car Hauler," *Washington Post,* September 9, 1995.

70. Interview with Fred Zuckerman, April 2020.

71. Ibid.

72. Tim Shorrock, "Business Groups to Fight Campaigns by Unions," *Journal of Commerce,* September 21, 1995.

73. Interview with Rand Wilson, August 2019.

74. Interview with Ken Paff, June 2015.

75. Sam Theodus who ran with Ron in 1991, originally threw his hat in the ring to challenge Ron, but instead joined forces with Hoffa, Jr.

76. Interview with Bob Muehlenkamp.

77. Interview with Paff.

78. Sharon Walsh, *Teamster Race Became a Dealmaker's Undoing,*

79. Interview with David Eckstein, December 2019.

80. Internal IBT Study, "James Hoffa Jr. Study of Connections to Corruption," 1996, Kennth Crowe Papers, Tamiment Library and Robert F. Wagner Archives at NYU.

81. Ibid.

82. Steven Greenhouse, "Once Again the Hoffa Name Rouses the Teamsters Union," *New York Times,* November 17, 1996.

83. Shelly Donald Coolidge, "Jimmy Hoffa 'Jr' Campaigns to Follow in Dad's Footsteps," *Christian Science Monitor,* March 18, 1996.

84. Interview with Eckstein.

85. Interviews with Muehlenkamp, Burke, and Eckstein.

86. Interview with Belk.

87. Frank Swaboda, "Hoffa Forces Disrupt Teamsters Convention," *Washington Post*, July 16, 1996.
88. James B. Jacobs and Kerry T. Cooperman, *Breaking the Devil's Pact: The Battle to Free the Teamsters from the Mob* (New York: New York University Press, 2011), 129.
89. Swaboda, "Hoffa Forces Disrupt Teamsters Convention."
90. Ibid.
91. Ibid.
92. Jacobs and Cooperman, *Breaking the Devil's Pact*, 130.
93. Frank Swaboda, "Democracy Takes Hold at the Teamsters Convention," *Washington Post*, July 20, 1996.
94. F.C. Duke Zeller, *Devil's Pact: Inside the World of the Teamsters Union* (New Jersey: Birch Lane Press, 1996), 356.
95. Glenn Burkins, "Teamsters' Chief Carey Loses Straw Poll of Delegates to Rival Candidate Hoffa," *Wall Street Journal*, July 19, 1996.
96. Zeller, *Devil's Pact*, 356.
97. Jacobs and Cooperman, *Breaking the Devil's Pact*, 130.
98. Interview with Moriarity.
99. Jacobs and Cooperman, *Breaking the Devil's Pact*, 132.
100. Steven Greenhouse, "Teamster Counterrevolution: Why It Nearly Won Election," *New York Times*, December 22, 1996.

7. The UPS Strike

1. Unknown source.
2. Rand Wilson and Matt Witt, "The Teamsters' UPS Strike of 1997: Building a New Labor Movement," *Labor Studies Journal*, March 1, 1999, 61.
3. Interview with Rand Wilson, August 2019.
4. Ibid.
5. Steven Greenhouse, "Yearslong Effort Key to Success for Teamsters' Fight for Good Jobs," *New York Times*, August 25, 1997.
6. Interview with Wilson.
7. Interview with David Eckstein, July 2019.
8. Ibid.
9. Ibid.
10. Interview with Wilson.
11. Interview with Eckstein.
12. Interview with Wilson.
13. Interview with Aaron Belk, August 2015.
14. Interview with Rick Gilberg, May 2014
15. Interview with Ed Burke, February 2016.
16. Interview with Eckstein.

17. Ibid.
18. Ibid.
19. David Levin, "The 1997 UPS Strike: Beating Big Business and Business Unionism," *Labor Notes*, August 15, 2017.
20. Bloomberg News, "UPS Pilots Vote to Authorize Strike," *New York Times*, May 1997.
21. John Russo and Andy Banks, "How Teamsters Took the UPS Strike Overseas," *Working USA*, January/February 1999, 76.
22. Interview with Eckstein; Joe Allen, *The Package King: A Rank-and-File History of UPS* (Chicago: Haymarket Books, 2020), 90.
23. Interview with Wilson.
24. Ron Carey letter, *Convoy Dispatch*, July/August 1997.
25. Teamsters' UPS Update, May 30, 1997.
26. Teamsters' Booklet, "Half a Job Is Not Enough," 1997.
27. Tribune News Service, "UPS Workers Asked to Authorize Strike," *Chicago Tribune*, June 28, 1997.
28. "One of the Best Organized Centers in the U S," *Convoy Dispatch 161*, July/August 1997.
29. Allen, *The Package King*, 92.
30. Wilson and Witt, "The Teamsters' UPS Strike of 1997," 60.
31. Ibid., 61.
32. Interview with Eckstein.
33. Steven Greenhouse, "Pension Plan Puts Teamsters' Chief in Tight Spot," *New York Times*, August 14, 1997.
34. Interview with John Calhoun Wells, August 2020.
35. Ibid.
36. Judith Evans, "UPS, Union Fail to Agree on Contract," *Washington Post*, August 1, 1997.
37. Staff, "Teamsters Set New UPS Strike Deadline," *LA Times*, August 3, 1997.
38. UPI, "Teamsters set to resume talks," August 3, 1997.
39. Interview with Wilson.
40. Steven Greenhouse, "UPS Struck by Teamsters as Talks Fail," *New York Times*, August 4, 1997.
41. Mark Chellgren, "UPS Pilots Stage Military Operation to Keep Up with Strike," AP, August 6, 1997.
42. Interview with Moriarity.
43. "Tempers Flare on UPS picket lines," CNN, August 5, 1997.
44. Steven Greenhouse, "For the Teamsters' Leader, UPS Is an Ancient Enemy," *New York Times*, August 7, 1997.
45. Steven Greenhouse, "Deeper Shade of Blue Collar," *New York Times*, August 10, 1997.

46. Unknown source (Harley Shaiken and he confirmed the quote).
47. Gallup Poll, August 23, 1997.
48. Steven Greenhouse, "Unions Plan to Loan Teamsters; UPS Warns of Layoffs," *New York Times*, August 13, 1997.
49. Greenhouse, "For the Teamsters' Leader."
50. Ibid.
51. David Bacon, "The UPS Strike: Unions Win When They Take the Offensive," *In These Times*, August 24, 1997.
52. Greenhouse, "For the Teamsters' Leader.".
53. NLRB, 1947 Taft-Hartley Substantive Provisions.
54. National Archives, Harry S. Truman Presidential Library & Museum, Independence, MO.
55. James Bennett, "American Airline Pilots Strike but Clinton Orders Them Back," *New York Times*, February 15, 1997.
56. The Gallup Poll: Public Opinion 1997.
57. Allen, *The Package King*, 95.
58. Interview with Eckstein.
59. "Labor Secretary Urges UPS, Union to Resume Talks," CNN, August 11, 1997.
60. Interview with Alexis Herman, September 2020
61. Staff, "Embattled Union Leader Takes a Risk," *Tampa Bay Times*, August 6, 1997.
62. "UPS, Teamsters to Resume Talks," CNN, August 6, 1997.
63. Deepa Kumar, *Outside the Box: Corporate Media, Globalization, and the UPS Strike* (Champaign: University of Illinois Press, 2007), 80.
64. Ibid.
65. Greenhouse, " For the Teamsters' Leader."
66. David Levin, *Labor Notes*, August 1997.
67. Bloomberg News, "UPS, Union Not Budging as Talks Resume," August 8, 1997.
68. Steven Greenhouse, "UPS and Union Break Off Negotiations," *New York Times*, August 10, 1997.
69. Interview with Eckstein.
70. Interview with Herman.
71. Ibid.
72. "Labor Secretary to Meet with Both Sides in UPS Strike," CNN, August 11, 1997.
73. Ibid.
74. Kumar, *Outside the Box*, 192.
75. Ron Carey Press Conference, CSPAN, August 6, 1997.
76. Steven Greenhouse, "Strike Slows UPS to a Standstill; No Talks in Progress," *New York Times*, August 6, 1997.

77. Greenhouse, "For the Teamsters' Leader."
78. "Labor Secretary to Meet with Both Sies in UPS Strike," CNN, August 11, 1997.
79. Interview with Herman.
80. Interview with John Calhoun Wells, August 2020.
81. Steven Greenhouse, "Labor Unions Plan a Teamster Loan to Sustain Strike," *New York Times,* August 13, 1997.
82. "UPS Strike Drags On," CNN, August 12, 1997.
83. Interview with Herman.
84. Ibid.; interview with Wells.
85. "UPS, Teamsters Try to Break Deadlock," CNN, August 14, 1997.
86. Steven Greenhouse, "Clinton Pressing 2 Sides to Settle the UPS Strike," *New York Times*, August 18, 1997.
87. Interview with Wells.
88. Steven Greenhouse, "Teamsters and UPS Agree on a 5-Year Contract to End Strike after 15 Days," *New York Times*, August 19, 1997.
89. Steven Greenhouse, "Long Hours Fail to Budge UPS Talks, Carey Says," *New York Times,* August 16, 1997.
90. NBC, *Meet the Press,* August 18, 1997.
91. Greenhouse, "Clinton Pressing 2 Sides."
92. Greenhouse, August 19, 1997.
93. Ibid.; Peter Behr and Beth Berselli, *UPS,* "Teamsters Reach Tentative Contract Accord," *Washington Post*, August 19, 1997.
94. Greenhouse, "Teamsters and UPS Agree."
95. Interview with Eckstein.
96. "Teamsters trickle back to their UPS jobs," CNN, August 20, 1997.
97. Ibid.
98. Wilson and Witt, "The Teamsters' UPS Strike of 1997."
99. Steven Greenhouse, "A Victory for Labor, but How Far Will It Go?," *New York Times,* August 20, 1997.
100. David Bacon, "The UPS Strike: Unions Win When They Take the Offensive," *In These Times*, August 24, 1997.
101. Dan La Botz, "The Fight at UPS: The Teamsters Victory and the Future of the 'New Labor Movement,' " *Solidarity*, March 1998.
102. Stuart Silverstein and Robert Rosenblatt, "Carey Loves Trouble, with a Capital 'T' for Teamsters," *Los Angeles Times*, August 16, 1997.
103. "A Wake-Up Call for Business," *Businessweek*, August/September 1997.
104. Kumar, *Outside the Box*, 192.
105. Ibid.
106. Interview with Wells.
107. Interview with Herman.

8. The Scandal

1. Barbara Zack Quindell, *The Election Officer's Report*, August 21, 1997.
2. Ibid.
3. Frank Swaboda, "Hoffa Demands Special Prosecutor in Teamster Case," *Washington Post*, August 25, 1997; *Meet the Press*, NBC, August 25, 1997.
4. Interview with Steve Early, April 2021.
5. Sharon Walsh, "Teamster Race Became a Dealmaker's Undoing," *Washington Post*, October 22, 1997.
6. Jere Nash was described as a folksy Mississippian. He once headed Mississippi Common Cause and managed the campaign of Ken Harper who ran against Trent Lott for a Senate seat.
7. Interview with Ken Paff, June 2015.
8. Interview with Bob Muehlenkamp, March 2022.
9. Walsh, "Teamster Race Became a Dealmaker's Undoing."
10. Steve Greenhouse, "Behind Turmoil For Teamsters, Rush for Cash," *New York Times*, September 21, 1997.
11. Ibid.; Brian Duffy and Jeff Glasser, "Justice Department Possible DNC, Union Deal," *Washington Post*, August 23, 1997.
12. Interview with Michael Ansara, July 2021.
13. Interview with Gene Moriarity, February 2014.
14. Ibid.
15. Interview with Ansara; Steve Greenhouse, "Behind Turmoil for Teamsters, Rush for Cash," *New York Times*, August 21, 1997.
16. Interview with Bill Hamilton, August 2019.
17. Ibid.
18. Conboy Report, November 1998.
19. Interview with Hamilton.
20. Interview with Muehlenkamp.
21. Interview with David Eckstein, Decembeer 2019.
22. A memo from Bill Hamilton to Ron on October 17, 1996, states that Project Vote, a progressive group that the IBT funded in order to increase voter participation in elections by minority voters, was "working hard in North Carolina where Harry Gantt is running very hard to defeat Senator Jesse Helms.... I can't think of a more important goal than to turn out a huge vote that helps defeat Helms." Another memo from Hamilton to Ron on October 16 states that an $85,000 contribution to the National Council of Senior Citizens would help get out the vote "in places like Florida, where we are trying to pick up a couple of congressional districts." Jeff Glasser, "Justice Department Probing Possible DNC, Union Deal," *Washington Post*, August 23, 1997.

23. Interviews with Aaron Belk, Bob Hauptman, Bill Hamilton, David Eckstein, and Doreen Gasman, August 2015.

24. Marilyn Vogt-Downey, "The Trials of Ron Carey, Teamster Politics and Its Meaning," *Labor Standard*, October 2001.

25. Interview with Hamilton.

26. Hamilton couldn't justify the amount, so he turned it down. Davis then went to Richard Trumka at the AFL-CIO for the needed $100,000. Trumka too denied Davis but offered that if the IBT gave the $150,000 to the AFL-CIO, Trumka would be able to send Citizens Action the funds. Nash then got Hamilton to agree to that request. Citizens Action then completed the swap with another $100,000 to Ron's campaign. The contributions to the National Council of Senior Citizens were used to turn out retired union members, and the Project Vote donation was used to turn out minority voters in North Carolina. Both were believed to be political donations for the congressional and presidential elections.

27. Ken Crowe, "The Vindication of Ron Carey," *Nation Builder*, October 24, 2001, 1.

28. Interview with Muehlenkamp.

29. Interview with Hauptman, April 2020.

30. Interview with Muehlenkamp. Bob's testimony at Ron's trial: "It was hard to get Ron's attention by the Fall of 1996. Ron had very little energy. He was emotionally, physically, and intellectually weakened by serving five years in that office....went from being the best questioner to an executive who wanted his trusted underlings to just do their jobs with as little input as possible from him.

31. Interview with Eckstein.

32. "Hoffa Cries Foul in Teamsters Vote Count," CNN, December 19, 1996.

33. Conboy Report, November 1998.

34. Mark Maremont, "Hoffa Operatives Used 'Moles,' False Identity in Teamster Probe," *Wall Street Journal*, December 23, 1997.

35. *US v. IBT*, 957 F. Supp 55 (1997).

36. Steve Greenhouse, "Teamster Voting That Chose Carey Declared Invalid," *New York Times*, August 23, 1997.

37. "FBI Investigating $95k Contribution to Carey Campaign," AP, March 9, 1997.

38. IRB Hearing, 1998.

39. Crowe, "Vindication," 18.

40. Ibid.

41. Steve Greenhouse, "Teamsters' Head Returns More Disputed Campaign Donations," *New York Times*, March 21, 1997.

42. Ibid.; Frank Swaboda and Brian Duffy, "Federal Grand Jury Investigating

Teamsters President," *Washington Post*, April 2, 1997. Charny resigned from CWS earlier in March.

43. An EO spokesperson said the inauguration will be allowed to go on. However, she noted that she had the authority to order a new election even after Carey is inaugurated. Steven Greenhouse, "Asserting Illegal Donations, Hoffa Challenges Balloting," *New York Times*, March 20, 1997.

44. Staff, "Carey Takes Oath as President of Teamsters Union," *Buffalo News*, March 23, 1997.

45. Steven Greenhouse, "US Investigates Campaign Gift to Teamster Chief," *New York Times*, March 27, 1997.

46. Interview with Hauptman.

47. Interview with Hamilton.

48. Interview with Ansara, July 2022; Steven Greenhouse, "Teamster Vote Under a Cloud in a Fraud Case," *New York Times*, June 7, 1997.

49. As Ansara related to me: "it was a classic kickback scheme. Martin was shaking down contractors and laundering money through them. My wife had nothing really to do with it. She trusted me and she did as I asked her." Ansara was also quite apologetic for his actions, which he described as "inexcusable." He went on: "I don't think Martin was being honest with anyone. But it was my obligation to understand what we were doing, and I take full responsibility for it. Employers couldn't donate and Martin said it was 'a minor technicality, can you help me get around that' and I inexcusably said yes. And used my wife." Also, Davis owned stock and was on the board of the Share Group. Nash worked for the Carey campaign and the November Group of which the Carey campaign was a client.

50. Greenhouse, "Teamster Vote Under a Cloud in a Fraud Case."

51. Interview with Hamilton.

52. Ibid. Hamilton recalls: "I was being dragged in front of the grand jury and my lawyer, Bob Gage, wanted me to be prepared to invoke the Fifth if necessary, which I couldn't do under the consent decree; it violated my Fifth Amendment but no one cared about that. So, I resigned because I really didn't have much choice and I wrote an indignant letter to Carey. I decided to use it as a way to vent my frustration with the whole fucking process, so I attacked Mary Jo White. I gave it to a friend of mine at the AP."

53. Kevin Galvin, "Teamster Officer Quits, Alleges Document Leaked in US Probe," *Washington Post*, July 31, 1997; Steven Greenhouse, "Teamsters' Chief Lobbyist Quits, Calling US Inquiry a 'Circus,'" *New York Times*, July 31, 1997.

54. Interview with Hamilton.

55. Ibid.
56. Elections Officer's Report, 1–2; Steven Greenhouse, "Teamsters Voting That Chose Carey Declared Invalid," *New York Times*, August 23, 1997.
57. Election Officer's Report, 114.
58. *Meet the Press,* NBC, August 31, 1997.
59. Interview with Barbara Zack Quindel, July 2019.
60. Frank Swaboda, "UPS Accuses Federal Officer of Favoring Union," *Washington Post*, September 4, 1997.
61. "Hoekstra had a theory that we rigged the accounting for the pension to make it look good for Ron," recalled Bob Hauptman. Bob was called to testify before the Hoekstra subcommittee. "I had been a staffer who had done all the work for that. It was the only time someone told me to 'give them a long answer.' It's when we changed the family plan to give rank-and-filers more credit. It used to be where local officers got more, so we tried to level that out and get more equality. Hoekstra says we 'cooked the books.' I said, 'No, we made the pension plan much more fair and we're following the accounting rules.'"
62. Jacobs and Cooperman, *Breaking the Devil's Pact: The Battle to Free the Teamsters from the Mob* (New York: New York University Press, 2011), 137; Glenn R Simpson, "Charges of Wrongdoing to Be Examined by Panel," *Wall Street Journal*, August 26, 1997.
63. Jacobs and Cooperman, *Breaking the Devil's Pact*, 135; Stephan Labaton, "Teamsters Election Monitor Is Reported Planning to Quit," *New York Times*, August 30, 1997.
64. Jacobs and Cooperman, *Breaking the Devil's Pact*, 135.
65. Steven Greenhouse, "3 Teamster Aides Make Guilty Pleas and Hint at Plot," *New York Times*, September 19, 1997. "They caught Nash and they twisted his nuts," commented Weingarten. Interview with Reid Weingarten, April 2020. He pledged to cooperate fully with the prosecutors. If he provided "substantial assistance" in the prosecution, the prosecutors would write a 5K1 letter to the judge who was presiding over Nash's case and recommend leniency.
66. Greenhouse, "3 Teamster Aides."
67. Steven Greenhouse, "Teamsters Chief Contends Aides Betrayed Him," *New York Times*, September 24, 1997.
68. "Judge Appoints New Overseer," *New York Times*, September 30, 1997.
69. Bill Mc Allister, "DiGenova's Triple," *Washington Post*, November 13, 1997.
70. Allen, *The Package King*, 113.
71. Interview with Paff; Joe Allen, "The Persecution and Vindication of Ron Carey," *Jacobin*, October 31, 2017.
72. Years later, Hoekstra would comment that "I am convinced that if this

subcommittee had not acted, Ron Carey would still be president of the Teamsters." He also referred to the Carey years as "the bad ol days." Hoekstra's "star witness" was Gregory Mellenholz, who was fired by the Teamsters for sending copies of financial records to Hoffa lawyers.

73. Allen, *The Package King*, 113.
74. CSPAN, *National Press Club Newsmaker Luncheon With Teamsters President Ron Carey*, October 20, 1997.
75. Ibid.
76. Ibid.
77. Ibid.
78. Ibid.
79. This might be a reason why Ron decided to take a leave of absence. He wanted others to have the ability to declare before the deadline.
80. Conboy Report; Thomas Edsall, Sharon Walsh, and Frank Swaboda, "Teamster Election Scandal: Liberal Activism Gone Awry," *Washington Post*, October 6, 1997.
81. *Decision of Kenneth Conboy to Disqualify IBT President Ron Carey*, November 17, 1997, 5.
82. Ibid., 32; Jacobs and Cooperman, *Breaking the Devil's Pact*, 136.
83. *Decision of Kenneth Conboy to Disqualify IBT President Ron Carey*, 32; Conboy was a corporate lawyer who once represented the Carlysle Group and was on the board of directors of Bristol, Myers, Squib and other conglomerates such as International Paper, Koch Industries, Getty, Big Tobacco, and many banks.
84. Frank Swaboda, "Teamsters' Carey Disqualified From Running in New Election," *Washington Post*, November 18, 1997.
85. The Conboy Report does not state that there was any direct testimony that Ron had any knowledge or role in the scheme. He was basically disqualified for approving contributions to Citizens Action that were perfectly legal. Again, it is legal and ethical to believe that a legal contribution can produce a legal side benefit.
86. Allen, "The Persecution and Vindication of Ron Carey."
87. Interview with Moriarity. Susan Davis had a baby late in the campaign. Her child had special needs so Susan was basically absent the last few months of the campaign. The junior lawyer of her firm was, in effect, in charge of the campaign and the vetting of the donors to TCFU.
88. UPI, "Teamsters' Carey Takes Leave of Absence," November 25, 1997. He took a leave from Local 804 as well.
89. Interview with Belk.
90. Interview with Eckstein. .
91. Interview with Sylvester.
92. *US v. IBT*, 22 F. Supplemental 2nd 135 (SDNY 1998).

93. UPI, "Teamsters' Carey Takes Leave of absence."

94. Crowe, "Vindication," 8.

95. Interview with Muehlenkamp.

96. Dan LaBotz, "Rank and File Teamsters Fight for Labor's Future," *Dollars and Sense*, September/October 1998.

97. Interview with Gasman.

98. Interview with Moriarity.

99. Interview with Paff.

100. Frank Swaboda and Sharon Walsh, "Overseer Named for Rerun of Teamsters' Vote," *Washington Post*, December 3, 1997.

101. Ibid.

102. Jacobs and Cooperman, *Breaking the Devil's Pact*, 140.

103. Bill Leumer, "Teamster Head Ron Carey Repudiates Charges at DC Hearing," *Workers Action*, January 29, 1998.

104. Steven Greenhouse, "Carey Denies Any Knowledge of Teamsters Fund Diversion," *New York Times*, January 22, 1998.

105. Ibid.

106. David Corn, "The Prosecution and Persecution of Ron Carey," *The Nation*, March 19, 1998.

107. Steven Greenhouse, "Teamsters Leader Presents His Case, but Enigma Remains," *New York Times*, January 25, 1998.

108. Ibid.

109. Steven Greenhouse, "Crucial Call Is Disclosed in Teamster Case," *New York Times*, March 12, 1998.

110. Conboy Report, 22.

111. Greenhouse, "Teamsters Leader Presents His Case, but Enigma Remains.".

112. Nash was working for the November Group for $8,000 per month from April through June and for $18,000 per month from August through November. Vogt-Downey, "The Trials of Ron Carey."

113. Greenhouse, "Teamsters Leader Presents His Case, but Enigma Remains."

114. Greenhouse, "Crucial Call Is Disclosed in Teamster Case"; IRB Report, July 27, 1998; Corn, "The Prosecution and Persecution of Ron Carey."

115. Greenhouse, "Crucial Call Is Disclosed in Teamster Case."

116. Crowe, "Vindication," 9.

117. Greenhouse, "Crucial Call Is Disclosed in Teamster Case."

118. Corn, "The Prosecution and Persecution of Ron Carey."

119. Ibid.

120. Interview with Moriarity.

121. Steven Greenhouse, "Hoffa Cleared to Run in Teamsters Election," *New York Times*, May 3, 1998.

122. Steven Greenhouse, "Judge Allows Hoffa to Stay in Union Race," *New York Times*, June 23, 1998.
123. Interview with Hamilton.
124. Steven Greenhouse, "Board Expels Ron Carey from Teamsters for Life," *New York Times*, July 28, 1998.
125. IRB Report, July 27, 1998; Crowe, "Vindication," 11.
126. Ibid.
127. Greenhouse, "Board Expels Ron Carey from Teamsters for Life."
128. Interview with Sylvester.
129. Greenhouse, "Board Expels Ron Carey from Teamsters for Life."
130. Steven Ginsberg, "Teamsters Chief Carey Expelled from Union," *Washington Post*, July 28, 1998.
131. Crowe, "Vindication," 2.
132. Interview with Gasman.
133. Davis was working for Terry McAuliffe at the same time he was working to get Ron reelected.
134. Michael Ansara: "One of my regrets is what it all did to reform of the Teamsters, which I really supported and winded up harming badly. But we were inexcusably wrong and doing what Davis asked us to do. It was totally and inexcusably wrong, and I wish I had never done it. But I was not told exactly what we were doing—being involved in a classic kickback scheme. Martin was shaking down contractors and laundering money through me. My wife really had nothing to do with it; she trusted me; she did as I asked her." Interview with Ansara.
135. Charny failed to confirm all of the donors he was tasked to vet to see if they were non-Teamsters and non-employers. He was counsel to the TCFU. Charny spoke with twelve potential contributors, or someone on their behalf, rejecting five and accepting seven contributors. His failure to vet those donors properly allowed the Hoffa people to find a way to overturn the election. Charny's personal trouble was that he went beyond what a lawyer should be doing. It doesn't seem he was aware of the nefarious scheme going on. However, he submitted a perjurious affidavit to the court-appointed EO. In October 1998, he pleaded guilty to one count of conspiracy to defraud the United States by making false statements. Charny was ultimately sentenced to time served and paid a small fine for his "stupid" misconduct. In re: Nathaniel K Charny, Supreme Court, Appellate Division, First Department, New York.
136. Interview with Hauptman.
137. Interview with Moriarity.
138. Interview with Hamilton.
139. Ibid.
140. Interview with Muehlenkamp.

141. Interview with Hauptman.
142. Interview with Sylvester.
143. Interview with Hamilton.
144. Ibid.
145. Interview with Belk.
146. Ibid.
147. Hamilton testified that he discussed the scheme with Judy Scott who then told Tom Sever that the union's board did not need to review the large contributions. Sever allowed the check to be issued on the condition that Scott produce a legal memorandum supporting her view. She did not produce that memo until three months after the contribution was made, in January 1997. Scott left the Teamsters in February 1997.
148. Interview with Belk.
149. Interview with Hauptman.
150. Interview with Eckstein.
151. Interview with Muehlenkamp.
152. Interview with Moriarity.
153. Interview with Sylvester.
154. Hauptman angrily went on to say that besides perjuring himself in the vetting of contributors, Charny "was totally knowledgeable about the swap and helped implement it! He claimed to have investigated, vetted things he never vetted because he knew the answer. Of course, he knew what he was doing was wrong. He got the checks as Martin Davis and Ansara testified. He was the go-between who communicated to both sides of the quid pro quo as to what checks had come in and which checks went out. He was the one communicating with people saying, 'We got the checks from the one side, it's OK to let the other checks go.'" Interview with Hauptman.
155. Ibid.
156. Interview with Early.
157. Interview with Moriarity.
158. Crowe, "Vindication," 4.
159. Lacey, a Republican, was appointed by President George H. W. Bush's attorney general, Bill Barr, to be an Independent Counsel who eventually cleared Bush of bungling an investigation into loans by an Atlanta branch of the Banca Nazionale del Lavoro in order to help arm Saddam Hussein during the Iraq-Iran War in the 1980s.
160. Interview with Hauptman.
161. Interview with Weingarten.
162. Interview with Hauptman.
163. Interview with Eckstein.
164. Stemming from these Star Chamber-like hearings, Mary Jo White took

Ron to trial over statements she considered lies. Ron won. They lost. They failed.

165. Interview with Moriarity.

166. Interview with Sylvester.

167. Crowe, "Vindication," 6.

168. Jacobs and Cooperman, *Breaking the Devil's Pact,* 147.

169. Steven Greenhouse, "A Third Hoffa Vice President Faces Charges," *New York Times,* December 18, 1998; Steven Greenhouse, "A Teamsters Leader Known for Honesty May Be Expelled Over Finance Reports," *New York Times,* January 10, 1999.

170. Steven Greenhouse, "New Candidate Joins Race to Lead Teamsters," *New York Times,* May 23, 1998.

171. Steven Greenhouse, "Hoffa Will Lead Teamsters after Chief Rival Concedes," *New York Times,* December 6, 1998.

172. For a brief synopsis of what a 5k1 letter is, see https://fastlawpc.com.

173. Crowe, "Vindication," 13.

9. The Trial

1.   Interview with Sandra Carey, July 2016.

2.   Ann Coulter, "Mary Jo White-Wash," *Jewish World Review,* March 1, 2001.

3.   Steven Greenhouse, "Ex-President of Teamsters Is Charged with Lying," *New York Times,* January 26, 2001.

4.   Interview with Reid Weingarten, April 2020.

5.   Ibid.

6.   Interview with Bob Hauptman,

7.   The statute of limitations was to run out by the end of 2001. It makes you wonder what might have happened if Al Gore had been elected president.

8.   Greenhouse, "Ex-President of Teamsters Is Charged with Lying."

9.   United States Code 1001.

10. United States Code 1623; Jacobs and Cooperman, *Breaking The Devil's Pact,* 270–71.

11. Robert Gearty, "Ex-Teamsters Boss Goes to Trial," New York *Daily News,* January 26, 2001.

12. Interview with Weingarten.

13. Interview with Ed Burke, February 2016.

14. Interview with Weingarten.

15. Greenhouse, "Ex-President of Teamsters Is Charged with Lying."

16. Devlin Barrett, "Ex-Teamster Boss Arraigned on Perjury Rap," *New York Post,* February 2, 2001; CNN, "Ex-Teamsters Boss Pleads 'Not Guilty,'" February 1, 2001.

17. Ken Crowe, "The Vindication of Ron Carey," *Nation Builder*, October 24, 2001, 1; Steven Greenhouse, "Ex-Teamster President Is Tried In a Case of Re-Election Fraud," *New York Times*, August 28, 2001.
18. Greenhouse, "Ex-Teamster President Is Tried."
19. Interview with Tim Sylvester, November 2019.
20. Ibid.
21. Interview with Hauptman, April 2020.
22. Trial Transcript, 40. *United States v. Ron Carey*, U.S. District Court building, 500 Pearl St., New York, NY 10007.
23. Crowe, "Vindication," 2.
24. Trial Transcript, 41.
25. Interview with Weingarten.
26. 5k1 Letter: see Fastlawpc.com.
27. Interview with Hauptman.
28. Crowe, "Vindication," 12.
29. Interview with Hauptman.
30. Crowe, "Vindication," 12.
31. Interview with Hauptman.
32. Crowe, "Vindication," 10.
33. Interview with Hauptman.
34. Crowe, "Vindication," 12–13.
35. Ibid., 4.
36. Trial Transcript, 63.
37. Interview with Hauptman.
38. Trial Transcript, Hulkower, 40.
39. Interview with Hauptman.
40. Crowe, "Vindication," 16.
41. Interview with Sylvester.
42. Trial Transcript, 64.
43. Ibid.
44. Crowe, "Vindication," 15.
45. Trial Transcript, 2241.
46. Interview with Hauptman.
47. Interview with Weingarten.
48. Interview with Ken Crowe, September 2014.
49. Crowe, "Vindication," 17.
50. Trial Transcript, 51.
51. Crowe, "Vindication," 24.
52. Ibid., 19; Interview with Hauptman.
53. Interview with Sylvester.
54. Crowe, "Vindication," 24.
55. Ibid., 22.

56. Interview with Bill Hamilton, August 2019.
57. Interview with Weingarten.
58. Crowe, "Vindication," 22.
59. Ibid., 23; Interview with Muehlenkamp, March 2022.
60. Trial Transcript, 45.
61. Crowe, "Vindication," 21–22.
62. Interview with Weingarten.
63. Interview with Hauptman.
64. Marilyn Vogt-Downey, "The Trials of Ron Carey," *Labor Standard*, October 26, 2001, 13.
65. Staff, "Former Teamsters Chief Acquitted," *Washington Post*, October 13, 2001.
66. Crowe, "Vindication," 2.
67. Ibid., 26.
68. Steven Greenhouse, "Former Teamsters President Is Cleared of Lying Charges," *New York Times*, October 13, 2001; "Former Teamster Chief Acquitted," *Washington Post*, October 13, 2001.
69. Greenhouse, "Former Teamsters President Is Cleared of Lying Charges."
70. Ibid.; Phil Hirschkorn, "Former Teamster Boss Carey Acquitted," CNN, October 12, 2001.

10. Legacy

1. The IRB prohibited IBT members from having any contact with Ron Carey. Kenneth Crowe, "The Vindication of Ron Carey," *Nation Builder*, October 24, 2001, 25.
2. Interview with Tim Sylvester, November 2019.
3. Interview with Bruce Carey, July 2018.
4. Interview with Pat Pagnanella, June 2014.
5. Interview with Bruce Carey.
6. Interview with Sandra Carey, July 2016.
7. Interview with Doreen Gasman, August 2015.
8. Interview with Gene Moriarity, February 2014.
9. Ibid.
10. Interview with Sylvester.
11. Meredith Kolodner, "Carey Looks Back: Ex-Teamster Head Still Driving Hard," *The Chief*, May 16, 2007.
12. "Ten Years Since the UPS Strike, Part 1," http://youtube/Q_-upPC7E7k,
13. Ibid.
14. Mark Brenner, "Labor Notes Interviews Former Teamsters General President Ron Carey on the UPS Contract," *Labor Notes*, October 31, 2007.

15. Ibid.
16. Ibid.
17. Interview with Sandra Carey.
18. Interview with Bruce Carey.
19. Interview with Sandra Carey.
20. Interview with Bruce Carey.
21. Interview with Sylvester.
22. "Remembering Ron Carey," http://youtube/DLYj3vfLcts.
23. Ibid.
24. Ibid.
25. Ibid.
26. Ibid.
27. Ibid.
28. Ibid. Though Tim Sylvester and Jim Reynolds were not allowed to have any official contact with Ron Carey, they nonetheless did maintain secret contact with their former boss and mentor. They even had a code for Ron's name in their phone contacts. They referred to him as "Tuna."
29. Interview with Bruce Carey.
30. "The Rank and File Remembers Ron Carey," TDU.org, December 13, 2008, Convoy Dispatch.
31. Steve Early and Rand Wilson, "A Teamster Apart: Ron Carey Remembered," *The Nation*, December 2008.
32. Deepa Kumar, *Outside the Box: Corporate Media, Globalization, and the UPS Strike* (Champaign: University of Illinois Press, 2007), 187.
33. Liz Rhoades, "Street renaming OK'd for northeast leaders," *Queens Chronicle*, December 31, 2009.
34. Kumar, *Outside the Box*, 194.
35. "Forgotten Teamster Speech," Teamster Convention, June 1991, Teamsters History Project.
36. Ibid.

Index